SEEKING PERFECTION

ABOUT THE AUTHOR

Jonathan Melville is a digital editor and arts journalist who has written for titles including *SFX Magazine*, the *Edinburgh Evening News* and *The Guardian*. As well as running Scottish online magazine, reelscotland.com, he has filmed content for WOW247.co.uk and STV.tv and produced audio features for BBC Radio Scotland's *Culture Studio*. Jonathan lives in Edinburgh.

Twitter: @jon_melville
jonathanmelville.co.uk

The author meets Michael "Burt Gummer" Gross, March 2015 © Jonathan Melville

SEEKING PERFECTION

JONATHAN MELVILLE

FOREWORD BY MICHAEL GROSS

Published by Fountainbridge Press

First edition, August 2015

ISBN 978 0 99332 150 4

Layout by Laura Kincaid
tenthousand.co.uk

For Claire

CONTENTS

FOREWORD

It was early in 1989 when my agent informed me of an audition for a new feature film, "a monster movie" he said.

I was, I confess, underwhelmed. As a child I had loved creature features, and had pored over articles in *Famous Monsters of Filmland* and other such publications. I was particularly drawn to the great Universal Studio classics like *Dracula, Frankenstein, The Mummy* or – still one of my all-time favourites – Warner Bros.' 1954 atomic age cautionary tale: *Them!* As an adult, however, I no longer thought of monster movies as "serious" entertainment.

On the other hand, I was eager for something new. My seven years as paterfamilias on the hit series *Family Ties* was coming to an end, and I was uncertain what the future would hold. Specifically, would audiences accept me as someone other than the kindly Steven Keaton they had come to know and love? With that in mind, I set aside my reluctance and agreed to take a look at the screenplay.

Contrary to expectations, I was immediately attracted to the material. While I had come to associate science fiction and horror with over-worn clichés, cardboard characters, and screenplays that took themselves far too seriously, screenwriters S. S. Wilson and Brent Maddock seemed almost to have reinvented the genre. Their story was set not in the dark of night, but in the bright light of day; their scenes were set not in some claustrophobic, abandoned house, but in the wide-open spaces of the American west. And while their characters were decidedly eccentric, they remained fully formed, likeable and – much to my surprise – funny. Not self-consciously funny, not the "funny" that comes from clownishness and jokes, but the more enduring humour of character and situation. The screenplay was a combination of bone-crunching, horrifying threat, mixed with subtle, sophisticated humour – and I was intrigued. Yes, I told my agent, I would very much like to meet with the director and writers.

A short time later I had the pleasure of meeting Steve Wilson, Brent Maddock and director Ron Underwood in person. Though all were unknown to me, I was not unknown to them, for *Family Ties* had not only catapulted Michael J. Fox to fame, but had made our entire cast household words. President Reagan had publicly announced that we were his favourite TV show. I had even been a clue on *Jeopardy!* America had taken the Keaton family into their hearts, which made me wonder if Wilson, Maddock and Underwood had mistaken me for some other actor. For while *Family Ties* had firmly established me as the kindhearted, gregarious, left-of-centre Steven Keaton, these gentlemen had tapped me for the role of an uncompromising, misanthropic, right-of-centre character named "Burt Gummer." Explaining my confusion, I jokingly put the question directly to them: "Why me?"

As I recall, they answered that they had seen other examples of my work, thought there was more to me and my talent than met the eye, and liked the idea of casting "against type". They were curious to see what I might do with the character of Burt.

To this very day, what I "did" in that room is a point of contention between director Ron Underwood and myself. While I remember presenting a spirited but rather straightforward audition, Ron still maintains that at some point in the process I ended up climbing on top of his desk, in imaginary mortal combat with what came to be known as "Graboids". While I would like to think of myself as an actor with enough bravado to have leaped atop his desk, I have no recollection of doing so. I remember only being "committed," while Ron seems to remember me as, well, a *candidate* for commitment.

Whatever the truth, I got the job, and just days after the *Family Ties* wrap party, I found myself on location in Lone Pine, California, in the shadow of majestic Mount Whitney, in the company of Kevin Bacon, Fred Ward, Reba McEntire and an equally majestic ensemble of actors, staff and crew.

Foremost among those creative spirits were Ron, Steve and Brent, who proved as open-minded in the making of the film as they were in casting me in the first place. Their work, their collaboration, their vision was as productive and as pleasant a time as I have ever had – so much so that I eagerly signed on for three more sequels and a short-lived television series. The monster movie I was reluctant to read was, of course, released in 1990 as *Tremors*, and the rest is cinematic history.

Steve, Brent and Ron not only assured me there would be life after *Family Ties*, but that it could be a life filled with captivatingly different characters. Burt Gummer, a comic masterpiece so well written that I needed do little more than recite the lines and avoid bumping into the furniture, was their creation. *Tremors* was their creation and, a quarter-century later, they are the gifts that keep on giving.

Michael Gross
November 2014, Los Angeles

INTRODUCTION

Growing up in the 1980s, many of my film memories can be traced back to Saturday afternoon screenings at Edinburgh's old ABC cinema, when the likes of *E.T.* (1982), *Ghostbusters*, *Indiana Jones and the Temple of Doom* (both 1984) and *Back to the Future* (1985) were the talk of the playground. With my imagination fuelled by time travel, aliens and high adventure, cinema trips would be followed by a purchase of the accompanying novelisation, sticker album and those packets of bubble gum with picture cards inside.

Fast-forward a few years, and I was living in the Scottish Highlands. The nearest cinema was two hours away by train, while news on the latest film releases came from Saturday morning TV, the occasional episode of Barry Norman's *Film* programme and issues of *Starburst* magazine ordered in to the local paper shop. It seemed I was the only film fan in the village.

By November 1992, like every normal 16-year-old*, I was a regular reader of the *Radio Times* and *TV Times* listings magazines, searching for information about TV and films coming up the following week. On Saturday 28 November 1992 at 9.25pm** I sat down to watch a film on BBC One that I'd have adored had I seen it on the cinema screen, one which transported me to another part of the world, to a community using their wits to battle underground worms in the desert. *Tremors* had it all:

---

* OK, so perhaps not that normal

** According to the BBC's Genome website genome.ch.bbc.co.uk humour, action, monsters, stunning scenery normally reserved for westerns, a dash of bad language and a guy in an Atlanta Hawks cap with some serious weaponry in his basement.

With no modern technology to help the Perfectionites, it wasn't immediately obvious when *Tremors* had been made or when it took place, lending it a non-glossy, low-budget feel that was, well, perfect. This was a B movie, plain and simple, a film that was impossible to stop watching thanks to memorable characters, fantastic creature designs and a self-aware script that didn't talk down to the audience. In effect, Val and Earl *were* the audience, just two regular guys trying to make the best of a bad situation. Was it science fiction? Sort of. Horror? A bit. Comedy? Well, it was very funny.

The downside of being a *Tremors* fan in 1992 was the lack of merchandise available to fans. No books, t-shirts, soundtrack albums, sticker books. Nothing. With no internet, it was impossible to know who else outside my immediate circle of friends recalled the plight of the good people of Perfection. I'd have to wait until the next BBC showing to revisit the town.

As it turned out, missing the original *Tremors* at the cinema wasn't much of a problem, as its relatively poor performance at the box office was part of the reason it went on to be so successful. *Tremors* arrived during the glory years of VHS, when going to the local video store was a weekly ritual experienced by millions around the globe. This was a film that demanded repeat viewing over a few beers and popcorn, its quotable lines and blue collar characters ensuring it appealed to the masses.

The sequels appeared sporadically in the years after. Summer 1996 found me on holiday in Toronto and discovering *Tremors 2: Aftershocks* at a Blockbuster video rental store. Kevin Bacon wasn't back for this bout of Graboid hunting, but Fred Ward and the comedy were. It was almost as entertaining as the original, the lower budget hardly a problem for a film that also took place in the desert and didn't rely on too many major effects. *Tremors 3: Back to Perfection* arrived in UK shops months after its US debut and bumped Michael Gross up to lead while introducing the Ass Blasters, though it wasn't quite as much fun as *Aftershocks*.

Tremors: The Series and *Tremors 4: The Legend Begins* followed in quick succession. The former, an attempt to capture the tone of the films with a new cast (and, of course, Michael Gross), was verging on greatness, while the latter cast Gross in a new role and decided to play with the franchise's rules by taking viewers back in time to Rejection, Nevada. While the TV show deserved another season to truly find its feet, the fourth film did feel like the end of the line for the film series in many ways. Where else could it go? *Tremors* in space?

I have no qualms about labelling the original *Tremors* a classic of its kind, the last great monster movie produced in Hollywood. The sequels are a bit more of a problem. Watched in quick succession, it's possible to pick up on the in-jokes and references to previous movies and to see the character of Burt Gummer rise through the ranks to become the franchise's star. Gross never delivers a bad line reading, knows exactly what is expected of him and is the glue that holds everything together. The budgets are lower and the effects get cheesier, but there's a tone that permeates through each film that tells viewers that they're being included in the joke.

Catching one of the sequels in isolation can be more of an issue. Without the first film acting as ballast, a stray viewing of *Tremors 4* can be disorienting. The town of Rejection is clearly a play on Perfection from *Tremors* and *Tremors 3*, but anyone not up on their *Tremors* lore immediately misses an important gag. Likewise, this film has an Old Fred like they did in *Tremors*, while Hiram's potential love interest has red hair, as did Burt's wife in the first film. These are all small points in isolation, but the film is full of references for the fans, while the growing bond between Hiram and the Rejectionites is actually very sweet compared to the find 'em and blast 'em nature of *Tremors 2* and *3*'s plots.

While it's understandable that casual viewers might dismiss any of the sequels as bad, that's to do them a disservice. Anyone reading this book probably doesn't need much to convince them to sit and watch the films in order again, but if you've only ever seen the first film, or stopped watching the sequels after you caught the second one during an AMC marathon, I'd urge you to buy/stream/download the others and have yourself a *Tremors*-fest. You'll start to notice things you didn't before, get the odd reference you missed the first time and, by the time you get to *Tremors 4*, you'll see that it's by no means a bad film, just ... misunderstood.

Hopefully *Seeking Perfection* will help the case for the sequels, allowing viewers to understand how and why they came to be. The first film was a passion project for a small team who wanted to create a high quality, hugely enjoyable and satisfying movie for a film studio whose main aim was to turn a profit. The follow-ups were driven by a studio with a desire to shift more videocassettes with the name *Tremors* from the shelves of Walmart. That the same writers, directors and producers remained with the franchise for three more films and a TV series is almost a happy accident; Universal would have continued to make the films without them had they refused and the fact there was just enough money left over to pay for their expertise is something fans should be forever thankful for.

This book started life as a 2,000 word article for UK sci-fi magazine, *SFX*, in which I spoke in-depth to *Tremors* co-creator, S.S. Wilson, and star, Michael Gross, for the film's 21st anniversary in 2011. Realising that there was a lot more to be revealed about the first film and its various off-shoots than could be covered in a magazine article, I decided to follow-up some of Wilson's comments and see who would be willing to discuss their time with the franchise in time for 2015's 25th anniversary.

My goal here is to report the facts behind the fiction, quoting as many of those involved in the first four films and the TV series as I could track down. I decided early on that I didn't want to simply rate the films out of 10, search for every blooper I could find or try to justify the science behind the evolutionary process of the Graboid. That's a perfectly valid approach to the films, and if someone else wants to write that book I'll be the first in line to buy it, but for the silver anniversary I felt it was more important to let the people who made the movies have their say at last. For many of the cast and crew, this was the first time they'd been interviewed about their work on the films.

As this book goes to press, a new entry in the *Tremors* saga is due to arrive on DVD shelves and in iTunes. *Tremors 5: Bloodlines* is an update of a 2004 script that finds Graboids in South Africa and promises a new version of the creatures last encountered more than a decade ago. On a personal level, having spoken to those involved in the original quadrilogy of films at both Stampede Entertainment (the company formed by the creators of the first film) and at Universal Studios Home Entertainment (the direct-to-video division who own the rights and funded the sequels), I'm torn about the fact that the creators aren't involved in this iteration. As you'll read in the book, the *Tremors* tone isn't something that comes pre-packaged and has never been easily replicated by others.

At the same time, Universal is a business that needs to turn a profit and perhaps the fifth film will succeed on Michael Gross' charms and an all-new production team that understands what makes a *Tremors* film work. We can but hope that the world of big business realises just what it is that makes the *Tremors* saga so unique and that events conspire to reunite the original team at least one more time. Keep watching the ground...

Jonathan Melville
July 2015, Edinburgh

PROLOGUE
FROM SMALL BEGINNINGS

A boulder in the heart of the Mojave Desert may seem an unusual location for a multi-million dollar film franchise to have its roots, but little about the complex history of the *Tremors* franchise could ever be considered normal.

Situated approximately 150 miles north of Los Angeles and surrounded by the Sierra Nevada, Cosos, El Paso and Argus Range mountain ranges, the Naval Air Weapons Station (NAWS) China Lake was opened during the height of World War II for the research, development and testing of rockets for the Californian Institute of Technology. At more than 1.1m acres, it represents the US Navy's largest single landholding.[1]

By the early 1970s, NAWS (then the Naval Weapons Center) was home to soldiers, scientists and technicians, while a filmmaking unit recorded activity on the base, from the creation of educational films for the cadets to the documenting of training missions and rocket tests. One member of the unit was Steve "S.S." Wilson, a young editor who had signed up for a summer job with a naval film company located at the Center. Wilson worked on the bustling base during the day, with occasional visits to the nearby city of Ridgecrest for rest and relaxation.

Used to the wide-open spaces of his native Oklahoma, Wilson explored his surroundings whenever possible, taking advantage of the opportunity offered by the Navy to roam the ranges around China Lake at weekends. Underdeveloped and home to more than 340 species of wildlife, the boulder-strewn landscape gave Wilson a chance to get back to nature, while dodging the occasional wild horse. Like many aspiring screenwriters in search of their next story idea, Wilson constantly had one eye on his surroundings for potential new material and had recently spotted tiny ant lions in the area, insects that make cone shaped holes in the sand. When an ant comes by they flick dirt up and the ant is sucked under.

"One day I was sitting out there on one of those boulders and thought how interesting it would be to have something that moved through the sand like a fish, and I couldn't get off the rock," said Wilson, thinking back to the ant lions. Without giving it any more thought, he scribbled the idea onto a scrap of paper under the title *Land Sharks*, pushed it into his back pocket and scrambled down the rock.

For now, the idea would have to wait.

CHAPTER ONE

CATCHING THE FILMMAKING BUG

Forget the great film studios of Hollywood and Europe: in the 1950s and 1960s suburban USA was where some of the most interesting filmmaking was taking place.

With expensive 16mm film being used primarily by professional filmmakers, the development of cheaper 8mm film in the early 1930s by Eastman Kodak allowed members of the public to purchase relatively inexpensive handheld cameras to capture family life in the back yard, from Little Johnny's first bicycle ride to family barbecues. By 1965, compact film cartridges had been introduced to most new battery-powered Super 8 cameras, replacing traditional 8mm film rolls and providing users with a better quality picture for their mini-masterpieces.

In Norman, Oklahoma, young Steve Wilson had been charged with taking over the family 8mm camera by his father, while encouragement from his uncle nurtured a lifelong interest in animation. "I was a huge Ray Harryhausen fan; all those films are wonderful and quirky in their way," said Wilson. "The stories aren't always the best, but to me as a kid they were absolutely unique."

Wilson was just one of many young boys fascinated with the work of Los Angeles-born filmmaker, Raymond Frederick "Ray" Harryhausen, who had displayed an interest in fantasy and filmmaking at an early age. Inspired by films such as 1925's *The Lost World* and 1933's *King Kong*, the teenage Harryhausen was actively encouraged by his parents to figure out how the big screen creatures moved. The results led to him becoming one of the world's most renowned proponents of stop-motion animation and the creator of Dynamation, a technique that saw miniature models moved millimetres at a time and each shot caught on film in classics such as *One Million Years BC* (1966) and *The Golden Voyage of Sinbad* (1973).[1]

Though enamoured with the fact that Harryhausen seemed to be the only filmmaker doing something different with his creations – they weren't simply lizards with horns glued to their heads as witnessed in films such as 1960's *The Lost World* – Wilson knew he didn't have the artistic skills to make anything as exotic as his hero. Wilson soon began animating objects rather than puppets, skills honed for one high school science project in which he created an animated dinosaur to explain persistence of vision, a theory used to explain why humans see moving images when they watch a film.

Despite his love of stop-motion, Wilson opted to study psychology at Pennsylvania State University in the late 1960s, much to the dismay of his father. During an early visit from Wilson Snr, he pointed out that his son had been making films since the age of 12 and promptly went to the teenager's counsellor, changed all his courses to film-related subjects and in the words of Wilson, "altered my life completely".

Following graduation, Wilson was drafted into the US Army in 1970, allowing him to remain stateside creating educational films, before he left in 1972 and made his way to the University of Southern California (USC) the following year to join the School of Cinema-Television (now the USC School of Cinematic Arts) graduate film programme. Although USC Cinema counts John Milius and George Lucas among its alumni and is today ranked number one in America, it didn't have quite the same prestige in the 1970s.[2] "At the time film schools weren't so much an anomaly, but they were a new thing," noted Wilson. "A degree from USC was openly mocked by producers in Hollywood."

Another arrival at USC was Brent Maddock, a native of Westchester County in New York who had graduated from Colgate University in New York State with a degree in English Literature and no idea what he was going to do with it. Directing and acting in college theatre productions, Maddock's experience making his own Super 8 films meant he was fascinated by the medium by the time he enrolled at Colgate. "There were no filmmaking courses, but I would go to the professor and say, 'Would you give me credit if I do a film rather than a paper?'"

Maddock applied to both film school and business school ("My father and grandfather were New York City businessmen, they were like those *Mad Men* guys") and was offered a place in both of them. Deciding to go with his gut, he set out to drive to California in his Toyota and reported to film school for a master's degree. Steve Wilson was the first person he met walking into the rustic USC film school, closely followed by Ron Underwood.

"We probably met in orientation, very early on in school," recalled Underwood, a medical student-turned-filmmaker who hailed from Los Angeles and who had started experimenting with 8mm in fifth grade, winning Eastman Kodak awards in junior high. "Steve and Brent were both graduate students and I was an undergraduate. We got together and showed films that we had made in the past and I loved Steve's stop-motion work."

The three men may have admired each other's work, but they also shared an interest in the films they had grown up watching in an era when vintage B movies were used as cheap filler by TV stations across America, in a similar way to their origins in cinemas in the late 1920s. Where once it had been enough to precede a silent feature film with some shorts and a live act, the introduction of sound in 1927 led to programmers adding newsreels, cartoons and a serial to a double helping of features in an effort to make a night out appear more value for money. While the first, or "A", film tended to be glossier and star well-known actors, the second, or "B", features were made on a smaller budget and often ran to just over an hour.

The Bs continued into the 1930s and 1940s, studios such as Universal and RKO enjoying a boom in B westerns, while by the 1950s there was a proliferation of big screen science fiction in which Small Town USA was the victim of regular infiltrations from alien beings determined to destroy the fabric of American society. Films such as *War of the Worlds* (1953), *It Came from Outer Space* (1953) and *The Monolith Monsters* (1957) terrified and entertained cinema-goers, while social commentators looked deeper to discover parallels with the xenophobia and fear that were being nurtured by the Cold War.

The traditional double feature had started to fade from cinemas by the 1960s, the term B movie now applied to films with lower budgets and simpler stories, often with roots in the science fiction or horror genres. These pictures began to thrive at drive-ins around the country, while late night screenings on television channels hungry for content brought B movies to a new audience in the 1950s and 1960s, allowing the likes of Steve Wilson, Brent Maddock and Ron Underwood to soak up otherwise long-forgotten cowboy epics and sci-fi creature features that were relegated to the small hours.

While Underwood spent the next few years of college life living in the LA suburb of Glendale with his wife, Wilson and Maddock became roommates in a variety of LA apartments. As they learned each other's screenwriting strengths and weaknesses, with Maddock specialising in snappy dialogue and Wilson focusing on plot, their shared love of animation led them to regularly watch *Looney Tunes* reruns and discuss writing a book on the subject. "I'd figure out how many frames Chuck Jones used to get Wile E. Coyote from point A to point B, trying to learn from his impeccable sense of timing," said Maddock. Their obsession paid off years later when, after submitting an unused script to animation legend Jones, he hired them to write jokes for several *Looney Tunes* cartoons featuring Daffy Duck and Road Runner.

From understanding the mechanics of cameras to directing and editing on film, the three men took an interest in all aspects of filmmaking as they worked hard to perfect their skills. Ron Underwood's big break came when a documentary he had made for class about the relatively new sport of hang gliding was released by Paramount in 1974, giving him an insight into the potentially lucrative educational short film market whereby film

film prints were sold to libraries and institutions. Steve Wilson's immersion in the world of filmmaking led to two summers spent editing at the China Lake naval base, where his *Land Sharks* concept became yet another addition to his growing collection of ideas for possible scripts.

The tail end of the 1970s found Underwood, Wilson and Maddock freshly graduated from USC and keen to find work in their chosen careers. At the age of 20, Underwood began working as an editor and cameraman in industrial films and commercials, before the American Film Institute awarded him a production fellowship.[3] Following completion of the fellowship, Underwood contacted Wilson and Maddock with an idea to join him in creating new educational films that would use Wilson's stop-motion skills to set them apart from their rivals. Funded and produced by Underwood for educational specialists Barr Films, 1978's *Dictionary – The Adventure of Words* was designed like a Ray Harryhausen film, with split screens shot in camera. The three filmmakers each took a share of the profits, which became their most successful film for the next decade.

The friends had realised that they could collaborate on a film project that was both creatively rewarding and financially lucrative, a discovery that encouraged them to continue working on new projects indefinitely.

Hoping to produce more mainstream films, Underwood next convinced his team to adapt a 1955 Kurt Vonnegut short story, *Deer in the Works*. The plan was to make a dramatic short that would be sold to schools and libraries. More expensive than their usual films and with a longer shoot, the adaptation was a steep learning curve for the writers. "Screenplays are ridiculously short compared to a novel or even a novella, and you're constantly trying to decide how you can do service to the feeling you get from a story or novel in thirty minutes," said Wilson. "It was an interesting experience, though I think what Brent and I did was probably a bit ponderous."

ENTER NUMBER FIVE

The trio's success with *Dictionary – The Adventure of Words* led them into the world of working for hire during the early 1980s, taking on educational projects for a flat fee while the companies that commissioned them retained ownership.

The team had a novel way of approaching their projects that ensured they shared the workload and continued to gain experience in different areas; Maddock and Wilson would write a script for Underwood to direct and produce, before they all swapped roles on the next film. "One of the films we made was about how to write a term paper for school, which was a very boring subject," said Underwood, recalling that 1983's *Library Report* was set in the future and featured a teenage girl and her robot. "When we were finishing it, Steve said to me, 'We should work on a feature with this robot character.'"

The two writers had collaborated on numerous speculative feature film scripts away from their educational work, but they still hadn't been able to interest anyone in their ideas and had no agent to represent them. Buoyed by the success of their robot-centric short, Wilson and Maddock began work on a script that would put a fresh spin on the well-worn concept of a robot coming to life and running amok, finally hitting upon an idea that was part-Pinocchio and part-Frankenstein.

"The thing that always got me about robot movies is that the robots are always alive; that's the joke going back to *Forbidden Planet*'s Robbie the Robot," noted Wilson. "The robot seems to have an attitude and to be alive with a sense of humour. In *Star Wars*, C-3PO and R2-D2 are obviously alive and nobody ever questions it. So we thought, 'What if we step way back from that and say the robot is alive?' Nobody would believe it; they'd try to trick it and prove it's not alive."

In 1983, George Lucas' epic *Star Wars* trilogy had ended with *Return of the Jedi*; studios were now determined to capitalise on the public's appetite for science fiction. From Gary Nelson's *The Black Hole* (1979) and Roger Corman's *Battle Beyond the Stars*

(1980) in cinemas, through to *Battlestar Galactica* (1978–79) and *Buck Rogers in the 25th Century* (1979–81) on the small screen, space opera, laser guns and robots were everywhere. Younger viewers (and their parents' wallets) were also targeted with the arrival of the *Transformers* animated series in 1984, a programme spun-off from the successful toy range. The walking, talking and fighting robots caught the imagination of children around the globe, who could watch their heroes battle it out on TV before recreating the scenarios on the living room floor.

Wilson and Maddock's idea revolved around the US military creating an experimental robot that accidently comes to life after being struck by lightning. The robot would be named Number Five and the plot would centre on it/him trying to convince people it/he was alive. Working on educational films with Ron Underwood during the day, the pair fitted writing duties into their spare time, getting together every other weekend and most evenings to discuss their script. "We were completely outside the system," Wilson said. "Our running joke was that we hoped somebody stole something from us as that would be a form of success."

Though the pair recognised that work on the robot script was a priority, they also took on the occasional solo commission to keep their finances flowing, one of which led Wilson to return to his passion for animation via an acquaintance from his early days in LA, writer and producer Terrence McDonnell. As well as penning scripts for TV series such as *The Six Million Dollar Man* (1974–78) and *Gemini Man* (1976), McDonnell was story editor on the original *Battlestar Galactica* and had landed a position on animated series *M.A.S.K.* (1985–86) by late 1984.

Inspired by the success of the *He-Man* (1983–85) and *Transformers* cartoons, toy manufacturer Kenner developed their new animated action series around underground task force M.A.S.K. (Mobile Armoured Strike Command), who were in constant battle with the evil V.E.N.O.M. (Vicious Evil Network of Mayhem). McDonnell was hired to oversee the writing of 65 season one episodes, each designed to shift thousands of toys from the shelves of Toys 'R' Us. "Terry hired everyone he knew with a typewriter because he needed an enormous number of stories," recalled Wilson, who wound up writing around a dozen episodes, working closely with McDonnell on various wacky ideas. "It was a gruelling period because I had to write them very fast and there were a great many strange rules – we weren't allowed to let certain characters ride in certain cars because they hadn't been designed by the toy company in the real world. The women got short shrift because their bikes hadn't been designed yet, so they had to ride with other characters."

While Wilson was busy crafting new adventures for Miles Mayhem, Matt Trakker and the other employees of M.A.S.K., Brent Maddock attended a screenwriting workshop at the University of California, Los Angeles (UCLA) in early 1985 and asked if he could use the script he and Wilson had developed about the living robot, originally titled *The Robot Movie* and now called *Short Circuit*, for class. One of his classmates was a friend of 25-year-old Gary Foster, son of independent film producer David Foster, whose credits included 1971's *McCabe & Mrs Miller* and the 1982 remake of *The Thing*. Aware that Foster was looking to include a robot in his next film to capitalise on the success of the *Transformers* toy range the previous Christmas, Maddock's classmate gave the *Short Circuit* script to Gary Foster, who in turn passed it to his father.

Impressed with their concept, David Foster let the screenwriters know he was keen to show it to Hollywood film studios, aware that he had to compete with six other robot films at various stages of development around town. With interest from a producer, the pair now had to find an agent to handle negotiations for the sale of their script. Enter talent agent, Nancy Roberts, who had begun her career as a freelance writer before starting her own independent production company that had worked on Hallmark TV specials and animated feature films.[4] Roberts founded The Roberts Company in 1981 and her client list included over 40 writers and directors. Said Roberts, "I wasn't going to take on any new clients, but I read the script and thought, 'Oh my God, these guys are really talented.'"

With a number of agents wanting to represent them, the writers chose Roberts because of her belief in their potential. "Nancy is a force of nature and as long as she's on your side you're fine," said Maddock. "She always got great deals for us, but more than that she always had a great vision for what we could do. We don't relate to the business part of the job; that's not our natural territory. The money guys make us feel creepy. We've been in rooms with a lot of creeps, some of them ragingly dysfunctional and hugely powerful and they seem to go together. Some of the most insane meetings I've had were with gigantically powerful film producers and you'd walk away thinking, 'This guy needs help!'"

Hollywood began to take notice of the *Short Circuit* script thanks to David Foster's efforts, with several studios engaging in a bidding war. A number of well-known directors showed an interest, including one who wanted to have a child added to the story, something Wilson and Maddock rejected due to concerns that their script would be rewritten for a younger audience. The screenplay was eventually bought by the short-lived Producers Sales Organization and released through Tri-Star Pictures.

The sale of *Short Circuit* was the big break Maddock and Wilson needed, putting them on the front page of *Variety* and launching them into the limelight. The story made news on two fronts: as well as coming from Nancy Roberts' small independent agency, which lacked the kind of leverage available to traditional larger agencies, the script was sold for the extremely high price of $360,000.[5] With the script rushed into production just three weeks after it was sold, the calls started flooding in and the writers were finally a hot topic in Hollywood.

"It happened amazingly fast," said Wilson. "Our thought was that we'd never break into Hollywood and that we'd make a low budget movie, that was until the kid gave the script to the other kid. We were kidded by more seasoned people that we would never have this experience again, and they were right."

* * *

In its original form, the 120-page *Short Circuit* script was a fantastical tale of a hi-tech machine created as part of a US government research programme, at a time when Russia was still the enemy. At the heart of the movie was the character of Number Five, a robot who was alive but who couldn't convince anyone of the fact. Though Steve Wilson and Brent Maddock were writing a fun adventure film, they were determined that characters surrounding the more whimsical Number Five should be as realistic as possible, including his creator, scientist Newton Crosby, potentially the robot's worst enemy as he built him and knew he couldn't be alive.

Wilson, Maddock and Ron Underwood had originally collaborated on the *Short Circuit* concept, with a view to making it as a low-budget film. Wilson would animate the robot, Maddock would write and produce and Underwood would direct. When Hollywood took a liking to the script and it morphed into a big budget production, it became obvious that Underwood's lack of feature film credits meant he wouldn't be in the running to direct a major studio picture. "I was just a hindrance to this project and wasn't adequately prepared for that kind of movie," admitted Underwood.

According to Nancy Roberts, as interest in the film began to pick up, Underwood knew he shouldn't get in the way of its development, with the agent unable to do what was required to kick-off her clients' careers by having somebody with little feature film experience attached to the project. At Wilson and Maddock's request, Roberts ensured her clients' contract included a "no re-write" clause, meaning the studio couldn't hire other writers to change the script in any way. "I can honestly say I did these incredible deals for my clients, I think part of that was because I had my own company and nobody could tell me I couldn't."

With Ron Underwood side-lined from the production of *Short Circuit*, the search was on for a director who could bring the script's quirky mix of comedy, science fiction and action to the big screen. The studio's choice was director John Badham, best known for techno thrillers, *WarGames* and *Blue Thunder* (both 1983). "When [I received] *Short Circuit* the thing I responded to was the character of Number Five," said Badham. "I thought [he was] a real character we'd never seen before because of the way he was created, and yet there was incredible humour ... that was what made me run around the house making noises thinking this would be a huge movie."

Despite the hard-won no rewrite clause being in place, TriStar and John Badham pushed Roberts to allow them to make script changes, going as far as to state they were going to hire another writer. Roberts responded by threatening to put an injunction against the picture. "This was really brass knuckles stuff," said the agent, who explained to her clients that it was in all their best interests to allow the studio to polish the script, aware that to have a big sale was what their careers needed and that to impede the film's development would be of no use to anyone.

Initially, Wilson and Maddock were asked to cut 20 pages from the script, though that wasn't the end of the changes. "John came out of TV, which is a real fast and furious business where you can't go over budget and he came in with that sensibility," said Wilson. "There's a long sequence where Number Five, in escaping from security forces, runs into a junkyard and realises he's about to be crushed in a car crushing machine. That was the only major piece that was cut. Lines of dialogue were trimmed here and there."

The decision to revise Maddock and Wilson's original script had major consequences for the finished film, significantly changing the motivations of the characters and subsequently affecting the studio's casting decisions. The role of Number Five's creator, Newton Crosby, was given to the star of 1984's *Police Academy*, Steve Guttenberg, while the female lead, Stephanie Speck, went to *WarGames*' Ally Sheedy. "It definitely was a very funny script and there was no way around it that the situation was funny," Badham said.

Convinced that Number Five was the film's protagonist and that those around the fantastical robot should be anchored in reality, the writers were disappointed by both the levels of humour being inserted into the script and the casting of an actor best known for broad comedy. "Steve Guttenberg's part wasn't changed or lengthened; unfortunately it was dumbed down," said Wilson, who made his feelings known to the director.

According to Badham, Guttenberg was able to bring credibility to the film's light tone. "We could believe him as a scientist serious about his robotics but he'd get so wrapped up in the reality of the fantasy that he'd be destroyed when the robot died, even though you could say, 'He's mechanical and we can put him back together.' If we believe the film, he was much more than the other robots, so there's a lot of suspension of disbelief that goes on to get us to believe that Number Five is real."

Another change was the introduction of an Indian character, Ben Jabituya. Written as a Caucasian in the script, Ben's race was altered following Badham's concerns during auditions. "Fisher Stevens came in and read and I knew he was a really good actor but something was wrong. I realised it wasn't the actors, it was the character."

Taking inspiration from Bronson Pinchot's scene-stealing performance in 1984's *Beverly Hills Cop*, Badham brought Stevens back for another audition. "I said, 'What if Ben was Indian and he's fighting the language but he's very bright?' We were having fun with it while at the same time being sensitive that we could be crossing the line, but it did bring such tremendous humour to it. I received a message from the producers saying 'Please don't do this' and there was a lot of worry that we were ruining the character. The minute we saw dailies we realised we were adding possibilities, Fisher's character was keeping scenes alive and adding humour to it."

"The irony of ironies is that the character we get no end of credit for is Ben," explained Steve Wilson. "Badham saw Fisher Stevens do this loony interpretation of an Indian scientist and loved it." Immediately all of Stevens' lines were rewritten, but not by Wilson or Maddock. As the drama in their script was gradually replaced by farce, the duo began to realise that the script was merely a blueprint for production and that their input wasn't as appreciated as they'd hoped.

"That was difficult for us," sighed Maddock. "Smart screenwriters realise that their job is to write the screenplay and forget about the movie, probably smart not to even go see the movie, but we'd been making movies all along. It was meant to be what Spielberg described as the importance of everything in a movie such as *E.T.* to be real; a real single mom in a real house with real kids with real problems and the only thing that's remarkable in there is an alien. So you ground the movie and it makes the miracle of this lost alien even greater. That's what we had been trying to do with *Short Circuit*, make sure everyone is actually real, real scientists and people, and the robot is the amazing miracle, but that got all diluted when the universe of the movie became farcical, so I think it was a lot less than it could have been."

The writers continued to offer their assistance after filming had concluded, getting involved in post-production when it became clear that the robot's lines could be altered due to the character having lights that flashed in sync with actor Tim Blaney's voice, rather than a mouth. John Badham soon realised that Number Five's dialogue could be improved with the addition of various one-liners in the final weeks of editing. Brent Maddock was charged with penning the film's most memorable zingers, including the oft-quoted "Hey laser lips, your mama was a snowblower", which made it into the movie just weeks before the picture was locked and prints were made.

Short Circuit opened in cinemas on 9 May 1986, grossing more than $6m at the US box office on its opening weekend and taking over $40m in total.[6] "We went to see it at the Cinerama Dome," said Wilson. "It was a dream come true. I'd come to LA, like so many people had, and found work in animation. I was thinking of leaving LA because I never liked it. It had been 10 years since I got there and I'd made my peace about where I was. And then to be on the red carpet surrounded by lights, it was staggering."

Although the film was a bona fide hit, Wilson and Maddock weren't satisfied. Used to being involved in every stage of their educational films, from writing and shooting through to editing and promotion, the pair were frustrated that the traditional Hollywood filmmaking process was shutting them out. Almost every part of the *Short Circuit* experience convinced them there had to be a better way.

Working on *Short Circuit* had been a mixed blessing for Wilson and Maddock, their excitement at being Hollywood's flavour of the month tempered by creative differences. As they considered their next move in 1986, a well-known figure in the film industry made it clear he wanted to meet them. "We were told that Steven Spielberg was annoyed that somebody at Amblin had passed on *Short Circuit* and he called us up; I still have his voice on an old answering machine," said Wilson.

THE SPIELBERG YEARS

Following some well-received stints on popular US television series in the 1960s, Steven Spielberg had worked his way up through the ranks to become one of Hollywood's hottest directors, establishing his own independent production company, Amblin Entertainment, based at Universal Studios by 1981. "At the time Amblin was a small house on the Universal lot, a little adobe building that they built for him," said Steve Wilson.

Much to the consternation of their agent, Nancy Roberts, Wilson and Maddock agreed to discuss rewrite duties for *Ghost Boy*, a script owned by Spielberg. Advised by Roberts that writers of their stature shouldn't do rewrites, the pair nevertheless headed to meet Spielberg at Universal. "He was shooting an episode of his *Amazing Stories* TV series," recalled Wilson. "We talked to him about *Ghost Boy*, shouting over the sound of a generator, and he told us he wanted us to rewrite it because he thought we had the right sensibilities for it. We went and read *Ghost Boy*, which became *Ghost Dad*, and visited Amblin regularly for follow-up meetings." Wilson and Maddock worked on the script in 1986, originally designed as a star vehicle for Steve Martin to be directed by *Short Circuit*'s John Badham, but the film didn't go before the cameras until 1989 (released in June 1990) with Bill Cosby in the lead, directed by Sidney Poitier.[7]

The 1980s was perhaps Spielberg's most prolific decade, a period that saw him variously write, produce and direct some of Hollywood's most successful films, including 1981's *Raiders of the Lost Ark*, 1984's *Gremlins* and 1985's *The Goonies*. According to Wilson, Spielberg had a hand in everything happening on the Universal lot. "If [*Back to the Future* director] Robert Zemeckis was working there then Steven was all over that. Matthew Robbins was directing *Batteries Not Included*, so he was all over that as well."

Batteries Not Included (1987) had originally been designed as an episode of *Amazing Stories*, but Spielberg was so enamoured with the idea that he decided it should be developed as a film script, with Wilson and Maddock tasked with helping to bring the story, about a group of New York apartment dwellers who encounter flying alien robots, to the screen. "It was one of those things where the movie was going forward rapidly and it was too expensive," explained Wilson. "One thing that Spielberg was always conscious off was how much things cost; he did not like things to go over budget and he didn't want them to be budgeted too high. The script that Matthew and Brad Bird had written was long and needed to be cut, but they were too busy in pre-production and they weren't able to write. We ended up doing so much rewriting on it we [shared] a credit. That's a Writers Guild of America decision, not a producer's decision, and it wasn't our goal going in."

Wilson and Maddock were also invited to contribute to 1988's animated dinosaur feature, *The Land Before Time*, directed by Don Bluth. Although executive producer Spielberg had promised writers Judy Freudberg and Tony Geiss story credit and Stu Krieger screenplay credit – something he could do thanks to animation not being under the auspices of the Writers Guild – he was keen for Wilson and Maddock to be involved. "He said, 'George [Lucas] and I would love you to work on this, we think it has problems and we're not sure what we should do, but you're not going to get credit.' We said that was fine and that we'd always wanted to do animation, so we ended up doing way more work than we thought we were going to. At the end of it there's an odd 'thank you to Brent and Steve', which I thought was nice, he didn't have to do that."

Steve Wilson's abiding memory of his time at Amblin was that Spielberg "was just non-stop energetic. It's hard to describe the sheer joy of storytelling you got with the guy. We'd be in the middle of a meeting for *Batteries Not Included* and he'd say, 'You should go over and talk to the director of *Harry and the Hendersons*, I don't agree with this, that and the other thing that he's doing and maybe you guys can convince him.' We'd run up to Spielberg's office and be interrupted by a call from Clint Eastwood telling him he'd become mayor of Carmel, then we'd go back to our meeting and talk about *The Land Before Time* before a conference call with George Lucas and run back to our office and work on *Batteries*. It was great fun, like I imagined it being on the Disney lot when Walt was alive."

Maddock also recalled Spielberg's love of filmmaking: "I remember Spielberg sitting in his office reading *Short Circuit* and saying, 'You guys really know how to cut a scene.' That was thanks to all those years sitting at an upright Moviola cutting movies, knowing when to hit the handle. He was very open to ideas and entertained everything. He seemed a real down to earth guy."

GETTING ITCHY FEET

Thanks to the success of *Short Circuit*, it was inevitable that Hollywood would expect a sequel. With John Badham unavailable due to his work on the 1987 crime comedy, *Stakeout* ("I needed four more weeks to finish *Stakeout* and they said we can't wait, so I sadly had to pass on it"), a replacement director was found in Kenneth Johnson (TV's *The Incredible Hulk*, 1978–82), while Wilson and Maddock were again approached for screenwriting duties. "In those days it wasn't considered a good idea to do them," said Wilson. "It was particularly frowned upon to do your own sequel. Nancy said, 'Guys, nobody does this, sequels are for hacks.' The studio gave us freedom; they just wanted more Number Five."

Determined to keep creative control over the characters they had developed, Wilson and Maddock went ahead and crafted a new story for their favourite robot that relocated him to New York. "We knew the overall arc; people accepted he was alive so let's go all the way and make him a citizen," explained Steve Wilson. "Then we thought that if he's in the big city and naïve, then probably we're in a story where he's misled, a Huckleberry Finn/Tom Sawyer kind of stuff, and that's how the story of the bad guys tricking him into helping them evolved." Inevitably, Number Five's progress was impeded at every stage, while he made a new friend in a con artist, Fred Ritter (Michael McKean). Fisher Stevens returned as Ben and was upgraded to co-star thanks to the absence of Guttenberg and Sheedy.

Though *Short Circuit* had come together relatively seamlessly, the sequel wasn't as painless. With a first cut that ran to over two hours in length, too long for a fun romp, the writers were asked by Kenneth Johnson to bring it down to a reasonable running time by cutting scenes. "Kenny was very headstrong about how he was going to do this," said Wilson. "I don't want to imply that he told us to get out of his office, it was just 'I know what I'm doing' and that was the director's job. If you wrote a script at Barr Films you went and hung out on the set and directed or pulled cables and went into the editing suite. The film industry is very hierarchical and writers are at the bottom of the totem pole. You're not expected, nor is it desired, that you have anything to do with production."

Alongside their duties on *Short Circuit 2*, Wilson and Maddock were still working at Amblin seven days a week on a number of projects, becoming increasingly exasperated at being shut out of the moviemaking system. Regular discussions with Nancy Roberts led to the agent suggesting the pair become producers on their next film, allowing them more say in all aspects of its production. Aware that their success with *Short Circuit* meant executives would pay attention to new material, Roberts encouraged the writers to search through their files to bring her material that could be presented to studios.

"As you do with any client, you ask them what else they have once all the dust is settled," said Roberts. "You want to go forward with other original material and they had always said that they were filmmakers. I asked them to just bring in material once all the craziness of the production was moving forward, something that they could present to studios." As a result of sifting through old scraps of paper in late 1986, Steve Wilson pulled out the idea he'd had while working in the desert over a decade earlier, a story of giant underground worms terrorising humans in a remote location. Labelled *Land Sharks*, the idea filled just three-quarters of a page. "I said, 'Why don't you go and flesh this out?'" continued Roberts. "They had the stature and the heat to make original material valuable and viable as well as these high profile assignments that they were being sought after for, as anybody does who has a big movie."

Convinced that the industry would take notice of the concept, the agent was dismayed to find that it would take a lot longer to bring it to the screen than *Short Circuit*.

CHAPTER TWO
SELLING PERFECTION

In the space of five years, Steve Wilson and Brent Maddock had gone from unknown screenwriters to the subject of trade press speculation thanks to the success of *Short Circuit*. While they had no problem securing meetings with studios and executives, they wanted more input into the creative process, helping to steward their own features from inception to release. They also wanted to bring their long-time collaborator, Ron Underwood, back into the fold after he had been side-lined on *Short Circuit*.

With Wilson's dormant *Land Sharks* idea now back in contention thanks to Nancy Roberts' requirement for a new project to present to studios, the team decided that a horror film would be perfect material for a first-time feature director to make his mark. The original idea was a simple one: what would happen if someone became trapped on a rock in the middle of the desert and couldn't get off because giant creatures were under the sand? Maddock, Wilson and Underwood began discussing the kinds of plot points that might help them evolve such a concept, thinking about the kinds of books and movies that already existed and what hadn't been done before.

The trio took their inspiration from the era often held up as the golden age of big screen science fiction, the type of films they'd loved as teenagers. They began discussing an idea reminiscent of the classic fifties science fiction dramas, harking back to a time when a scientist or sheriff was the only person standing between humanity and certain destruction. Once the story had been outlined, Wilson and Maddock took over the writing of the script.

As the sci-fi buff of the writing team, Wilson had spent hours poring over comic books and watching B movies as a boy, while Maddock came out of a different artistic school and had written a book exploring the work of French director, Jacques Tati.

The script examined what would happen if a typical small town was attacked by unknown creatures and the scientists were replaced by two handymen whom the locals always hire to solve their problems. The idea developed during regular meetings: opening on the outskirts of Perfection, Nevada (population 14), the story quickly established the characters of Valentine McKee and Earl Bassett, two hardworking handymen dissatisfied with their careers and determined to leave for the neighbouring town of Bixby. Following an encounter with a visiting seismologist, Rhonda LeBeck, who is monitoring activity in the area, the pair discover the body of local resident, Edgar Deems, atop an electricity pylon, seemingly dead from dehydration.

Steve Wilson, Brent Maddock & Ron Underwood attend a *Beneath Perfection* script meeting © Ron Underwood

Val and Earl's attempts to leave Perfection are soon thwarted by the arrival of giant underground worms, dubbed Graboids by storeowner Walter Chang, that are hell bent on wiping out the townsfolk. Following the death of one of the creatures, the residents realise that Graboids track their prey by sensing their vibrations. The Perfectionites begin to fight back, with survivalists Burt and Heather Gummer killing one in their rec room before another is destroyed in the desert with the aid of Burt's explosives. The final creature is killed after Val lures it over the edge of a cliff, leaving the cowboy to commence a relationship with Rhonda.

Land Sharks was an old-fashioned science fiction adventure story infused with a liberal helping of scares. The quirky cast of characters who populated Perfection ensured the audience had plenty to root for, while a hefty dose of humour confirmed this wasn't a straightforward horror film.

While encouraging the pair to write their treatment, Nancy Roberts privately had questions about the viability of the package with Ron Underwood as director. Although Underwood had directed many successful educational films and a 1986 ABC Afterschool Special, *The Mouse and the Motorcycle*, Roberts was aware that these wouldn't interest executives who could take their pick of hotshot talent graduating from USC with exciting student films. The agent may have had her concerns, but the small team of Wilson, Maddock, Underwood and Roberts began hawking their concept and around Hollywood, hopeful that the combination of talent, memories of *Short Circuit*'s success and a detailed 25-page treatment would interest a studio.

However, as they talked about 30-foot long worms burrowing underground and terrorising a community in a sci-fi/horror/western/comedy, the quartet were met with various studio executives staring blankly back at them. Nobody was biting. "Now people talk about the *Tremors* tone, but at the time nobody knew what it was, it was too odd," said Wilson. "Ron would go to the pitch meetings and that was in part Nancy's elaborate plan to get the film made."

As the pitches continued without success into 1987, with the film's title briefly changed to *Graboid* before it was decided it might give away the surprise of the underground creatures too soon, another collaborator joined the project for a short period. Tony Garnett, a veteran English writer/producer of films such as Ken Loach's *Kes* (1969) and the BBC's acclaimed *Play for Today* strand, was working on the Warner Bros. lot, reporting to the studio's Executive Vice President of Worldwide Production, Lucy Fisher. "I thought it was original and interesting," recalled Garnett of the script that had now been retitled *Beneath Perfection*. "It only needed a few adjustments. I was only involved a little in development because movie people of all kinds interfere with writers to "help", only for their big boots to crush the creativity out of their work."

Beneath Perfection's mix of horror, science fiction and comedy was baffling to studios whose marketing teams relied on familiar hooks to sell their films to the public. Horror franchises such as *A Nightmare on Elm Street, Halloween* and *Friday the 13th* could be produced cheaply and sold on their similarities to each other, but Wilson and Maddock were trying something new, with their large-scale monsters potentially requiring a higher budget. While sandworms had featured in David Lynch's 1984 film, *Dune*, there were few similarities with those planned for *Beneath Perfection*. "A lot of people have asked us if *Dune* was an influence and other than worrying about it, it wasn't," Wilson said.

"I put it up to the studio, but they passed," continued Tony Garnett. "No one got it. They pass on most projects, especially the ones showing some originality. They promote the predictable and the hackneyed, something which doesn't interest me. I was philosophical. I liked Ron, got on well with him and thought he was original and very talented, attributes that guarantee a difficult time in Hollywood."

Their script treatment wasn't winning them any fans at the studios, but the team still felt they had something in *Beneath Perfection*. Sensing that the quirkiness of the tone wasn't coming through in the pitch document, Roberts decided to approach the problem from a different angle. "Brent and Steve write what are called "genre crunchers", hybrid horror/comedy, and I said to the guys, 'If you really want this to happen, you're going to have to write a script and do the same thing that was done with *Short Circuit*. If you believe in it, take the gamble.'"

The decision to invest their time in a non-commissioned *Beneath Perfection* script would be the tipping point for the project, allowing Wilson and Maddock's combination of horror and humour to come to the fore through their characters. "Here we were, highly paid Hollywood scriptwriters who could meet almost anybody in town and we had to write seven drafts of the script," said Wilson. "However, that's where we discovered the *Tremors* tone."

The pair worked from their respective homes in different parts of the Los Angeles area to craft their screenplay, Wilson in the San Fernando Valley and Maddock in Santa Monica. With email still a long way off, they would each write on their computers and talk regularly by phone. The writers outlined the script together, before Maddock wrote the first half and Wilson the second. They'd then meet up, put them together and read the script as a whole, before dealing with loose ends and tangents that occasionally arose.

The original script opened with a short sequence featuring Edgar Deems and Old Fred; in the finished film, Edgar is introduced halfway up an electricity pylon and Fred is seen tending his land. Edgar, described as "a weathered desert rat of a hermit", is walking his stressed donkey, Justine, around in circles outside his cabin. After a visit from Fred, who explains that his sheep are apparently being eaten by coyotes (even though there's no sign of any), Edgar places Justine in the barn. On closing the doors, Edgar hears strange noises inside, but finds the donkey has vanished. The scene was excised from the final film.

Beneath Perfection's tone continued to develop with each rewrite. "Steve is a monster movie fan, he was one of those kids who'd watch the film three times in a row," explained Maddock. "I had no interest in sci-fi and thought that if this idea is to work, and if I'm to have any interest in doing it, let's put real people in this movie, not the kind of people you see in all those cheesy sci-fi movies. Let's have some natural comedy and see what we can come up with."

Character introductions were kept to a bare minimum in the *Beneath Perfection* script, but Wilson and Maddock had a strong idea of who Valentine McKee and Earl Bassett were from the outset. The script introduced the "smart and good-looking" 25-year-old Val, who had "nevertheless managed to underachieve brilliantly". Despite successfully coasting through life and winding up "on the edge of civilisation", Val had recently wondered why he hadn't accomplished more. Earl, 43, was said to be "A good-ol' boy who has lived his life just like Val, drifting from job to job." Unlike Val, Earl had long ago worked out why he hadn't accomplished much and regularly attempted to offer life lessons to his friend and colleague.

The script may have been a work of fiction, but the writers were keen to cement it in reality wherever possible, including references to seismology, the branch of science concerned with the study of earthquakes. For their research, the pair approached Dr. Kate Hutton, staff seismologist at the California Institute of Technology (Caltech) in California, who had been friends with Steve Wilson while at Pennsylvania State University. "It was clear from the beginning that it was a monster movie and not a disaster movie, so there was no question of getting the seismology correct, the question wasn't really relevant," noted Hutton. "I did advise on the instrumentation. The Public Relations office was even okay with my working with them in my own private capacity, as long as the Caltech name was not used on a monster movie."

Though the science may not have stood up to too much scrutiny, Hutton was pleased with the end results. "It was a fun movie and the instrumentation looked very plausible. I did enjoy the Graboid being beat up on with a sensitive seismometer, that made me laugh. Did Rhonda inspire any seismology students? I haven't met anyone who will admit to it, but you never know."

The structure of the story remained consistent with each rewrite, though tonal changes resulted from the gentle push and pull between humour and drama that came from Wilson and Maddock's differing sensibilities. "Brent has a natural tendency towards comedy and I tend to make things more straight ahead," mused Wilson. "If I'm doing a monster movie I want some things to be genuinely scary, so there was give and take between the four of us, myself, Brent, Ron and Nancy, and in the last few drafts we were pulling comedy out."

The writers ended up leaving in only the humour that was rooted in the situation, with lines such as Burt Gummer's "You broke into the wrong rec room" resulting in a huge laugh, but remaining genuine in the sense of who he is and what he believes. They also maintained a strict rule that they wouldn't have characters spouting one-liners or indulging in slapstick, while the script avoided making fun of the monsters. Early drafts also included exchanges between characters that would later be excised, such as a moment in Walter Chang's Market when Val spots a decorative bleached-out cattle skull on the counter displaying a $29.95 price tag. Val points out to Chang that they sell them to him for just $3.

"After we had written a few drafts we spent a long time sitting with Ron storyboarding the movie," said Maddock. "We thought it was important to know what we were doing and what effects shots were needed. We took it to the studios with the proviso that we would produce it and that Ron, who had never directed a feature film, would be the director."

THE ROBERTS MASTER PLAN

Acutely aware that a proposition involving a first time feature director and a script about giant underground worms would be difficult to sell to a traditionally risk averse industry, Steve Wilson and Brent Maddock's agent, Nancy Roberts, set about creating a plan that would lead her to the offices of Hollywood's studio heads.

The first stage in her campaign was to find somebody who would give the studios some confidence in *Beneath Perfection* and steer it through the choppy waters from script to screen. By chance, one of Roberts' acquaintances, Amy Pascal (who would later go on to become the president of Columbia Pictures and co-chairman of Sony Pictures Entertainment), was working for producer Tony Garnett, who had been part of the early pitch process. After reading the script, Pascal asked if she could pass it to one of her friends, Ellen Collett, who in a stroke of luck, worked as a development executive for one of Hollywood's most respected producers, Gale Anne Hurd.

Hurd's career had begun as an executive assistant to legendary low-budget filmmaker Roger Corman, before moving up through the ranks at his New World Pictures production company. She later worked with fellow New World alumni and future husband, James Cameron, on 1984's *The Terminator*, leading to a number of successful collaborations including *Aliens* (1986) and *The Abyss* (1989). Hurd had a commitment to make films for $10m or under through her own company, Pacific Western, a budget that would work for *Beneath Perfection.*

Nancy Roberts didn't want a repeat of the *Short Circuit* situation, which had seen Ron Underwood effectively jettisoned from the project due to a lack of feature film experience. Roberts was convinced that the only way to keep him attached to *Beneath Perfection* as director was to find somebody with enough clout to convince the studios that he was the best – and only – person for the job. "I knew that Gale's deal was at Fox and if they passed she would have to go to Disney," said Roberts.

"I think Nancy got in touch with me," recalled Gale Anne Hurd. "They were looking for someone to 'Godmother' the project. Up until that time I had an overall deal at 20th Century Fox and then I was approached by Universal who said they wanted me to go and make films for them. I had a number of screenplays in development and they were looking for me to do films in the sci-fi, fantasy and horror genres, so this obviously fit with that mandate."

Hurd's agreement to come aboard the project was the boost Roberts needed. Studio concerns about Ron Underwood's lack of experience would be allayed by Hurd's presence, the unspoken agreement being that she held the reins and would step in to help if the new director couldn't handle the job. Her first step was to offer the script to Fox, who declined, with Disney the next on her list. "I knew that Disney's Michael Eisner would pass because he had two peeves; ice and dust," said Roberts. "If you were working on the agency side on a regular basis you kind of knew peoples' idiosyncrasies. Sure enough, he passed."

Meanwhile, Roberts was working hard to ensure the project would receive a sympathetic ear at Universal Studios, somewhere she felt would be a good fit due to Steven Spielberg being housed there and his prior connection to Wilson and Maddock. It also helped that Universal had a long history of creating classic monster films, stretching back to 1923's *The Hunchback of Notre Dame* and 1925's *The Phantom of the Opera*, while titles such as *Dracula, Frankenstein* (both 1931) and *The Invisible Man* (1933) had cemented the studio's reputation in the genre. "I also knew Casey Silver [vice president of production], Sean Daniel [president of production], and Tom Pollock [chairman]," said Roberts. "Before the script had even reached Gale, I had made a concerted effort to get to know Jim Jacks at Universal."

Described by Roberts as "a kind of curmudgeon but a quintessential movie-lover", Jim Jacks was renowned in Hollywood for his unrelenting support of filmmakers. Jacks had quit his career as a Wall Street analyst in the 1970s to become a screenwriter, before going on to take up executive positions at Universal and nurturing the careers of filmmakers such as the Coen brothers, Richard Linklater and Kevin Smith. At a time before sequels and remakes were so beloved of Hollywood, Jacks revelled in finding interesting projects and championing them to the studio. With his eclectic tastes in cinema, Nancy Roberts was sure Jacks would understand that *Beneath Perfection* was a modern spin on fifties sci-fi features.

"I knew Gale Anne Hurd and she had given us the script," said Jacks, who at the time was Universal Studios' senior vice president of production and head of acquisitions. "We really liked it; it was fun, funny and had the potential for scares. Steve and Brent had made *Short Circuit*, which had been a hit, and we felt they had a sense of what audiences wanted to see."

"Jim was notorious for pounding the desk and screaming at people," said Wilson. "He did exactly that and we finally got in to see the studio heads."

Following an early meeting in which he wasn't vocal enough about his plans for the film, Underwood's suitability for the task was questioned by Universal and Brent Maddock mooted as a potential replacement director. "To his credit the chairman of the studio, Tom Pollock, who had been an entertainment attorney before then, said, 'My client George Lucas would've been the same way in a meeting; we can give him another chance.'" said Underwood. "I met Jim before the meeting and he gave me some advice about how to jump around and up and down. I did, and it worked."

Tom Pollock may have "got" the script, but his primary concern revolved around what type of film it was. Knowing that both studios and audiences tend to segment films into defined genres, Pollock wondered if *Beneath Perfection* was a comedy adventure or a monster movie? "The answer was that it was both," laughed Maddock. "It's a comedy-adventure, it's a cowboy movie, more of an adventure film than a comedy but it's also a monster movie. I think that scares people away because everybody who's in a position of power in Hollywood is thinking, 'How do I market this movie?'"

By late 1988 *Beneath Perfection* had found a home at Universal Studios, with Jacks and Gale Anne Hurd now acting as powerful advocates for the film as it moved through the corporate machine. "It was Ron's first movie as director and we liked him and his take on it," explained Jacks. "I was willing to go with filmmakers who hadn't made many previous movies. It was a good group of people leading the movie and it had to be done for a price and they had a plan how to do it. It came down to the fact that they had a really good script."

As she had done on *Short Circuit*, Nancy Roberts negotiated a no rewrite clause for her clients' script, also ensuring that Underwood's contract guaranteed two weeks of shooting without being fired, no mean feat for an ambitious low-budget film helmed by a first time director. "She was very good at getting us all into secure places so that we could do our work without fear of what was going to happen," Underwood said. "You have to be able to create without a lot of fear or it starts inhibiting your work." Though she had orchestrated its progress, carrying out many of the tasks of a film producer, Nancy Roberts refused a producing credit on the film, concerned that as Wilson and Maddock's agent she could be perceived as interfering in her clients' careers.

Discussions next took place around *Beneath Perfection*'s budget, which was dependent upon the contractual requirements necessitated by Wilson, Maddock and Underwood's decision to retain more control over the project. Universal agreed that the film would be produced as a negative pickup rather than a traditional, in-house picture, meaning the filmmakers had more freedom over the script content, director and day-to-day production but that there was now more pressure on Gale Anne Hurd. The deal ensured Universal would pay the producers on the day the negative was delivered to them (hence the term "negative pickup")[1] and required that the filmmakers had to have a completion guarantee (an insurance policy for investors that the film would be completed on time and to budget), which they wouldn't have required as an in-house Universal film.

"We got a completion bond from Film Finances and they wanted to make sure we had another executive in production management involved," said Hurd. "I had meetings with Jim Brubaker, an outside consultant for them, who had to sign-off on budget. We ended up with a $10m budget and revisions had to be made to accommodate the shooting schedule and what we were able and not able to do on that budget." A side effect of the need to keep the budget at the $10m mark was that cost savings had to be found around the production, one major area being its crew budget. *Beneath Perfection* would need to become a non-union production.

The unionisation of Hollywood's below-the-line workers (those in craft and technical positions) has a long history stretching back to the end of the 19th century. By the late 1980s, unionised productions were under threat: while more than 90% of permits issued by the Los Angeles Film Office for film work in 1979 went to companies that only hired workers covered by union contracts, by January 1989 only 40% of permits were for unionised productions.[2] A combination of the film industry attracting more workers than it could comfortably employ, plus unions not opening their doors to this huge workforce, meant that any studio keen to keep production costs down (and to avoid dealing with unions sometimes perceived as difficult) could choose to make their movies with a non-union crew.[3]

Becoming a non-union feature meant crew salaries and overtime payments could be negotiated on a case-by-case basis, while regulations restricting the hiring of additional non-unionised crew on location could be overlooked. With Universal perhaps aware of a situation in early 1988 that had seen the Teamsters Local 385 union picket the comedy *Ernest Saves Christmas* (1988) as it filmed in Orlando, Ron Underwood recalled that shooting of *Beneath Perfection* began under the alternative title of *Dead Silence*.[4] "The studio wanted to keep the film hidden due to it being a non-union production, although they were involved at an arms-length distance with the picture being a negative pickup as opposed to a studio picture," said Underwood. "They wanted it to be under the radar."

In addition, rather than making the film with her Pacific Western company, Gale Anne Hurd created her No Frills Films production company for *Beneath Perfection/Dead Silence*.

CASTING THE PERFECTIONITES

Casting can make or break a film. Hire the right lead and a production could almost guarantee huge audiences, rave reviews and an Oscar nomination. Get it wrong and, no matter how strong the script, a film could be a flop. "I was incredibly involved in everything, from helping put the crew together to casting, because my name was on it," said Gale Anne Hurd. "Universal was not looking to Steve, Nancy or Ron to deliver the film, they were looking to me. I was much more involved than an executive producer would normally be."

As pre-production on *Beneath Perfection* edged closer, Universal was determined to keep an eye on the end product, aware that they had to market a film about giant underground worms to an unsuspecting public. One way to bring audiences through cinema foyers was to sell the film on the star names in the cast list. "We knew it was going to be good, and that's why we made it," Jim Jacks said. "But it was always going to be a tough movie to sell because when it comes down to it, the film is about man-eating giant worms and when you say that people say, 'Maybe I'll catch it on video.'"

Casting agent Pam Dixon was hired to compile a strong roster of talent for the producers' consideration. Dixon knew she needed to populate the small town of Perfection with some big personalities and worked closely with Gale Anne Hurd during the casting process. "Gale was a very big producer and that's a very important piece of the puzzle," said Dixon. "She had done *Aliens* and people knew who she was, she had a great track record and she was very involved. When people spoke to Ron Underwood, Gale was part of the conversation."

Casting *Beneath Perfection* was Underwood's first time dealing with the politics of studios; he soon witnessed how easy it was for a film to go astray because of pressure from agents and studios to use their clients. "You have to be careful not to get pulled into casting the wrong people for your film because of some prior relationship, or something else that's going on with the studio."

For the part of "smart and good looking" Valentine McKee, Ron Underwood's first choice was a 22-year-old actor who was making his name in teen comedies. "I met with John Cusack first and I remember him saying he had just worked with a first-time director and that he didn't want to do that again right away. That was *Say Anything...* with Cameron Crowe, which became a big hit for them."

Pam Dixon knew it was important to fill the cast with established actors who could take the pressure off the first time director, giving him as little to worry about as possible. During the first casting meeting, she mentioned Kevin Bacon's name for the role of Val. Philadelphia-born Kevin Norwood Bacon had left home aged 17 to pursue an acting career in New York, leading to theatre roles and a film debut in 1978 comedy, *National Lampoon's Animal House*. Bacon would cement his horror genre credentials with a part in the 1980 slasher film, *Friday the 13th*, before taking on a number of supporting roles in other features and the lead in the fondly-remembered dance drama, *Footloose* (1984).

Dixon's next step would usually have been to send Bacon a copy of the director's previous feature films, but with Ron Underwood she only had shorts to pass on to the actor. As the casting director knew Bacon personally from New York theatre, she suggested sending him the script before bringing him to LA to meet with the director and Gale Anne Hurd. Soon after the meeting he was offered the role and accepted. "When I met with Kevin he was very supportive, totally got the tone of the film and I really felt like we made the right choice," Underwood said.

"I was a little reticent," laughed Kevin Bacon, with reference to the underground worm script being presented to him by his agent. "But there was something fun about that character and the relationship between those two guys, grown men who were kind of losers. When you have two losers who are put into the situation of having to rise to a level of heroism, I think it can be kind of fun. So I was really taking a flyer on it, but I can't say I was feeling, 'Oh wow, this is the one.'"

"It was a nail biter to get him to commit," recalled Nancy Roberts. "That was the beginning of the real heavy numbers crunching in the studios and how they would justify the budget for each film. They give you something called "breakage", which means the budget can't change, but if they want a certain level of cast member to justify their marketing, and the budget, [they'll pay more]. So a person of Kevin Bacon's level was really critical."

Universal Studios had their own ideas for the casting of Earl Bassett, with James Garner (*Maverick*, 1994) the first actor to be recommended for the role. "There was a lawsuit going on by Garner against the studio because of his television show *The Rockford Files*," said Underwood. "He was suing for profits or profit participation and Universal wanted us to offer him the part of Earl to help clear up that lawsuit. We didn't know why they wanted him so badly, but it shows you the kind of politics involved and remaining true to what is right for the film is very difficult." Other names considered for the part of Earl were Michael Caine[5] and actor Louis Gossett, Jr. (*An Officer and a Gentleman*, 1982), with Dixon sending a copy of the script via the latter's agent, only for them to decline on his behalf. Gale Anne Hurd later discovered Gossett had never been shown the script.

"We got Kevin quite quickly," Jim Jacks said. "Fred Ward came into it later. We had a couple of other people we went to first and Fred ended up doing a great job and we were very happy with him, but he wasn't what you would call a big box office name at the time."

Born Freddie Joe Ward in San Diego, California, Fred Ward spent the early part of his acting career in Italy, making his screen debut in Roberto Rossellini's 1972 mini-series, *The Age of the Medici*. Roles in a number of high profile features, including *Escape from Alcatraz* (1979) and *Southern Comfort* (1981), led to him being cast in cult action movie, *Remo Williams: The Adventure Begins* (1985). "With Fred, I'd just been such a fan of his work," said Underwood. "When he said yes it was perfect, but I didn't know how perfect it would be until we got the two of them on set together and started rehearsing."

"I loved Fred," recalled Kevin Bacon. "We made friends right away and he's a fascinating guy, kind of eccentric. He's really into interesting philosophies and is very well read. I never read books and he was constantly talking about books. He was obsessed with Django Reinhardt and was studying really hard at playing jazz guitar."

"The character actors in that film were well known to the acting community but not necessarily the public," said Dixon. "The person nobody had seen for a while was Kevin Bacon. After *Tremors* he didn't stop working; it kind of reminded people about him." With the two leads in place, the casting of Perfection's other residents now got underway. "We decided if we could get an ensemble that was interesting we'd do that," said Jim Jacks. "That's how people like Reba McEntire ended up in the movie, she was wonderful."

Born in McAlester, Oklahoma, singer Reba Nell McEntire released her first single in 1976, finally securing a Top 20 hit in 1979. By 1988, McEntire had released her thirteenth album through MCA (another Universal company) and was considered one of country music's biggest stars. The singer was being considered for the role of Heather Gummer, one half of the married survivalist couple who, according the script had "settled in Perfection to await the coming apocalypse."

"The interesting person for me was Reba McEntire, who had never done a movie," Pam Dixon said. "I started my career working for Robert Altman and I'm a very big music person, so in a lot of the films I've cast I've incorporated someone from the art or music world. The great thing about Reba was that she was on the Universal label, so they loved that idea."

"My agent sent me the script," said McEntire. "Half way through reading it I called him and said I loved it. I had to audition twice, once for the writers and once for the producers. I made two trips to LA for that." Ron Underwood was impressed with McEntire's outgoing personality during the audition process. "She had a great attitude character-wise, had grown up with guns and wasn't afraid of that kind of world and life. She responded well to the character and it became clear that she would be a real asset to the film."

Each of the actors who read for the role of Heather had to handle a deactivated shotgun during the audition, something McEntire managed with conviction. "She's a true redhead and when she came in she was made up as a country music star,"

Steve Wilson said. "Ron asked if she was comfortable as a survivalist and looking more natural and she said, 'There are a lot of freckles under here honey, but if that's what you want.'"

"They were worried how I would react to not being able to wear make-up or having my hair fixed," admitted McEntire. "I told them I was fine with no make-up and a ponytail and that I'd grown up on a working cattle ranch so was used to being hot and dirty."

At the same time as his on-screen wife was being auditioned, actor Michael Gross was being short-listed for the small-yet-memorable role of her husband, Burt. The Chicago-native's acting credits stretched back to 1975 TV movie, *A Girl Named Sooner,* but it was his seven-year stint on the NBC (part of Universal) comedy, *Family Ties* (1982–89) that had brought him to the attention of US audiences. Gross was keen to challenge stereotypes, having been a regular visitor in millions of viewers' living rooms every week for seven years. "I think a script had been delivered to me and there was also some indication of the scenes we'd be covering," he said. "They were rather short but sweet. Burt comes in, does his business and he goes out. It's a plummy part and I thought to myself, 'Oh my God, this is the role, he's just so wonderfully outrageous.'"

"Michael Gross I really had my doubts about because I only knew him from *Family Ties*," explained Underwood. "It was such a different kind of character. I remember him jumping up on the desk and making me believe that there were going to be monsters coming out of the floor of my office very shortly. I thought 'This guy is amazing', the level of commitment he was willing to make."

"I present something very different, perhaps more civilised than Burt Gummer when I walk in a door, more the attorney or the senatorial type," said Gross. "I thought 'Wow, chance takers, how much fun is that? A major motion picture and these guys are willing to try something different.' Ron claims I was on the top of his desk, pretending to shoot monsters with an imaginary gun and I swear I don't remember this. I think his memory's faulty and he thinks mine is, but so much for first-hand accounts on what happened in a certain room at any given time. That's why I don't trust eyewitnesses in court."

Playing seismologist Rhonda LeBeck was Mississippi-born actress, Finn Carter, who had recently enjoyed a three-year stint on the CBS daytime drama, *As the World Turns* (1956–2010) and was appearing in a staging of Terrence McNally's *Up in Saratoga* at the Old Globe in San Diego in March 1989. Carter regularly took the train to Los Angeles for auditions, one of which was for *Beneath Perfection.* "I was on, under and around the table," recalled Carter with reference to the energetic audition process, "and I didn't know there was any humour or comedy in the script. I took it deadly seriously and maintained that for most of the shoot; at one point we were filming something and I turned to Kevin and said, 'Are we in the same movie?' I didn't get it at all."[6]

Carter may have been bemused, but her audition was strong enough for the producers to fight with the studio for her to be cast. "Finn was not really well known, but we fought for her because we thought she just so embodied Rhonda and her sensibilities," Underwood said. "It probably wasn't who the studio envisioned in that part, they would have liked some unbelievably gorgeous blonde, but we really fought for Rhonda being the right person."

The role of Perfection's Earth mother, Nancy Sterngood, went to actress Charlotte Stewart, best known to audiences at the time for playing Eva Beadle Simms in the long-running NBC drama, *Little House on the Prairie* (1974–83). "We had a chat about the character and what she would be like. She's kind of an old hippie and single mom living in the desert doing her sculpting and pottery. I had to go through two more auditions with the executive producers at Universal." After she was cast, Stewart had an encounter with another member of the production team. "I was going to Universal for a table reading and there was this very nice lady wearing black and white striped shoes, and I looked at her and said 'The Wicked Witch?' and she said 'Occasionally', and it was Gale Hurd!"[7]

Pam Dixon cast her net wider to find Nancy's young daughter, Mindy, with eight-year-old actress Ariana Richards arriving to the audition with 50 other girls. "Getting the role of Mindy started my tradition of playing a young person who becomes a survivor while being attacked by monsters," laughed Richards, with reference to her future role of Lex in Steven Spielberg's 1993 film, *Jurassic Park*. "The producers met me and asked, 'Ariana, can you pogo stick?' Being the consummate imposter that every actor needs to be, even at age eight, I said, 'Absolutely'. That afternoon my mom took me to buy a pogo stick."

Actor Tony Genaro came to auditions fresh from success in Robert Redford's 1988 film, *The Milagro Beanfield War*. "I knew someone who had read for one of the roles and did not get it; he'd read the script and thought of me for Miguel. He told the casting people and they invited me in. When I walked through the door Ron Underwood said, 'Oh, you're the guy from *The Milagro Beanfield War*, the role's yours.'"

The part of Perfection's resident teenager, Melvin Plug, went to 15-year-old Bobby Jacoby, who today acts under his real name, Robert Jayne. "I was kind of a terror when I was a kid. I was shooting *Meet the Applegates* when one of the crew members said he was doing a movie with a rotten kid in it and that I'd be perfect for it. I came back to LA and met with Ron Underwood for about five minutes and he said, 'Wanna do it?' Next thing I know I'm with Kevin Bacon and we're shooting this movie."

Cast as the short-lived Dr. Jim Wallace, veteran actor Conrad Bachmann was a familiar face from TV series such as the 1970s *Mission: Impossible* and 1980s soap *Falcon Crest* when he auditioned for *Beneath Perfection*. "When I first went into the reading and got to the part where the Graboid was eating me I started screaming and went to the floor," said Bachmann, who then received a callback to meet Brent Maddock, Steve Wilson, Ron Underwood and Gale Anne Hurd. "Just before I went in the casting director said, 'When you get to the part where you die screaming can you do me a favour; I've got a really severe headache today, so can you not scream?' That was the whole role!

So I went in and got to the point where the Graboid was eating me; I was due to scream and I had to say, 'Excuse me, the casting director told me not to scream because she had a headache.'"[8]

Chinese actor, Victor Wong, known to film audiences for appearances in 1986's *Big Trouble in Little China* and 1987's *The Last Emperor*, was cast as canny storeowner, Walter Chang. "He was a wonderful actor," recalled Underwood. "In the script, the character was named "Fandam", which is Vietnamese. Victor said, 'You know, we should come up with a Chinese name, since I'm not Vietnamese.'"

The small cast was completed by Richard Marcus as Nestor; Bibi Besch as Megan, the wife of Dr. Jim; Michael Dan Wagner as Old Fred; Sunshine Parker as Edgar; with John Goodwin and John Pappas as road workers, Howard and Carmine.

SOUNDS OF THE UNDERGROUND

Another member of the production brought aboard before shooting commenced was composer and songwriter, Ernest Troost, who had worked with executive producer, Ginny Nugent, at New World Pictures. "It was one of those scripts that you just couldn't stop turning the pages; it was fun and had just enough tension to it," said Troost. "I really love character movies and for me that was the strong suit of this movie that took it away from just being another horror or sci-fi movie. The characters were so down-to-earth and funny but they weren't overly broad."

The mix of genres informed discussions between Troost and the film's producers. "I suggested that for the characters we go in the direction of rootsy blues and use the orchestra for the horror or action scenes. The roots ensemble included drums, a couple of guitars, a reed organ, a harmonica and bass guitar. It had a little bit of funkiness to it so that it's not slapstick comic but it has that effect on screen of being kind of light."

BUILDING THE GRABOIDS

Used to performing most of the production roles on their educational films, from building the sets to cranking the camera, Steve Wilson, Brent Maddock and Ron Underwood found themselves working with a larger crew on *Beneath Perfection*. From location scouts to dirt wranglers, assistant editors to key grips, hundreds of people made up the complex eco-system.

A major consideration for the production team was how to bring the creatures at the heart of the film to life. Cinematic history is littered with unconvincing monsters that have left audiences laughing rather than screaming, usually thanks to a lack of budget and time. Everybody involved with *Beneath Perfection* knew the credibility of the film lay in the believability of their creatures and from the outset they opted to use practical model effects rather than computer-generated (CG) effects shots.

CG had its roots in computer animation experiments of the 1970s, with 1977's *Star Wars* revolutionising the use of visual effects thanks to the work of Industrial Light and Magic (ILM) and introducing audiences to 3D computer animation in the Trench-Run Briefing sequence.[9] The 1980s saw the increase of CG, with the Genesis Effect in 1982's *Star Trek II: The Wrath of Khan* notable for being cinema's first entirely computer-generated sequence and the same year's *Tron* making use of 3D graphics for its backgrounds.[10]

CG was still an expensive proposition for a $10m film in 1988, with *Beneath Perfection*'s production sandwiched between the release of James Cameron's $70m *The Abyss* (still in production in late 1988) and 1991's $100m *Terminator 2: Judgment Day*, both of which revolutionised the industry and shared a producer with the former in Gale Anne Hurd. Aware of the rise of CG, Steve Wilson was still keen to use practical model effects and stop-motion animation to bring the Graboids to life. "There were many things that would have made CG impossible on our budget, not least that it was before they developed all the particle simulation technology which allows them to do water, dust and all the chaotic things. We knew that the film was going to be all dust all of the time."

Beneath Perfection's behind the scenes roster of talent benefitted from Gale Anne Hurd's lengthy list of prior connections, mainly stemming from her work with Roger Corman and James Cameron. Practical effects designers, Alec Gillis, who had worked on Corman's *Battle Beyond the Stars*, and Tom Woodruff Jr., who had been part of the effects crew on Cameron's *The Terminator,* joined *Battle Beyond the Stars*' miniature effects experts, Robert and Dennis Skotak, to create the Graboids.

Gillis and Woodruff had recently branched out from their positions at Stan Winston's legendary effects studio to form their own company, Amalgamated Dynamics, Inc (ADI). Their first project for ADI was an effects-heavy TV series called *Monsters* (1988–90), and around the same time the pair were called in for a meeting with Hurd. "We later heard that she had originally gone to Stan Winston to do the creature stuff, and he had her call us," said Gillis. "We got off to a good start because of that reference."

One problem faced by Gillis and Woodruff was that their new company had no studio to house vital equipment such as spray booths, a foam room or giant ovens in which they could cure their latex creations. Rather than admitting they were still searching for premises, ADI met Underwood, Maddock and Wilson at a variety of Los Angeles restaurants to discuss the project, always under the pretence that it was "more convenient" for all involved.

ADI had gleaned brief descriptions of the Graboids from the script and were aware they had "spines on their body that would help propel them" and that "their mouth opened like a grotesque flower". Settling on the idea that the creatures would resemble giant sandworms, Gillis and Woodruff looked to nature for inspiration, poring through reference materials and sketching elements they felt best represented their shared vision of a creature that could have been of either alien origin or natural evolution.

As the film's producers picked out portions of different sketches, ADI reworked different combinations and added more ideas, finally agreeing on a design that they sculpted in clay before moulding in fiberglass, with the skin cast from latex. Woodruff and Gillis built their own bespoke oven, heated to 200° for six hours, to cure the skin of the 8-feet tall Graboid head. "In some places we'd also use a nylon rod that was formed into hoops," Woodruff said. "The rod gave a nice bounce to it and the weight of the rubber would create this bouncy quality that looked kind of fleshy. In our minds we imagined it like a sea lion coming ashore, all that blubbery shake."

ADI had not yet progressed to working with hydraulics or computer-controlled systems so every part of the Graboid body was hand-leveraged, with long pipes protruding from the back of the head. Built on pivots and levers, the operators could move the head and open the jaw and side mandibles with cable controls when the creatures emerged from the ground. Due to the shape of the Graboid, the levers required to move the mouth were all inside the head. "There was a big open section right behind the beak and we would have all our mechanisms in there," said Woodruff. "Sometimes when a creature would burst out of the ground and then flop down, depending on how they'd positioned the camera, we could hide the crew behind the creature itself by getting down low and ducking out of camera view."

Despite the complex build, the goal was to have a system that could be operated very simply by a small team. The operators had built one main "hero" creature, with a fully operating mouth and mandibles that had to be moved from place to place. To complete the effect of the creature bursting through the dirt, the plan was for the art department to dig a pit at each location that would allow four or five men to be sunk down into the ground with dust masks and safety goggles, closely followed by the Graboid head. They would then shore up the sides with wood to make everything safe.

Woodruff and Gillis were determined to perfect their full-scale creatures, but they were also aware that a lot of on-screen performance would be carried out by the visual effects supervisor, Robert Skotak, and his quarter-scale miniature models. "We started our company, 4-Ward Productions, with the film," explained Skotak, who worked closely with his brother, Dennis, and partner, Elaine. "We got a call from Gale and she asked if we'd be interested in working on this film on the miniatures. Elaine and I were driving around after our meeting with Gale and said, 'Why are we always doing these films for other people? Why don't we form a corporation and do this film ourselves?' We bought some tables and rented a space at this huge building in Atwater Village."

ADI and 4-Ward worked on the principle that the majority of sequences requiring a Graboid to break through the ground would be a filmed as a miniature. If the creature had to interact with people, it was filmed full-size. ADI planned to take simpler full-scale puppets on location to get the minimum shots needed alongside the actors, before embellishing them with tabletop miniatures created by 4-Ward.

With their cast and crew falling into place, the producers turned their attention to finding somewhere to lay foundations for the town of Perfection, Nevada.

CHAPTER THREE
FILMING TREMORS

Founded in New York on 30 April 1912 by German émigré "Uncle" Carl Laemmle and a team of partners, The Universal Film Manufacturing Company soon became Hollywood's biggest studio, known in the early years for shooting hundreds of low-budget westerns, horror pictures and melodramas on the 230-acre Universal backlot in Los Angeles.

Audiences couldn't get enough of the western in the silent era, with the likes of Hoot Gibson and Jack Hoxie starring in action packed productions such as *Rustlers* and *Told in the Hills* (both 1919). It was in 1920 that studio executives won their fight for a change to the locations used in their cowboy pictures, as most of them were still filmed on Hollywood sets. Granted larger budgets by Laemmle, producers could now take their crews 60 miles north to Lone Pine, where they were surrounded by the stunning Alabama Hills, located near the eastern slope of the Sierra Nevada Mountains in the Owens Valley.[1]

Lone Pine had been a favourite location for film and TV crews for decades – *A Star is Born* (1939), *Gunga Din* (1939) and *Bad Day at Black Rock* (1955) all shot sequences there – but by the late 1980s its glory days had waned. In late 1988, *Beneath Perfection* director Ron Underwood added Lone Pine to a short list of possible locations for his desert-set horror comedy, boarding a studio-rented private jet alongside co-writer/producer Brent Maddock, line producer Ginny Nugent and associate producer Ellen Collett to scout Red Rock Canyon, Nevada; Moab, Utah; Tucson, Arizona; and Lone Pine, California. In the end, Lone

The town of Perfection was built in the shadow of the Sierras

Pine won out thanks to the stunning rock formations at the foot of the Sierras.

The Sierras were also home to Owens Lake, a section of dry land that had once been a source of water for a thriving farming community before it was diverted into the Los Angeles Aqueduct in 1913, causing the lake to desiccate. "There's a layer of arsenic that was left over from that and I can just imagine what we were breathing each time it was windy, which was a lot," said Gale Anne Hurd. "Half the time catering served lunch we'd be eating the sand along with our food."

Cinematographer Alexander Gruszynski, who had worked with Hurd and Ginny Nugent on 1988's *Bad Dreams*, had been briefed that the film should have the look of a classic western. "Instead of these two cowboy types, Fred Ward and Kevin Bacon, fighting your classic western villains, they're fighting those worms. And of course there's also an element of comedy there."

TOWN PLANNING

The person responsible for overseeing the design of Perfection was Ivo Cristante, who had moved to Los Angeles from Canada in the late 1970s and been interviewed for a job at education specialists, Barr Films, by Ron Underwood. Recalling that Underwood had originally turned him down due to a lack of skills, Cristante arrived at Universal a decade later to discuss the role of production designer on *Beneath Perfection*. "The first thing I said when I got through the door was, 'Well Ron, you may not remember me but I have some skills now.' I think it was because of my enthusiasm for the script I got the job."

Cristante created his concept drawings for the town in Los Angeles before moving to Lone Pine in February 1989, where he set up a drafting table in his motel room due to the lack of space for a traditional foreman's shack. "We were kind of like the bastard child of Universal at that time because they were putting all their efforts into Sam Raimi's *Darkman*," said Cristante, with reference to the cult 1990 film that paid homage to the studio's 1930s horror output. "They let us alone and we didn't cause them any problems: it was, 'Shut up and make a movie.' We were also trying to stay away from filming at the studio because we were worried we would be attracting the union; we were a little bit on the lam, so to speak."

Plans were soon underway for the building of Perfection close to Lone Pine, but there was a hitch with the location selected for the construction of the buildings. At a meeting with the Bureau of Land Management, it emerged that they controlled all the open land and that it was protected. "They said, 'How are you going to do your construction, because you can't touch any of these plants out here?'" said Underwood. "All these tumbleweeds were out there and we couldn't use any kind of equipment or vehicles, let alone put a road in to town."

The shock of losing their chosen location led to a frantic search for private property that could be used to erect the town, with the producers and Ivo Cristante settling on an area near the town of Olancha. Their territory was marked by a few small buildings grouped along Highway 395, with a turnoff leading up to a borax mine. Perfection was built on two empty parcels of land. "In the east you had the entire crest of the Sierras, which was breathtaking," Cristante said. "In the morning you could stand in the middle of the flats and watch the shadow of the mountains creep along the ground beside you; the only thing that would drag me out of bed is knowing that that phenomenon occurred. It was beautiful, the taste of the air, the cleanness, the dew on everything that lasted all of 45 seconds before it evaporated."

Cristante had initially assumed that the remote location would mean a lack of materials and provisions, though he soon learned to trust in local resources by sourcing welders, carpenters and painters from towns such as Keeler, on the edge of Owens Lake, while materials such as lumber were also bought within the area.

Now that Steve Wilson and Brent Maddock had achieved their goal of having more responsibility over a feature, Nancy Roberts made sure they were involved in all aspects of production, with

Wilson also becoming *Beneath Perfection*'s second unit director. "On the set there was [a] huge commitment to it, and you could feel that it had a really good energy," noted Roberts. "But it was also a really tense energy because the budget was extremely tight and it was extremely ambitious. That meant if an explosion didn't rig correctly you waited a half a day, a half a day that money is churning."

While the majority of horror films take place at night and in enclosed locations, most of the action in *Beneath Perfection* was set to occur in broad daylight in the middle of the desert, a concept that caused major concerns for cinematographer, Alexander Gruszynski. "You go into a movie with the understanding that it's budgeted to shoot for a finite number of days, which you cannot extend. Usually you schedule a film in such a way that when you lose daylight you can continue shooting inside. We had very few opportunities to do that because of where the story takes place, with few interiors."

An early arrival to Lone Pine was production coordinator, Cristen Carr Strubbe, whose job it was to take care of many daily tasks required on the set of *Beneath Perfection*. "I went up with the art department while we were building Perfection. I arranged to have electricity brought up there, phone lines (this is before cell phones), took care of the paperwork and had the film shipped back to the lab. I also had to make sure that when the crew came up they had places to stay."

Strubbe was responsible for getting not only the actors and crew on set, but also the Graboids. Aware that in many ways the creatures *were* the movie, she spent much of her time dealing with the transportation of the full size Graboids from the mechanical effects house in Los Angeles up to Lone Pine, before sending them back down for any repairs. "I had to hire a kid whose sole job was to ride in the back of a 40-foot truck for three-and-a-half hours each way with the Graboid. Whenever they'd take breaks in the truck he would call from a pay phone and tell me what was going on. We used to liken it to Bruce the shark from *Jaws* that Spielberg always talks about, although the animatronic guys were simply amazing."

"I think we probably had two or maybe three bodies," said creature designer, Alec Gillis, who ensured there were back-ups for the main hero body. "We didn't have a huge budget on the film, so we had to be careful with manpower; we didn't want to overbuild things that couldn't be operated on set. A lot of it was miniature, which is cheaper to do and you get more dynamic movement out of it."

Transporting the Graboids was a challenge, but filming them proved to be even more of an issue for Gruszynski. "You never knew if they were going to work. It took forever to put them underneath the surface and they were only good for one take because after the first take you had to clean up all the pistons as the dirt and the sand got into them. All that took time and I had no control over that aspect of it. I was just looking at the sun getting lower and lower and that was really hard. It remains the most stressful movie I've ever made."

"It was all an adventure, being on set and seeing the worms for the first time," recalled the film's youngest star, Ariana Richards. "They were not very scary in real life, but I got the sense that the special effects guys created it as they went along. Depending on what a scene might call for, they would manipulate the worm and drag it through the sand or dump goo and special effects blood on it."

While Cristen Carr Strubbe organised transport and construction, Lise Romanoff arrived on set to coordinate the various special effects teams who were collaborating on the film. "They brought me in to handle the $3m worth of special effects; we all had to keep on budget because there was just no room for error. It was a negative pickup so there was only so much money to work from, with no deep independent pockets in case they went over budget. We spent so much time on the coordination, getting everything all lined up."

* * *

Beneath Perfection's cast was also preparing for life in the desert, with Michael Gross the first to arrive as he transferred directly from the set of *Family Ties* following the end of production on the series and a wrap party at LA's Gene Autry Museum, a venue devoted to western art and lore. "Autry was there that night with his wife," said Gross. "The very next day I drove up to Lone Pine to report for duty. By that time I had shaved off Steven Keaton's beard and kept the moustache for Burt."

Along with Burt's military look, Gross wore an Atlanta Hawks baseball cap ("They had a deal where they sent us what seemed like a million caps") and ensured he had the correct reading material to help him prepare for life as a survivalist, swotting up on books including *Improvised Munitions* and *The Survivalist's Retreat*. "Burt was just so wonderful because at his core he was always thinking Armageddon, it was going to be nuclear or biological and he was going to be ready. From the very beginning I caught what they wanted, which was a marvellously comic paranoia."

Tony Genaro was working on the film within a month of being cast and arrived in Lone Pine after the town set had been built. "Because of the rattlesnakes in the area they had to make sure that the actors weren't going to be attacked, so we had rattlesnake wranglers. I had just gotten off this very artsy film and when I saw the Graboids for the first time I thought, 'Oh my God, what have I gotten myself into?'"

Cast as Heather early on in pre-production, Reba McEntire was still under the impression that actor James Garner had been awarded the role of Earl Bassett when she got to the Lone Pine set. "I said, 'Where's James Garner?" They said, 'What do you mean, James Garner?' I said, 'They told me it was going to be Kevin Bacon and James Garner.' 'Oh, no, he pulled out a long, long time ago.' Nobody told me, and that was a huge disappointment. I didn't know who Fred Ward was. Met him – liked him – but James Garner, good lord, I'd been a big fan of him since *Maverick*!"[2]

For McEntire, the filming of *Beneath Perfection* was in addition to her already hectic weekend touring schedule. "I flew commercially to LAX and took a puddle jumper to Inyokern,

California. Then I'd drive to Lone Pine, get to the hotel and sleep for a few hours before they came to take me to the set out in the desert. The "star" trailer was anything but glamorous and I did more sitting around than acting. It was cold in the morning, hot in the middle of the day and then cold again when the sun went down. My first words to film were 'Stinks too', and that was it for the day; I jumped up and down that I had finally been filmed in a movie."

Co-star Tony Genaro described McEntire as "very salt of the earth, and talented. I remember Finn Carter said to Reba, 'Reba, now what kind of name is that, that sure is a strange name.' Reba said, 'And Finn's just a regular ol' name? Every other girl's named Finn?' I said to Reba, 'I know you make millions of dollars in concerts and I understand the contract on this film, because pretty much everyone's getting about the same, how much money are you losing doing this movie?' She said, 'Tony, you don't wanna know.' She was a hoot."

SHOOTING IN LONE PINE

Beneath Perfection's initial shoot lasted for 54 days, longer than Ron Underwood had spent on any previous production. "When I started I thought I'd have a little more time than on those short films, but for what we were trying to do it was just as hard as the shortest shoot I'd ever had. Gale Anne Hurd gave me confidence as she was able to say, 'You've got good stuff here, don't worry about the fact that it's not always working the way you want it to, you're getting good footage.'"

Said Hurd, "Huge credit to Ron, this was a movie where the tone was incredibly difficult to get right. You want it to be fun but you want to care about the characters and be invested in them, laughing and afraid for them, but not laughing at them. That was one of the reasons it was so difficult to get it made, because people wanted either a horror film or a comedy, not a little bit of both."

Before his arrival on set, Underwood had planned his camera angles and was prepared for the searing heat of the desert sun, which he was sure would fatigue his cast and crew. Lone Pine had other plans. Rather than soaring, the temperatures plummeted, with the first day of principal photography affected by the sight of snow in front of the cameras. "You could go into your trailer for your break and it'd be nice and sunny, you'd come out and it'd be snowing," said Tony Genaro. "They'd whip up a huge tent and light it like a bright, sunshiny day, but it was snowing outside."

"The conditions were ghastly," concurred Steve Wilson. "We lived through temperatures below freezing to over 100° with snow, rain and dust storms. No phone worked on the set except one radio phone."

The water tower and Chang's Market are erected
© Ivo Cristante

Extreme weather also caused problems for Ivo Cristante and the construction team as they built Perfection's houses and shacks either side of Cactus Flats Road in Olancha. Mini-tornadoes known as dust devils would regularly rip through town, with one storm picking up Chang's Market and moving it 20-feet, forcing Cristante to devise a method of moving it back into place. He settled on a rod with a handle at the top and a helix at the bottom that was screwed into the sand. "All of our sets were tied off until the camera needed them and then we'd untie them, shoot it and then tie them back on again, almost like tying the reins of a horse."

Working at high altitude in the mountain rock formations hampered the construction crew's progress, as they took time to acclimatise to the change in elevation. Unable to work at the same pace as in the lower part of the valley, precious time was lost as they fought to combat altitude sickness.

Shooting in the town of Perfection offered the crew an opportunity to hide camera equipment behind buildings, but when the action moved to wide open desert things became more complicated. One of the most exciting aspects of the location was the ability to turn the camera 360°, but the crew soon discovered that at least 180° was needed to hide their trucks and equipment. "What slows you down is that whenever you need to turn around, you see the whole area that now needs to be moved to the other end of the angle you just photographed," said Alexander Gruszynski. "You had to move all the equipment there, then we would shadow things back-and-forth and stay in smaller vehicles and vans."

The vast amount of sand in each shot meant that the cinematographer had to work hard to ensure the landscape appeared pristine, with little sign of human presence. "Imagine that I have a crew of 150 people and I'm trying to photograph the ground where supposedly nobody has ever put their foot on," explained Gruszynski. "We had people whose only job was to brush off any prints or any signs of human interaction. There was a lot of brushing involved in the film."

Due to the tight schedule, location issues and varying weather conditions, tensions sometimes flared on set. "One time we had trampled all the vegetation as we had built the town and the dressers had spent a day and a half putting it all back together," said Ivo Cristante. "As they were finishing up, this fellow with a tractor drove right through it." After shouting at the perpetrator, physical effects coordinator, Art Brewer, Cristante suddenly found himself facing the man, who had ripped off his glasses, put up his fists and was preparing to battle it out in the middle of Perfection. To both their relief, the crew pulled them back from the brink before a punch was thrown.

Safety was a priority on set, but that didn't stop accidents occurring elsewhere, as Ron Underwood discovered on the first day of the shoot. As he left his motel and drove along Lone Pine's main street, the director spotted a member of the props team hanging over the edge of his truck, attempting to start the engine. "As we were passing, his truck started moving, with him hanging in that position and it crashed into a wall. I look back on it as the beginning of being in total shock throughout the making of that film."

As production coordinator Cristen Carr Strubbe prepared to leave *Beneath Perfection* early to work on another film, a slew of accidents occurred that delayed the transition. As well as the prop man being pinned against a wall, Kevin Bacon's eardrums were perforated as he fired a gun and the camera crew fell ill due to food poisoning from shellfish. "I had six or seven crew members in the hospital and I wasn't going to leave them there. Sara Spring, who took over as coordinator, came up and I ended up doing all the insurance and dealing with the people I already knew while she started taking over all the paperwork. It was a bizarre moment in time."

Around the set, members of the crew were taking stock of their new location, applying their problem solving skills to each new scenario. With many scenes filmed over a period of hours, a key part of Alexander Gruszynski's role was to ensure that the continuity of light remained consistent as the day progressed. "The sun moves and the whole of the Owens Valley is sandwiched between two ranges of mountains to the east and west, meaning that for the first couple of hours the whole valley is in the shadow. At the end of the day, before the actual sunset, it again envelops the valley in shadow. You're shooting a single sequence throughout the day where the quality of light changes."

Ron Underwood may have been the person ultimately responsible for the film's look and feel, but he couldn't be everywhere at once. Helping him was a small team of assistant directors and second unit directors, each given their own sequences to shoot that would slot in with Underwood's style. *Beneath Perfection* co-creator, Steve Wilson, was the director of the second unit, often following the main crew to capture shots that didn't feature the principal cast, including a number of explosions and sequences including gunshots. The unit also had its own script supervisor and assistant director, plus a separate cinematographer/director of photography in Virgil Harper.

Graduating from the Brooks Institute of Photography, Harper had worked as a stills photographer for the Encyclopaedia Britannica Company before moving into the area of filmmaking on educational shorts for Al Higgins Productions. "Educational films were big back then. I worked as a camera assistant on a film called *The Life of a Two Dollar Bill*, and one of the people on that was Ron Underwood. I stayed in touch with him, and then he started working for Barr Films. I worked with him for 15 years as a director of photography. I'd known Steve Wilson and Brent Maddock before working on *Beneath Perfection*."

As second unit director of photography, Harper had to ensure that his angles retained the same look and contrast to that of the first unit. "This film had the natural beauty of the desert going for it anyway, but I went in to see the editor along with the director and he gave us a list of what he wanted. He'd show us a scene and we'd figure out when it was shot. If he had shot the scene backlit you definitely don't want to go out and shoot an insert that's front lit."

Special visual effects coordinator, Lise Romanoff, was charged with running the second unit. "The main unit wouldn't take time to shoot all the close-ups and all the cutaways, so the second unit was 100% physical effects. I was out in the field every day, I only checked in the office in the morning and at the end of the day. I had a long list of which effects were scheduled on what day and who was doing them." As with the rest of the production, careful planning ensured that the second unit ran smoothly.

Universal Studios' Jim Jacks was also a regular on set. "You let them make their movie, but I watched dailies and I went up to Lone Pine several times during the shoot. I'd talk to either Gale or Nancy every day or two, so we were on top of it. We weren't saying, 'Why did you shoot this scene this way?' – they were doing a good job and I knew what they were going to do. There wasn't what I would call micro-management of that film."

FROM SCRIPT TO SCREEN

As with most productions, the film was shot out of sequence to make the best use of locations, cast and crew. Where possible, the following chapters will detail scenes chronologically as they occur in the finished film.

The opening sequence called for Val McKee to urinate off the side of a cliff, the only issue being that there was no such cliff in the area. The problem was solved with the aid of a matte painting, an image painted onto glass and placed in front of the camera by Robert Stromberg, a member of the team at LA effects house, Illusion Arts. "That was still when you painted with real paint and that was the first movie that I had done where it's called Original Negative Matte painting," Stromberg explained. "You're painting blind in many ways. I did all of the matte painting of the cliffs and stuff where the worms come out, but it was pre-digital."[3]

In Virgil Harper's opinion, the characters of Val and Earl were written with reference to Steve Wilson's own life experience. "I grew up in small communities and those personalities are based on people that he probably knew and ran into. The shot where you first see Fred out there sleeping in the truck, the way he wakes up, opens one eye and looks out? That's something that would happen on a range and I think that's the personality of Wilson coming through."

The actors may have closely followed the script, but improvised elements did creep in during filming, including the moment during the opening credits where Val attempts to hammer in a nail but keeps missing, much to Earl's bemusement. "That was real, Kevin was really trying to pound that thing in," laughed Ron Underwood. "We realised at the time it was funny, and so Fred did his reaction and everything in that shot."

A recurring element of the film is also seen in the opening moments, the game of rock-paper-scissors, referred to as "The Challenge" in the script, played by Val and Earl as they make important decisions. "Most of the comedy, particularly the quirky comedy, tends to come from Brent and it was probably his idea which seemed to fit the characters," said Wilson.

For much of the shoot, solutions were found as problems arose, including the scene filmed along Lone Pine's Whitney Portal Road when Rhonda is taking seismograph readings and the camera begins to follow her movements. One challenge facing Virgil Harper was how to show visually that the Graboid had heard her, something he solved with the use of a "pogo cam", a pole with a camera hanging down at the bottom. "We laid the camera on its side and as the creature becomes aware, it all of a sudden tips right, levels the plane a little bit, and then it moves."

"I took a lot of heat for putting the camera low from certain actors that didn't necessarily enjoy being photographed from down below," recalled Alexander Gruszynski. "It was in the spirit of the classic western, having all these kind of extreme low angles that we tried to incorporate in telling this story visually."

Although actress Finn Carter had sunblock on her nose and wore shorts for the seismograph sequence, ensuring it looked like another sunny day in Perfection Valley in the finished film, the reality was quite different. With the temperatures plummeting, Carter was enveloped in a large fur coat between each take to keep her warm.

Shots of Val and Earl discovering Edgar Deems hanging from an electricity pylon were part of the second unit's workload, under the direction of Steve Wilson. "I think it was Kevin that climbed up the pole and later Steve and I shot the close-up of the old guy up in the tower to cut with that," Virgil Harper said. "Another great shot is when they come to Old Fred's place. I remember they shot across all the massacred sheep and the corral, then they follow over and lift up on the crane and go all the way through the little shed and out to the garden."

For the sequence that saw Carmine the roadworker (John Pappas) insert a jackhammer into an unsuspecting Graboid before being dragged away, Ivo Cristante created a fake surface on Tuttle Creek Road that could be destroyed for filming. The production had been given permission to dig a trench in the real public road, on the proviso it was filled back in after filming. "We put the track with the mechanism in the trench then backfilled everything with vermiculite [a substance used to resemble dirt] and then paved it with Plaster of Paris, which breaks very easily. We got the colour as close as possible then threw dirt on everything as a final disguise and that's what gets broken. I think the County repaired the road themselves."

Next, Cristante had to show the jackhammer travelling up the hill, being pulled by the retreating Graboid. "Most of the hill beside the road is fake, with the winch hidden behind it. I made these large bins like sandboxes, 10-feet by 10-feet, filled them up with dirt from the immediate area and then punched little cavities into the dirt as if they were little rocks sticking out, then sprayed it with AV foam. Once that was set up, I peeled off the foam and the dirt stuck to it, then nailed it into position and spackled the gaps. That gave us a way to create a façade. We put our mechanism behind all that and it hid what needed to be hidden."

Actor John Goodwin, whose character of Howard the roadworker was subsequently killed by a rock fall after Carmine's gruesome death, recalled filming a scene with Fred Ward and Kevin Bacon that was ultimately deleted from the finished film. "On the first take [the guys] pull up and Fred Ward throws a beer to me; I'm supposed to grab it and open it up," said Goodwin. "I looked at Fred Ward and he looked at me and we were both panicked – he was afraid to throw it at me and I was afraid that I wasn't going to catch it. We did it five or six times and on the last take they shook it up and it went all over me."[4]

Though it takes place less than a third of the way into the film, the final sequence to be shot was the attack on Dr. Jim Wallace (Conrad Bachmann) and his wife, Megan (Bibi Besch), culminating in the sinking of their station wagon. It may have been one of the earliest moments of real terror in the picture, showing just how much of a threat the Graboids were to the Perfectionites, but the sequence was almost scrapped early on in the planning process when it became apparent just how expensive the stunt was going to be. It wasn't the only part of the script in jeopardy, with the fast pace of filming occasionally leaving other shots by the wayside.

"[The Universal executives] were looking at dailies, [and they were] fantastic," explained Nancy Roberts, with reference to the footage being shipped back to Los Angeles from the first few weeks of filming in Lone Pine. "Initially, a director can't fall more than two days behind without the studio having the ability to fire him, so making your days, on time and on budget is critical. As you go along, sometimes you have to drop things, and the question is are you dropping things that are significant? Is the budget impossible? If the filmmaker is proving in the raw footage that they're getting the movie, then the begging process [for more money] becomes less arduous because [the studio] can see it."

Thanks to the need to continually juggle laughs and scares in the script, all involved saw the station wagon scene as vital to the flow of the film, but the restrictive $10m budget wasn't going to stretch far enough. For Nancy Roberts, this meant an element of "creative begging" was required.

"It's [about] making a viable creative argument for why you need the scene, what the scene will do, and what will happen if you don't have the scene," said Roberts, who had to explain to the Universal executives that the film would be missing important moments without extra budget. The agent took the fight to Universal's Jim Jacks. "Jim was really helpful," continued Roberts. "I remember riding out with him to Universal because we needed another $1m and it was Jim and I who were going to make the case to Tom Pollock. And they granted it."

"I seem to remember we did give them some money, perhaps not as much as they asked for," recalled Jacks. "They've always been pretty responsible."

Now that the budget had been raised, the station wagon scene was back on track, but the problems didn't end there. "The first night we were out there shooting, they'd dug this big deep hole and had this air bag in there," said actor Conrad Bachmann. "As I stepped on my mark the air would release, the bag would go down and Bibi would be trying to save me. The first time we tried it, they lost all the air from the bag and I went crashing down into the hole and all that dirt came down on me."[5]

The next issue came with the sinking of the car on the last day of filming, on a night shoot in the desert outside the San Fernando Valley, where shooting had moved to reduce costs. As scripted, the sequence saw the station wagon pulled three quarters into the ground, with the doctor's wife dragged to her death by the Graboids. To achieve this, the crew had dug a hole and buried a giant hydraulic rig under the ground, attaching it to the station wagon. The hole was then filled with water and topped with vermiculite, which floated on the surface to look like the desert floor. The car would be pulled down in jerks and remain part-submerged, with clever editing used to indicate it had been pulled down the rest of the way. The rig had barely started before it unexpectedly stopped.

"We were surprised at times by things that didn't work," admitted Ron Underwood. "We were about to shoot the scene and the physical effects head of department came to me and said, 'Ron, this car's not gonna sink.' We didn't realise how absorbent that vermiculite was; it absorbed the water so strongly that it became a solid surface. This was the last day of shooting, the last opportunity for this to work."

Physical effects coordinator Art Brewer had pointed out to Underwood that the stunt wasn't going to work, before promptly leaving the set. "I asked Art what happened, he said it was to do

MFS car sinking - Dust - Meg stops her futile kicking at windshield

CU fire extinguisher under glove compartment - her hand grabs extinguisher as glove compartment flies open and stuff falls out

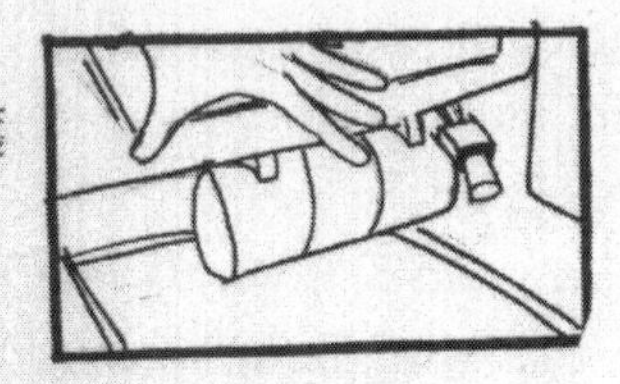

MCS Megan through windshield as she smashes glass with extinguisher

FS Megan crawls through windshield and balances on window frame - Dust fills the air

Jim and Megan Grabbed - Scs. 43-46
15 of 17

Unfilmed shots from the station wagon sequence can be seen in Michael Davis' storyboards © Ron Underwood

with the 'water or something,'" added Brent Maddock, who was watching events unfold. "I said, 'What are you gonna do?' and Art said, 'I dunno, it doesn't work', and he walked off. [Someone told me] this was his last movie, his last shot, and he was quitting the business. It was amazing."

CU sinking driver's side window - her foot sinking into frame - coming closer to dirt; her foot exits frame

Close on underside of car, Megan's hands come over bumper and pulls herself up

FS sinking car - Megan gets up onto bumper Dust - Dirt flying - Megan screams

CS Megan (lit from below) screaming - Dust Megan screaming

Jim and Megan Grabbed - Scs. 43-46
16 of 17

Unfilmed shots from the station wagon sequence can be seen in Michael Davis' storyboards © Ron Underwood

Standing in the desert at 3am, the team came up with a plan to use a montage of cuts to give the illusion the car was sinking, also placing a mound of dirt in front of the camera to make the ground appear higher than it was. The end result was a terrifying scene of death and destruction, with little evidence of camera trickery.

"I do remember [the car scene] being very problematic, there was an awful lot of discussion about that," said Cristen Carr Strubbe. "The ground was unstable out there. You're on the San Andreas Fault and things would shift and disappear. Luckily on that one I didn't have to have the money discussion."

Though the scene was hugely effective, it originally had an even bigger climax, one that survives in storyboard format if not in the final script. As detailed by storyboard artist Michael Davis, the sequence would have would have ended with Megan breaking the front windshield during the Graboid attack and climbing onto the hood of the car, before balancing on the front bumper as the Graboids pulled the car under the surface. In pre-production, it was discovered that the idea would be too expensive to film, even with the increased budget later awarded to the producers. "It's a bit painful looking through the storyboards and remembering all the compromise that goes into the making of a movie," said Ron Underwood. "It truly is a humbling and exhilarating experience to direct."

CREATING COMMUNITY SPIRIT

Named after the single pine tree that once stood at the mouth of Lone Pine Canyon, the town of Lone Pine was founded in the 1860s with the purpose of supplying the gold and silver mining communities of Kaersarge, Keeler, Swansea, Cerro Gordo and Darwin with food and equipment.[6]

After suffering an earthquake in 1872 that wiped out most of the town and killed 26 of its 250 residents,[7] Lone Pine's growth continued during the 19th and 20th centuries, its economy boosted by the arrival of the film industry in 1920. By 1989, there were just over of 1,800 residents[8] in Lone Pine and tourism was one of its biggest industries. "Lone Pine is basically one street; there are motels and a pub on one side, restaurants on the other," said Tony Genaro. "It's a stopover for people that are going up to Mount Whitney or heading on up to Reno."

Lone Pine's population swelled during the filming of *Beneath Perfection* as motel rooms were filled with hundreds of cast and crew, while some stayed in holiday homes on the outskirts of town. Though the actors, visual effects crew, carpenters, electricians and other members of the production were busy on location during the day, by evening the bars and restaurants were filled as they caught-up with colleagues from other departments in a less formal atmosphere. "It was absolutely happy," said Gale Anne Hurd. "It's rare to have an experience where the cast and crew get on so well."

"We lived in a little house in the main street just outside of the town, as much as there was a town," said Kevin Bacon, who arrived in Lone Pine with his pregnant wife, actress Kyra Sedgwick. "There was very little there; there was a pizza parlour and a bar called the Double L. I think it's still there with pictures of us on the wall."

"One night we went out dancing to a bar in Lone Pine," added Charlotte Stewart. "To see Kevin and Kyra out there dancing was hysterical. I wish I could've taken a picture, because they were boogyin' down. We were always doing something to keep us together, because there wasn't a whole lot else out there."

In a period before digital filmmaking became the norm, reels of film stock were transported back to Los Angeles for developing each day, before being returned to Lone Pine to be watched by Ron Underwood. The director hired the back room of a Lone Pine bar and hung a sheet upon a wall to project scenes. "We would get together every night and watch dailies, all of the cast was invited as well," recalled Underwood. "It really helps a movie to have that kind of environment, to see what's been done and where things are going."

"We'd shoot for days and end up having a little party when the dailies were being shown," added Genaro. "Steve Wilson was a beer connoisseur and he would bring out a big sampling of all the beers that he liked and everybody would get three cold ones."

Life wasn't always quiet in the town, with Robert Jayne, the set's resident teenager, recalling that he "was kind of a troublemaker back then, though you have to remember I was 15. I had an issue one time, I don't remember what I did, but there were only two motels in the town of Lone Pine and they said, 'Well he can't stay in the motel, what are we going to do with this 15-year-old bratty kid?' I was going have to stay in Ron's room. They decided to check me into the other motel in town and they were saying, 'We've got to give him a last name so we can check him into the motel and they won't know who he is.' They booked me in under the name "Melvin Plug" and that's how the character got his surname."

The sense of collaboration generated from Underwood and the production team filtered down through the production, with Michael Gross enamoured of the tone on set. "They were clearly having a good time. There were challenges, but nobody seemed like a neophyte or as if they were overwhelmed. There were no screamers on the set."

"There was definitely a community feeling; Ron was a new director, Brent and Steve were new writers and we were all out in the middle of the desert to make this monster movie," said Jayne. "It was an interesting challenge. We were in this small town of Lone Pine and every day we'd get in the van and have to drive 45 minutes to the middle of the desert where they'd constructed the set. It was very laid back and mellow."

With a need to maintain the illusion of vast empty spaces in almost every scene of the film, cast trailers and film equipment were stored far away from where shooting occurred, meaning there were few amenities for the actors during the day. "Sometimes we'd just all sit in our chairs and read while they were setting up," Charlotte Stewart said. "I think we shot six days a week and had Sunday off, so we would do something communal like go horseback riding. One weekend we went to the rodeo, it was up in the next town. It was a pretty close cast because we were together all day, every day."

"Lone Pine has a series of rock formations that you could hike up into and there's a really high elevation with cattle grazing and pastures; it's a spectacularly beautiful place," recalled Bacon.

"We'd go up there at weekends and climb around these rocks. They were famous because there used to be some westerns shot up there in the fifties. They were also looked on as places for hallucinogens, LSD and spiritual enlightenment. It was a very trippy place."

Brent Maddock recalled that each night he'd return to his motel and empty his shoes of sand into a small pile beside the door, with the pile getting higher and higher as the shoot went on. "Across the way you'd see Ariana and her little sister using the big double bed in their room as a trampoline after each day's filming."

As a minor on set, Ariana Richards was allocated a teacher responsible for ensuring she received her allotted time each day for schoolwork, while also watching out for her general welfare during filming. "We'd play baseball occasionally, well I didn't know how to play baseball but I'd try to catch things and throw them in-between. There were a lot of great people to hang out with and a lot of things to do. I remember Lone Pine being quite a stunning location. Worms weren't the only creatures we had to deal with; there were also rattlesnakes and scorpions."

The communal spirit also stretched to the film's lead actors, Kevin Bacon and Fred Ward. "Fred was a fun guy, quieter, but just a sweet, warm man," said Michael Gross of his co-star. "They played off each other so beautifully," added Charlotte Stewart. "Fred is one of the most artistic, poetic and well-read people I have ever met, he's fascinating to talk to."

"He was a little older than me," said Bacon of Ward, "and had at least one kid at that point, so I was looking to him for some, if not specific advice, then an example of being an actor and having a child. I liked him and we had a really fun time working together."

"I have such fond memories of working with the actors," said production coordinator, Cristen Carr Strubbe. "Kevin was great because he had this beautiful dog, I think its name was Lucy, and he would hang out in the production office. We were all up in the middle of nowhere and there was one coffee shop and one bar and we were all in a Best Western with a pool."

To Tony Genaro, Kevin Bacon was "just one of the guys", happy to make use of the former's pool in Lone Pine with Kyra Sedgwick. "I hung out a lot with Fred Ward, I liked his sense of humour and I respected him a lot as an actor. I also got a kick out of Robert Jayne."

"What I remember most about Kevin is that he and his wife were having their first child," said Gross. "She was huge; to say she was "showing" was an understatement. When I first saw his wife on screen years later, I think it was in *The Closer*, I didn't know who she was, because she bore absolutely no resemblance to the person who was walking around on our set, heavy with child."

For Bacon, his wife's pregnancy was both exhilarating and daunting, with impending fatherhood the cause of much stress during the Lone Pine shoot. "Kyra was nine months pregnant and would drive down to LA every once in a while to check with the doctors," said the actor. "She could've given birth in Lone Pine, where there was no hospital, and I think we'd have had to go 45 minutes north to another town where there was possibly a midwife. Plus, the idea that I was about to become a father was overwhelming; I was a sleepwalker back then and I'd wake up and be carrying her through the house because I had to get her away from monsters. She was shouting, 'Put me down, put me down!' It was a wild but kind of magical time."

Ivo Cristante's wife was also pregnant during the shoot, meaning the father-to-be spent his weekends in LA before he drove back to set on Monday mornings. "Kevin and I were racing to see whose child would be born first. He won by a week. I have great admiration for Kevin, I think when his son was born he gave out chocolate cigars and he said, 'Maybe we should be handing out condoms instead.'"

One notable aspect of the *Beneath Perfection* set was its wholesomeness, something Cristante had rarely encountered on a Hollywood production. "It was kind of remarkable because it was the 1980s and there was a certain wildness to film crews back then, but it wasn't present on that film. One of my construction team did have a drinking problem and I had to fire him halfway through the production, but there wasn't the kind of wild cavorting one associated with that era of filmmaking."

Thanks to there being children in Perfection, including Ariana Richards and her sister, plus the offspring of various crew members, those present recall it being relatively free of bad language and rowdy behaviour. "It proved to me that it's possible to have a reasonably civilised lifestyle and still work in the movie business," said Ivo Cristante.

CHAPTER FOUR

GOING DEEPER UNDERGROUND

It may have taken Hollywood executives years to fully comprehend the tone of the film that would ultimately become *Tremors*, with its mix of horror, sci-fi, western, comedy and romance, but one thing that was absolutely clear from the script was the sense of community generated by the ensemble of characters.

The film introduced viewers to just 17 people, although road workers Howard and Carmine are only seen briefly, Edgar is dead when he's discovered, Old Fred doesn't last long and the doctor and his wife are more Graboid fodder. That leaves 10 Perfectionites and the visiting Rhonda LeBeck to rally round when disaster strikes, each one given their own character tics to make them appear more than just potential monster bait. It doesn't matter that those tics are superficial – Walter is always after a fast buck, Melvin is an annoying asswipe, Burt is paranoid – the important thing is that Perfection feels like it's been there for a long time and these people want to survive.

"I think it was *Time* magazine that said, 'The cast was an ensemble that seemed like they actually lived in this little town and had known each other almost all their lives,'" stated Tony Genaro. "That's the great thing about *Tremors*, it's all about character," commented Gale Anne Hurd. "You fall in love with the characters."

"I couldn't really tell the tone from reading the script; I got it from Fred and Kevin and how they reacted to certain scenes," explained actress Charlotte Stewart. "There's a scene in the store when we're all sitting around trying to figure out how we're going to get out of there, and they say, 'OK who can ride horseback?' We all turn at the same time and look at Kevin and Fred. That is a definite comic move. We were definitely aware of it. But our timing had to be just right in everybody turning together."

"I thought [the script] was odd, it was hard for me to put my finger on what the tone of it would be," admitted Kevin Bacon. "It has a tone that's not often accomplished with success, that is to make something scary and humorous at the same time. Examples of [similar movies] are *Shaun of the Dead* and *An American Werewolf in London*; when those movies work well they can be really cool, but they're tough to pull off."

Though *Tremors* is variously labelled a horror and science fiction film, evidence of Lone Pine's western genre connections can be found in the scene that saw Val and Earl riding into the sunset in slow motion as they attempt to visit the town of Bixby for help. "It was just a little control we had on the camera that changes the shutter and the speed at the same time so that you can slow down the film," said Ron Underwood. "That horseback ride was fun to do because of the whole cowboy part of the story."

"It's the closest I've ever come to being in a western," stated Bacon. "Riding a horse is one of the few things I do well. There are a lot of skills I've had to learn for films, but I have a feeling *Tremors* is the only time I've been on horseback in one." Just before filming of the long shot of Val and Earl galloping across the desert from Perfection, Bacon was told he had to go home for turnaround, a legal requirement which releases an actor from the set for 12 hours before they start shooting again. "The sun was going down so it was a whole scheduling thing. On my way out I was watching the guy doubling me and thought, 'Jesus Christ, this is the only thing I can do and I have to have a double doing my horseback riding!' So I was frustrated by that, but it was good to do a little bit of it."

After discovering the doctor's submerged vehicle, Val and Earl's horses are attacked and killed by Graboids. "In those shots you can see the wires, you get the sense that it was pre-digital filmmaking, especially in that scene with the horses being eaten," continued Underwood. "We had the Humane Association involved and it was no problem for the horses as they were just lying down and we didn't hurt them in any way."

This sequence was the first time the Graboids were shown on screen, previous scenes only hinting at what lay beneath the desert floor. The combination of actors, full-scale models from ADI and miniatures from 4-Ward Productions typified the teamwork required to convince the audience that Val and Earl were under attack. "Any shot where you see a full size worm break-up and go in the ground and debris in the air, those were certainly not things that they could do full size and they'd have to be a miniature," explained 4-Ward's Robert Skotak.

After realising that the Graboids kill their victims from under the ground, the earth beneath Val and Earl begins to crack and the pair are thrown off balance as a creature breaks through the dirt. At the same time, Robert and Dennis Skotak were standing behind the camera with their own still camera, taking the photos that would help them replicate the moment in studio. "For every take we shot pictures of the clouds in the sky and wrote down what stills corresponded, so take two is still number 12, take four is still number 14, and so on," said Robert Skotak. "We then found out from the editor which take he used and we'd choose the appropriate still and use that for our backing, which was beautifully painted by a guy named Rick Rische."

Using the stills, Rische created a 15-foot long backdrop, replicating the cloud positions and landscape as it was seen on location to match the take. "I'm not sure that's done very often, but it's so we could guarantee that there's no question about continuity," Skotak continued. "We built a pie-shaped miniature, maybe 4-feet wide at the front and 15-feet wide at the back, on wheels so it could be moved around, and shot that outside. We had our backing set-up and we used natural sunlight for all of those shots. I think it was maybe a little higher than waist height and had a big space underneath it so we could operate things. For the shots where Val and Earl are shooting at the Graboid, with those little hits on the sand, that was me firing a BB gun at the ground."

Following the appearance of the first Graboid and its decision to chase Val and Earl, the Skotaks considered how they would create the effect of the creature moving under the ground as it approached its prey. "The way the worms were described is that they moved through the ground almost like a sea creature would move through water," said Skotak, who first inserted a foam rubber membrane under the surface of the miniature set before covering it with fake dirt. A pipe was then moved along the underside of the membrane to create the illusion of a worm pushing through the ground. "We also devised a mixture of microballoons and Fuller's earth, sand that was so soft you could set a feather and it would leave a dent. Microballoons are almost microscopic glass beads that are hollow, like little tiny balloons, and they tend to float a lot. It kicks up sort of a pretty realistic cloud that looks like a large-scale cloud of mist. Dust doesn't scale very well in miniatures."

Digging the ditch that will become the aqueduct © Ivo Cristante

From here, the action swiftly moves to an aqueduct that Val and Earl have to jump to escape the creature. With no such aqueduct in the area, one had to be created especially for the film near the Dolomite marble quarry, with ADI's Tom Woodruff and Alec Gillis taking time out from creature building to help dig a trench in the middle of the desert. "We'd have goggles on and bandanas across our face because the wind was whipping across the dry lake bed at us," said Gillis. "There was only one backhoe and it was being used across the valley setting up some other shot, so we're out there hand digging a trench for the scene where they uncover the Graboid after it smashed into the concrete and killed itself."

Building the trench proved to be anything but straightforward. "There was something called sugar sand, pockets that look like regular sand but it's almost like talcum powder," said production designer, Ivo Cristante. "When we were building that trench there were lots of pockets of that sugar sand and you'd suddenly find a section of the hole collapse on you. We didn't have time to find another location so we just had to hope that we could shore it up so that the set pieces were in position and that they'd hold it all back."

For the final part of the scene, after Val and Earl realise the Graboid is dead and discover "the ass end", second unit director Steve Wilson made it clear he wanted to film some shots of the creature, only to discover that permission had to be obtained from higher up the production chain. "I came from a background where you just get stuff done on the smaller films," said second unit director of photography, Virgil Harper. "I said, 'Why in the hell can't we just drive out there and shoot that? It's a simple shot.' Oh God, it started a hailstorm. I didn't think in terms of the producer saying, 'Well what if you go out there and break something, what if this or that happens?' If we were doing a Barr Films we'd just go out there and shoot it but in features it's like an army."

Chris Langley, a Lone Pine resident present for the shooting of the sequence, recalled that the scene was shot "at least 15 different ways" before director Ron Underwood was satisfied. "It was probably the first time I'd been on a set and it was then I began to realise the glamour of filmmaking was pretty tedious," said Langley. "I don't remember there being stand-ins. I was sitting next to Fred Ward and he and Kevin Bacon were talking about what they were going to do next; Fred had nothing lined-up and was going to return to his ranch."

Langley was impressed with the actors' ability to fall back into character after taking long breaks between shooting. "Fred said he entered himself both in the character and the posture, so that when they were ready to film he'd simply walk there, resume the posture and regain the mood. He was happy to sit and talk with people."

* * *

A recurring trope in horror films is the moment where the history of the antagonist is explained to the audience, either via exposition, a pre-title sequence or a flashback. For *Beneath Perfection*, Steve Wilson and Brent Maddock ignored the genre's unwritten rules and avoided explicitly stating the Graboids' origins.

"I came to realise early on in the scriptwriting process that there were only four possible explanations," explained Wilson. "They're created by radioactivity! They're supernatural demons! They're from outer space! They've always been here and we've just never seen them before! The studio winced at all of those and we compromised, so there's a scene in the movie where the three main protagonists are sitting on a rock and we run through them all."

The rock scene provided one of the film's most memorable lines as Fred Ward states that "No way these are local boys", but Universal wasn't happy to leave things so vague. "We were told we had to explain where they're from and we absolutely fought it," said Gale Anne Hurd. "We felt it was important that if the characters don't know, the audience shouldn't know. We can't know more than the characters."

With pressure from Universal to insert a new sequence into the script explaining the Graboids' extraterrestrial origins, Wilson and Maddock wrote a scene in which Burt and Heather discover a crashed spaceship and open pods in Perfection Valley, before radioing town to let them know they're dealing with aliens. The new pages were first revealed at one of the regular production meetings. "We put out a new script to 20 or 30 department heads and the first thing that came up were the new pages," Wilson said. "I took a vote and nobody liked the idea. I called Tom Pollock at the studio and told him the entire staff stood up against it." To everyone's relief, the sequence was excised from the script.

Though there were disagreements during the production, Wilson knew that the studio had the film's best interests at heart. "You could argue with Casey Silver and Tom Pollock, have a discussion. They had a lot of input and were concerned, but to their credit they understood it was an unusual movie and were working with us not against us to make it as successful as possible. You win some, you lose some."

Attention now turned to shooting Val, Earl and Rhonda's pole vaulting escape back to their truck. Filmed in the Alabama Hills, close to the area used to film the bridge sequence in 1938's *Gunga Din*, the scene required the filmmakers to enhance the local scenery with their own prop rocks. A platform was built to give the stunt performers a level surface to take off and land on, before fake rocks were placed in front. "They were a bitch to paint," stated Ivo Cristante. "It was basically one master and some close-ups, with the actors stepping off a stepladder onto a real rock for the inserts. Some of the wildlife would eat the foam rocks that we'd built. For some reason they found that spray-on foam very appetising and we'd find major chunks gone. We had to post people to shoo animals away."

"When Fred, Kevin and Finn end up pole vaulting from rock to rock, in the film you can hear the bass drum thumping of people walking around on hollow things," added Maddock. "We went up the day before we shot the pole vaulting, on a really windy day, and the gigantic boulders were rolling around the desert like tumble weeds. It was just the most amazing image." According to local resident Chris Langley, the rocks remained a part of the Lone Pine landscape. "For years people would take pieces of wood from inside them to build their houses. I had one I used in plays at the local school. One day a woman arrived from Glendale to buy a lot of them for her garden."

The pole vaulting sequence allowed the audience to root for the characters as they finally outwitted the Graboid, but it originally had a darker tone. "Tone was a very difficult thing with this movie, we didn't know exactly what it would be until it was done," said composer, Ernest Troost. "That scene is a perfect example of the challenge, because in an earlier version there were one or two shots of a tentacle coming out of the ground and the discussion was, 'How do we play this scene? We need to keep the tension going.'"

Troost scored the scene with an orchestra, ensuring the drama was sustained as the creatures lurked in the sand below. "I think at some point Ron said, 'This scene has to be kind of a celebration, the real fun moment.' They took out the shots of the tentacles and asked me to rescore it. I went in a completely different direction, back to the sort of the funky rootsy blues music, and it fit perfectly." The result was a sequence that's a triumph for the characters, a moment of elation as they're allowed to safely jump from boulder to boulder. "That's an example of how a scene evolved, we all went one way and then we went another way and ultimately, I think it makes people recognise that it's a fun movie."

The next shot, as Val, Earl and Rhonda attempted to escape from the Graboids in the truck, almost lost a moment of tension when cinematographer Alexander Gruszynski took exception to filming as the light began to fade. "There's a moment when Finn goes through the back window, looks over and a tentacle breaks the window," said Brent Maddock. "It was late in the day, you lose the sun around 5.30pm, and we had to get the shot. Alexander said it was too dark to shoot it and refused, but we had to get it. It lacks a little saturation, but the moment is in there, it's fine."

THE WORMS TURN

The film's next set piece took place back in Perfection's general store, combining the levity of Walter Chang attempting to name the mysterious creatures with the drama of the Graboids stepping-up their attack on the residents, both outside and inside the shop. As the townsfolk discuss how they'll confuse their enemies, Val leaps over the counter before ripping a map of the valley from the board.

"Something that really surprised me with Kevin, that wasn't in the script, was the way he crossed the room," said Ron Underwood. "He was looking at the map and he jumped over the counter. I thought he would just walk around and he flies over it. I love those surprises when working with actors, something that's not necessarily mentioned in the script but has a great power in it and says a lot about the character."

For the scenes outside Chang's Market, as Val comes face-to-gaping maw with one of the creatures following Melvin's attempts at crying wolf, full-size Graboids were utilised alongside more miniatures. "The Graboids feel real because they're mechanical creatures, they affect you more," said second unit director of photography, Virgil Harper. "If you look at movies like *Anaconda* with Jennifer Lopez, that snake looks so phony, it didn't scare you because it didn't have any reality. With *Tremors*, those weird tentacles weren't digital, they had a quality like a cobra."

Physical effects expert, Art Brewer, was tasked with ensuring the entrance of the Graboid was as realistic as possible. "The only bit of hydraulics on the movie was Art's elevator, where they dug a hole straight down into the ground and put this hydraulic ramp down in the bottom," said Alec Gillis. "We then loaded our worm with Tom in it, dressed it over and helped Art direct the breakaway. That was sort of between physical effects and set dressing. We would jump in and lend our expertise wherever we could."

Once the front half of the Graboid was placed nose up in the 8-foot deep hole with Woodruff inside, the elevator could be primed to quickly emerge through the ground. "The beak of the worm would punch through this thin polyurethane foam shell that had been placed over the top of him," continued Gillis. "It was covered with dirt and there were air cannons inside to blow big plumes of dirt and debris into the air. It was going to be this huge hyperkinetic explosion of ground opening up and the worm shooting out of the top, but I think on the first take it only came up a foot or two."

Woodruff then entered the lift before it was dropped down, with the next 40 minutes spent dressing the lines and putting the shell over the top before it was covered with dirt. "On the first take it came up about a foot and everything jammed up. The urethane foam had jammed the working somehow and it just didn't work. So we cleaned it all up, did another take and went back into the dark for another 40 minutes. This time the elevator came all the way up but it was so slow."

With the Graboid containing Woodruff now above ground, the creature's mouth opened to reveal tentacles, all of which were hand operated cable mechanisms. "The idea was that we wanted these tentacles to have a lot more performance ability; they had to hold themselves out straight when they weren't supported on the ground. They had to look like they had their own character; the worm was the big bold monster that would burst out of the ground, then the tentacles would be the feelers that would go around and look for prey."

Woodruff and Gillis had carried out a number of early tentacle tests at their LA workshop, rolling a worktable out into the sun before erecting a fake background of some bricks that they covered with dirt. "We had some pretty cool footage where they would snake along the ground and start working their way up the side of this brick façade," said Woodruff. "We also had some reverse shots where somebody would climb up on the worktable and we'd shoot a close-up of their legs walking. A tentacle would suddenly lurch forward and wrap around their leg, which was all done in reverse, so we would start with the tentacle coiled around. The guy would take some steps backwards and it took some performance work to figure out."

Pleased with their tests, the pair showed Wilson and Maddock the results. "We had some floppy tentacles that were just strung on wires and Steve and Brent kept asking, 'Can we have a hand puppet tentacle?'" added Gillis. "We put it together and it went up to about your elbow. We ended up using that thing a lot more than we ever expected. A guy could slip it on, usually Tom, hide next to the pickup truck and just pop it up. Or there were times where Tom was laying in kind of a ditch that had a piece of plywood over the top of it with a hole in it and some latex rubber across the hole. We'd fill it lightly with dirt and he could shove his hand out with the tentacle on it and it would look like a tentacle popping up out of the ground."

"Both of the screenwriters and Ron had lived with the story for a long time, so they knew exactly how these creatures should behave," said Alexander Gruszynski. "Most of the time Kevin and Fred were reacting to the creatures that were not there, so Ron's other very important role was to be the creature. He would be sitting down on the ground making all kinds of noises to help them work, and he couldn't even make the noises once the dialogue started so he kind of just had to shoot his arms in the air and make faces to help them out."

The sight of a creature churning the dirt on the surface as it headed for its prey occasionally preceded shots of Graboids exploding through the ground. "Art Brewer was trying to figure out how to get the Graboids to move correctly," said Cristen Carr Strubbe. "He finally decided to go totally old school. They dug a trench and put a buoy on a chain and covered it with dirt and just yanked the buoy. It worked better than all the big gizmos and millions of different things we tried."

Ivo Cristante, the man responsible for adding the finishing touches to these shots, was concerned with how they would look on screen. "I went to the effects guys and said, 'You're going to dig a trench, get one of the plastic buoys from the marina, attach a rope and drag it with a tractor. What are you going to put so we can dress it with the dirt and the bushes?' The effects guy said, 'I don't know, that's your job.' I said, 'But keeping the dirt up is a special effect,' and the reply was, 'No, it's dressing.' From past experience on horror films, undulating walls is part of the whole repertoire. There's a thin rubber called dental dam, it comes in three-foot wide sheets in rolls, and we lined the trench with that, put the dirt on it and it worked fine."

Cristante repeated the effect on the pits housing the elevators that pushed the Graboids through the ground. "There were moments when you had to cut as you couldn't sustain it for too long as the dental dam couldn't hold it and the sides burst and the dirt fell in and got in the hydraulics. That had to be thought through at some point and once you work out where it could go wrong I'd travel to the various mechanical guys' shops and solve the problem."

The crew's next challenge was to prepare for the Graboid attack on Mindy outside Chang's Market, the creature attracted by the vibrations of her pogo stick. It soon became clear to Ivo Cristante's team that the dirt road wouldn't be suitable for Ariana Richards to pogo stick on and that around 1,500-feet of roadway would need to be hurriedly paved, with the new surface also needing to be aged. "We quickly got a bunch of shovels and started throwing dirt before the steam roller came over, suddenly ageing the road exactly the way we wanted," said Cristante.

"Once I won the part of Mindy I practiced on the pogo stick," recalled Richards. "It actually took quite a bit of time to get the hang of it, but I was up to about 500 counts when I started filming the movie. Ron was really communicative and I always felt safe whatever they were doing when it came to stunts or special effects."

The next scene saw Val jump on top of his truck to avoid becoming Graboid fodder, with the vehicle rocked from underneath by hydraulics built into the set and placed under the ground. Explained effects coordinator, Lise Romanoff, "Each one of those would be tripped as they happened, in real time with the actors in the same shot, with a little dust flying up at the same time."

Following another Graboid attack on Rhonda that led to her losing her trousers to some barbed wire, the Perfectionites ran back into Chang's Market, chased by another creature that shook the wooden porch from underneath. "Those steps that land right into the store jumbled up as you ran, it seemed like something was under there coming to get you," said Tony Genaro, "but it was just a guy running along with a stick under the wood. It was very low-tech."

The interior of Chang's was now the focus of a major Graboid attack, again masterminded by Tom Woodruff and Alec Gillis, who rebuilt the store on a studio set in Valencia, Los Angeles. The first part of the scene saw the chiller cabinet start to vibrate, causing Kevin Bacon to jump on top in order to reach behind to unplug it. Following the first shooting of the scene, word came through to Bacon that Kyra Sedgwick had gone into labour, causing him to leave the set and head to a Los Angeles hospital to be with his wife and new son, Travis.

Painted Perfection backdrop used for interior filming © Ivo Cristante

After the birth, the production reconvened in Valencia. "The stage had a big basement level trench, so they supported the floor and built the whole set-up of that," explained Woodruff. "We had our big hero creature head mounted on the front of a heavy-duty dolly. We had linked in some of the pivot arms so that we could rock it from the back and make it break through the flooring as it's moving forward and then flatten down on the ground. We had a very energetic explosion of creature coming up from under the floor."

This was one of the film's most intensive sequences, combining the skills of the mechanical, construction and practical effect teams to coordinate all the shelves falling over and being destroyed as the Graboids appeared. "The floorboards had to be scored just the right way so that the creature could push up, then the stuntmen had to be involved for when Walter gets dragged down," said Romanoff. "I think that was probably the most amazing feat of the movie."

The scene saw the death of Walter Chang, proving to viewers that nobody was safe in Perfection. "Before Victor Wong had his death scene he said, 'Whatever you have to do, it's fine. Stick me in the jaws of the thing and just throw me around. Whatever makes it exciting is good with me' – he was just a real great guy," said Ron Underwood. The scene was more violent in the original script, with Walter's leg getting caught on the edge of the hole and "bent hideously backwards" before bones snap, ribs crack and his foot is folded back behind his head as he vanishes into the ground.

The action now moved to the roof of Chang's, a scene that found Kevin Bacon, Fred Ward and Tony Genaro working together. "That was kind of frightening," admitted Genaro. "Fred and I had to lower Kevin down into this window to get the walkie talkie and we actually did it, we each grabbed a leg and lowered him down. I thought, 'My God, what if we dropped this guy? He's the star of the movie!'"

Robert Jayne recalled: "It was a long shoot because we were in the desert and on rooftops, even if you weren't in the scenes that day. Say they were shooting two people, they never knew if they saw you in the background of the shot, so you'd have to be on set for 10 hours, just sitting in your trailer waiting to see if they were going to use you."

The next death was that of Nestor, with the character thrown from the roof of his trailer onto the ground, before he scrambled to the supposed safety of a large tyre. According to actor Richard Marcus, Ron Underwood was convinced the death scene was relatively simple to achieve. "When it came to my turn to be swallowed by the worm, Ron said, 'I think you can do this on your own, you're just going to have to squeeze yourself into the tyre; crush yourself like a pancake and somebody will be along to pull you down below.' I looked at it and said, 'OK, I'll try it, I don't know if can I fit through that hole and do a jack knife.' You never want to say to the director you won't do it, but at the last second the stunt coordinator walked over, looked at the situation and said, 'Ron, this isn't gonna happen.' At that moment Ron immediately said, 'OK, bring out the dummy!' I was grateful for the stunt coordinator, I can tell you."[1]

Underwood's desire to maintain a sense of momentum throughout the film saw him using a number of crane shots, something particularly noticeable after Nestor (or the dummy) is pulled under the ground, as the camera travels across the ground, through a fence and up to Melvin. By watching the sequence closely, it's just possible to see the fence being pulled apart to allow the camera past. "Because it was about the ground, I felt high and low angles were very important, so we had a crane all the time," said the director. "The shot where the camera focuses on Nestor in the tyre and then moves to Melvin was storyboarded. It was kind of hard with the technology of the time, speeding up the camera without making it totally wacky."

WRECKING THE REC ROOM

As with the earlier aqueduct sequence, the attack on Burt and Heather Gummer's recreational room required the skills of both ADI and 4-Ward Productions. "For Burt's basement in the attack, that was all miniatures once we had the initial full-scale creature

CU cartridges stuffed into gun barrel

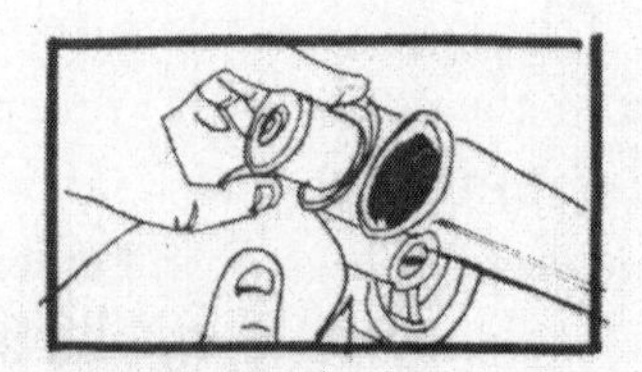

Over creature - Burt & Heather are
cornered - Burt closes chamber

Wide lens down barrel as gun swings up and
Burt pulls trigger

WS over creature as it takes two hits -
with creature guts flying out of a large
cavity in its backside - very loud shrieks
OOZE splats across lens

Burt Blasts One - Scs.99-103
16 of 17

Planning the rec room scene with Michael Davis' storyboard
© Ron Underwood

go through the wall," said Ron Underwood. "The great thing about the effects in the film was mixing it up so that you couldn't tell exactly what was going on."

"The pièce de résistance was that huge Graboid head on wheels that came through my basement wall," Michael Gross said. "That was full-size and they had fake concrete walls and

Creature drops to ground, tentacles go limp - forced heavy breathing sounds

2-SHOT Burt & Heather stagger together and hug - they stare dumbfounded at the creature, Burt suddenly shouts
B: "Broke into the wrong goddamn rec room, didn't you, you BASTARD!"

Burt Blasts One - Scs.99-103
17 of 17

Planning the rec room scene with Michael Davis' storyboard
© Ron Underwood

it needed to be a one-take wonder because setting it up again would've taken them a day or two. A lot of cameras were rolling when that thing came through the wall. You sweat as an actor because you say, 'There's so much counting on this one take. I don't want to be the one to make a mistake or discover I've left my glasses on.' They're literally running like six or eight cameras because they have to get it once, and everything's got to happen perfectly. That's when I get as paranoid as Burt."

The original plan had been to shoot the entire basement scene as a full-scale effect, but after realising that it couldn't easily be replicated for reshoots, 4-Ward Productions' Robert Skotak and his team were called upon to rebuild the set as a miniature. "We built three walls, the floor and the ceiling opposite where Michael and Reba were, so we had to build the whole end of the basement, the stairway, all the tools, etc. There was a point where we went down to where the prop people were assembling that set and counted something like 220 individual items that we would have to make, which is far more than was discussed. I think there was going be 10 or 12 things we'd have to build as miniatures; ultimately we made around 125."

Everything in the original scene had to be replicated in miniature, including floor tiles, ceiling tiles, the windows, the peg board and the telescope. Larger items included shelves of books and filing cabinets, plus the machine used to clean the bullet shells. Even the Pepsi can was recreated in miniature. "I think we laser copied the label on the Pepsi can and wrapped it around," said Skotak. "The one thing that I really should have eliminated was the office stool. We duplicated the texture of the cloth and went really careful on every possibility because we thought quarter-scale's kind of the minimum to get away with. So we really had to be dead on the money and we were very obsessive about the level of detail."

Only one element of the scene jars on repeated viewing, a shot of Burt Gummer from behind as he shoots at the Graboid. A stand-in was used due to Michael Gross' unavailability. "The live action was shot by Gene Warren, so he did the composite," said Skotak. "We shot the background and he put the composite together. I think we were off the film at that point and it's not perfect, unfortunately."

Part of the reason the rec room scene became a fan favourite was due to the reveal of the wall lined with guns that allowed Burt and Heather to take on their invader, proving just how prepared the Gummers were for all eventualities. "Steve Wilson always had this fascination with mechanical things; big trucks, big guns, watching stuff blow up," said second unit director of photography, Virgil Harper. "There are a lot of Hollywood directors who make movies with guns and machine guns and they don't have a clue, they've never shot a gun in their life. They have people walking around shooting a thousand rounds out of an M-16 in the street and no one gets hit. Steve, on the other hand, he knows what weapons do."

The sequence was also a chance for Reba McEntire to show she was more than just a singer. "I remember Reba saying one time how acting was 'more boring and harder than you think' because you spend a lot of time waiting," Harper said. "That's true, for every set-up you've got to change something. You can get a master shot lit and the talent will come in and you'll have them rehearse and all of a sudden you see you have to change something a little bit, because talent may improvise slightly, and so then you've to tweak. It's not an instant turn and shoot."

* * *

For the scene in which Val, Earl and Miguel celebrate the Gummers' destruction of the Graboid in their basement, the use of bad language became an issue for the filmmakers. "Kevin and Fred came on and said they wanted to talk like real cowboys and we were so heady doing our first movie that ratings weren't even on our radar," admitted Steve Wilson. "The unspoken rule was you could have two uses of the f-word and you'd get by."

Burt and Val's reference to the Graboids as "motherhumpers" has led many viewers to assume that over-eager TV censors were to blame, when in fact the decision to use the term was that of the producers. "This was an area of filmmaking I really didn't know about since I hadn't made features before," said Ron Underwood. "To get a PG-13, which we wanted, you could only say "fuck" once. When they're on the roof, Burt originally says over the radio 'We killed one of the motherfuckers' and then Val, when the thing is going off the cliff at the end, also used the word "fucker." It was weird that nobody told us 'You can only do one', but we found out from the ratings board when we sent the film in. It was obvious which one we wanted, because it was such a big moment in the film."

The scene also gained some notoriety, albeit a few decades after the fact, thanks to Robert Jayne's delivery of the line "Way to go dudes!", in reference to Burt and Heather's rec room success. Thanks to the internet, fans have since taken to re-editing Jayne's line into music videos and emailing them to the actor. According to Jayne, his somewhat lacklustre script reading was due to being a typically sullen teenager on the day. "When I had to do that line I said, 'Ron, c'mon man, I can't do this line, it's not cool' and he said 'Just do it one time, we probably won't use it.' So I said, 'Way to go dudes' and he said, 'Great, print!' Then it's in the film. Now it's on YouTube, about 10 or 20 different incarnations with about 50 to 100,000 hits, and there's a Sparta remix, to techno music, for two minutes, with [Richard Marcus] going, 'Yeah, yeah, yeah!' My lesson was, when you're on set and the director asks you to do a line, you do it 100%."[2]

Ivo Cristante's ingenious "rock and roll" roof made its debut in the scene, with the contraption required to show the effects of the Graboids' attempts at demolishing Chang's Market from under the ground. "We were almost ready to start shooting and realised that nobody was contracted to make the roof," said Cristante. "I had done this awful wrestling movie a year or two before and one little trick they use is how they construct the ring. It's just four plates that join in the centre, and in the centre there's a large coiled spring they usually take from motor homes and that gives the floor enough cushion to protect the performers. Because it's broken into four plates it gives it places to flex."

Cristante worked with the mechanical effects and construction teams to build two scaffold towers inside Chang's Market, placing a coiled spring on top of each one, before creating the roof as a series of six odd-shaped plates hinged together with roofing material, though not tarred or nailed down so it remained flexible. "We attached ropes to the appropriate corners of each plate, ganged them down, put a chair beside it and had a production assistant stand there and move the ropes up and down. You went on the roof and the whole thing undulated. I had told the assistant director that there was to be the camera crew and the principal actors but nobody else on that roof because I couldn't vouch for its safety. I went back there later in the day and there were 30 people on that damned roof. I was freaking out; the make-up artists were sunning themselves and nobody had any qualms about the safety."

The "rock and roll" roof of Chang's Market is slotted together
© Ivo Cristante

Said Underwood, "That roof would collapse and you could reset it so easily, it was ingenious what he did in designing the buildings for that town; to be able to design a roof that main actors could stand on and undergo that falling, dropping roof beneath them."

The "build it up then knock it down" mentality is a way of life on a film set, where nothing is designed to last longer than the duration of the shoot. "Whatever gets built is not built to be architecture, all the camera sees is the paint and we just care that the paint stands up long enough to get the shot," said Cristante. "If the grip needs to cut a chainsaw hole into the wall, so be it.

My philosophy is that if you really fuck up, paint it red and people will think it's a feature."

GUNS VS GRABOIDS

The next sequence followed Val as he ran to the Caterpillar, planning to drive the Perfectionites to safety. Determined to vary the Graboids' point-of-view, Ron Underwood employed the skills of visual effects supervisor Gene Warren, who had worked with Gale Anne Hurd on *The Abyss* through his company, Fantasy II. "I felt like we needed more than just the little pogo-cam shots that we did with a camera on a stick," said Underwood. "Gene had this really inventive idea about how to get a point-of-view through the dirt, which you physically can't do. He set a camera looking up at a plastic tube; we just dropped dirt on the camera and it looked like it was moving through the ground."

The escape from Perfection on the Caterpillar was a combination of work from both the first and second unit. "We did the shots with the big Caterpillar leaving Burt's home after they're up on the roof and they get rescued by Val and Earl," said Harper. "I did that hand-held, I just grabbed the camera, held it down below and walked backwards alongside it."

For the only time during filming, the cast and crew looked to the skies during this sequence, with Charlotte Stewart explaining that they "were shooting way out in the desert when we first took off on the tractor. We were in the middle of nowhere and all of a sudden this bat-winged plane came streaking through the desert. We were sitting there like aliens had just struck us, dumbfounded that this thing had flown by. We didn't figure it out until much later that it was the Stealth Bomber and they didn't know we were shooting out there."

One feature of the cult following that has grown up around *Tremors* since its original release is its high recognition among younger viewers thanks to broad humour, energetic action sequences and a smattering of bad language. *Tremors* also has a high level of gun violence, with numerous explosives, rifles and hand weapons used for comic effect within the film's heightened reality. The issue was alluded to during the Perfectionites' last stand against the Graboids upon a rock high in the Alabama Hills.

Actor Michael Gross was acutely aware that Burt Gummer's stance on gun use could confuse some viewers' perceptions of the character, leading him to insist that if his truck was going to have bumper stickers they couldn't be from the National Rifle Association (NRA), an organisation he was opposed to promoting. "I wouldn't exactly call myself a pacifist; I know there are reasons for war, sometimes good and probably most times very bad. I had actually been a member of a gun control group and of the NRA at one point, but they became too strident for my taste. The saying amongst the NRA is 'Guns don't kill people, people do' and my answer to that is, 'Guns don't kill people, they just make it easier.'"

Gross' personal views ensured he would not have been comfortable making a film that was violent for violence's sake. "Burt never turns his gun on another human being, ever," continued the actor. "It's about the monsters. Kids are fascinated about it, 'Look at Burt and his guns'. I say, 'Do you notice how Burt never aims the weapon at a human being?' There's one point where he gives the gun to Melvin, who makes a noise and Burt turns around and notices he's pointing a gun at a human being. He puts it down and says to Melvin, 'You came that close, that close, don't screw around when somebody's got a weapon in their hand.' So it's not funny. I took gun safety lessons and I have the greatest respect for weapons, I just think there are too damn many of them."

"Obviously there were a lot of guns for the Michael Gross character, and we had a gun expert [on set]," said Kevin Bacon. "I remember they took us into the desert with a whole collection one day, shooting things, thinking we'd never have to use them in the movie. It was kind of fun shooting into the side of a wall."

The sequence that saw Burt admonish Melvin upon the rock led to one of the Graboids being blown up with high explosives.

A recurring visual gag through the *Tremors* films is that once a Graboid is blown up and a shower of slime has rained down upon the heroes, a final slab of dead Graboid lands on somebody, usually causing them to raise a weary eyebrow. "It's timing," said Maddock. "It's the idea of you do it, you do it, you do it, you do it ... everything's fine ... you get your laughs, you get your gross out ... we're OK ... splat! In the first film, people liked the big Graboid explosion near the end with the stuff exploding over the rocks. I remember standing there with everyone throwing things at all the people hiding on the rocks."

The final set piece saw Val luring the remaining Graboid off the end of a cliff, the same one seen in the opening shot of the film. As before, the wide shot was a matte painting rendered by Robert Stromberg, placed in front of the camera on location and filmed from a height of more than 30-feet.

"I'd finished on the film by that point but they had me come in to do a few scenes with Kevin, where he's lighting the fuse to blow the monster up that's coming at him," said Virgil Harper. Harper requested that the crew laid out around 140-feet of dolly track for the camera beside the trench where they had buried the Graboid, before asking that they pull the buoy under the ground on a rope tied to a Jeep.

"It was like an E Ticket ride at Disneyland; the grips were pushing me as fast as they could on a doorway dolly with a camera on a high-hat camera mount," continued Harper, who was attempting to keep the camera's focus on Kevin Bacon. "They couldn't stop me, so we ran off the end of the dolly track as it was coming to mow them all down. Then we jumped onto a crane and I put the camera down and I had to get it slung underneath. I was trying to figure out how to shoot the darn thing, because I needed the camera nose almost on the ground. They swung me right into the close-up of Kevin, right at the end, just before it blows. That kind of stuff was so much fun."

For the shot of the creature crashing through the cliff face and plummeting to its bloody death, the Skotaks were called upon to build a quarter-scale model of the cliff based on photos taken of

Red Rock Canyon, near Lone Pine. Robert and Dennis Skotak recreated the cliff face as a 20-foot by 30-foot wide model made from wood, chicken wire and cheesecloth sprayed with urethane foam in their LA studio. A hole was cut into the side of the model and a ramp placed behind it, allowing the model makers to push the Graboid through.[3]

"We made a polyurethane skin that was prescored and draped around a core section made of rope, inside that we filled condoms with orange methocel blood," explained Woodruff. "We thought we were playing it safe by making the creature strong enough to sustain three takes, but the one that ended up on screen was take number nine."[4]

In the finished film, Kevin Bacon can be seen standing atop the cliff looking down on the splattered Graboid, with Fred Ward and Finn Carter behind him. This effect was achieved using some clever camera angles, with a scaffold built behind the cliff model and shot from below. For the long shot from below, two members of the effects crew, Steve Lebed and Mitch Coughlin, stood in for Kevin Bacon and Fred Ward respectively, while director Ron Underwood replaced Finn Carter as Rhonda.[5]

"It was such a happy experience working on the film," said Gale Anne Hurd. "I remember we didn't have enough money for a crew gift, that was one of the things that had cuts in the budget and as I recall Kevin Bacon and I split the costs personally. It's rare you'll find an actor who's so generous, committed and appreciative to fellow cast and crew members. That was just one more remarkable thing about the project."

With location filming completed, Perfection torn down and cast and crew dispersing from their temporary homes, Lone Pine was left in peace once more, with rattlesnakes now the only slithery menace the locals had to worry about.

Back in Los Angeles, Ron Underwood had bigger problems to deal with than Graboids: studio executives.

CHAPTER FIVE
RESHOOTS, RE-EDITING AND RELEASE

Still working under the title of *Dead Silence* to avoid union problems, Ron Underwood began his 10-week editing period away from the Universal lot at the historic Warner Hollywood Studios, once home to the original United Artists and Samuel Goldwyn Studios. The director settled down to cut the film alongside his editor, O. Nicholas Brown, the first time the pair had worked together. "I really liked Nick's sensibilities, his take on the film," stated Underwood. "He wasn't trying to manipulate the audience but just really 'what's right from your heart' for these characters and what's going on."

The director was glad to be away from the more demanding side of shooting in Lone Pine. "My time in the editing room was just blissful. The nature of shooting a film outdoors, out in the desert, it takes a lot of physical endurance. I think of shooting like shopping for ingredients so that you can make your feast in the editing room. You're not under that same amount of pressure time-wise and you're not dealing with 100-and-some people. The most important time that we spent was working on character. The actors were all so good, the nuance that they all brought to their roles, and finding those moments in the editing so that you're really along for the ride and you believe they're this community, that was great to bring about."

"While you're shooting, the director circles his favourite takes and that's what the editor takes into account and he assembles these sequences," said cinematographer, Alexander Gruszynski. "After the principal is done, the director sits in the cutting room and is very hands-on from the beginning to the end of the movie, sequence by sequence, and tries to chisel at the story. I'm involved once the film is edited and locked; that's when I sit in the lab and make sure that the visual continuity is there as far as the colour scheme and all that stuff. That's my job, to make sure that it looks the way it was intended, that within the sequence the colour matches from one angle to the other."

The film's soundtrack was now a priority for Underwood, with sound work supervised by an old USC classmate, Steve Flick. "Our re-recording mixers were also very talented and all went on to huge success," noted Underwood. "Our dialogue re-recording mixer, Kevin O'Connell, has been nominated more than anyone in Academy history without a win, while Greg Russell was the effects re-recording engineer and Jeffrey Haboush was the music mixer."

According to the director, one of the important elements of the sound mix was the roar of the Graboids, achieved by combining the flush of toilets, mechanical groans and various animal sounds, including the trumpet of elephants. Determined that cinema audiences should feel the rumble of the ground and the shrieks of the creatures, Underwood convinced the studio to let him mix the film in the relatively new Dolby SR format.

With his first edit completed, the director initiated a "friends" preview screening comprised of an audience of trusted associates, including Gale Anne Hurd's then-husband, James Cameron, and some of those who had worked on the film. One of those present was Hilbert Hakim, a friend of Hurd's who would go on to become a second assistant director on 1996's *Tremors 2: Aftershocks*. "Gale called me and four or five other editors and visual effects producers to watch a cut of *Beneath Perfection*," said Hakim. "Ron was there along with the producers, writers and the editors. Gale had catered the screening and said, 'After you eat I'm going to give you each a legal pad and by the time you finish watching the film I want that completely filled with notes as to how you think this film should be changed.'"

"This is something I have done on all my productions since then, even when I do movies for television, as you want to put your best foot forward when showing the film to the studio for the first time," said Underwood of the screening. "It allows you the confidence of knowing that the picture is working before you show it to the studio since it is so difficult once you're so close to the material to know for sure if you are communicating what you intend."

Hakim's initial reaction was that the film wasn't in perfect shape. "We could feel the beats that were missing. The visual and physical effects were kind of cheesy to begin with, not that they were meant to be very high-tech. The comedy was very flat and it came across as like a kind of cheesy sci-fi film. Gale had the courage and the confidence not to have her ego hurt and took our notes."

The screening led to some additional editing work taking place before the film was shown to Universal's studio heads. Underwood's desire to make it a faster ride led him to trim some scenes along the way, with one cut made to the Graboid naming sequence in Chang's Market. A close look at the film's trailer shows that Melvin originally mentioned "Mega worms, or suckers, or suckoids", but in the finished film that's trimmed to just "suckoids".

Once the studio had seen the cut, they were willing to put more money into effects to bolster the film, allowing Underwood to finally add shots of the creatures tunnelling through the ground. "I wanted both clean points of view travelling through the dirt and a pass-by of the creature travelling underground," noted the director.

The crew at 4-Ward Productions were hired once again to complete some additional photography for the film. "They wanted underground shots of the Graboid," explained Robert Skotak. "One was a shot where the worm comes up and hits the underside of a trailer. They're sprinkled throughout the movie, a shot here, a shot there."

With new effects completed and inserted into the film, this early cut of *Beneath Perfection* was finally screened to a general audience, with studio representatives in attendance. Though the majority of the film seemed to go down well, the beginning and ending caused some consternation. The original pre-title sequence, featuring Old Fred and Edgar Deems discussing a mule, was deemed to be too slow, while the final moments of the film caused an audience outcry. As originally written and filmed, Rhonda walked away from Val before he and Earl headed to Bixby in their truck. With Earl disgusted at Val's inability to sort out his love life, when the latter realised Rhonda still had his lighter, they turned the truck around to return to Perfection and Rhonda.

"At the end Val and Earl are talking at the truck and Val has this conversation with Rhonda; the audience started chanting, 'Kiss her, kiss her, kiss her' because he was fumbling around so much," Underwood said. "The president of the studio said, 'Well if we have them kiss at the end, that's what the audience really wants.' This was the first note given in regards to the reshoot that was later scheduled after this first preview." Though convinced that the original ending was right for their film, all concerned agreed it was not a battle worth fighting. "Nancy was talking regularly with the studio and warned us that this was not something we would be able to win, that the studio was definite about this," said the director.

Another note that came out of this screening was from the studio chairman, Tom Pollock, who wanted the script to explain the origins of the newly found Graboids. "Around this time Universal was in negotiations to be purchased by Matsushita in Japan," said Underwood. "Earthquakes are such a big deal in Japan that the studio thought that adding the element of an earthquake unleashing Graboids from the centre of the Earth would strengthen the Japanese market for the film. That would also please the company now in line to take over Universal. Brent, Steve and I had always loved the fact that no one could figure out where these monsters came from and we were not happy with this idea. However, we were told it must happen."

"Tom Pollock, after it was all done and cut, decided that he wanted a different ending and everybody sort of didn't agree," commented Nancy Roberts, "but Tom was the head of the studio and he authorised it to be shot. He was really generous, I can't say enough about the Universal team on this. It was just one of those happy circumstances."

FURTHER RESHOOTS AND ABORTED OPENINGS

With the order received from Universal to shoot a new prologue to the film, Wilson and Maddock hastily wrote a new short script and assembled some of the original crew to return to Lone Pine in October 1989. "We now had a much bigger daily shooting budget since the studio was 100% behind the film," said Ron Underwood. "It was bittersweet having all this money for what we didn't really want to shoot after struggling so much with our budget as we shot the film."

"They'd come up with the idea that maybe the creatures came from outer space," said Virgil Harper. "I remember we got a helicopter and flew over this kind of San Andreas Fault area in the desert. Then we did another shot where we came down like we were falling out of space in the helicopter, right down to a blacktop road out in the desert with yellow lines. We came flying right down as close as we could, then cut to a moving shot on a camera car and shot that in reverse, starting on a dead rabbit. As the camera left the rabbit, I started tipping up and then you saw a billboard in the desert at a cross in the road with a blinking yellow light. We had built a billboard with a Las Vegas dance girl that had just little tassels on her nipples. There was also a monument mentioning it was a gold mine area."

In what would have been the full sequence, the camera zoomed down from the sky and hurtled along the road before stopping dead centre on a close-up of the rabbit, all in one move. Suddenly a coyote came running out of the desert and grabbed the rabbit, before what sounds like an earthquake causes the tassels on the billboard to spin and the monument to fall apart. As the coyote howls and runs away, a puff of dust in the distance is the tell-tale sign that a Graboid has just eaten it.

The film's romantic finale was also reshot near Lone Pine, with Kevin Bacon, Fred Ward and Finn Carter taken back to the original site of the town in Olancha. Thanks to the set having been torn down months before, the crew assembled a street sign and some set dressing to allow the shots of Val kissing Rhonda to be filmed. "They really wanted me to kiss Finn," Bacon said. "Movies always have to end strong and I guess that was the idea. Luckily my hair was still long."

"I was in New York and got a call I had to come back out," said Carter. "So I was flown out and basically spent a day kissing Kevin, from every angle, and in between kisses he'd tell me how his newborn baby was doing. That's how romantic it was."[1]

Armed with new opening and closing sequences, Ron Underwood returned to his editing suite and set about cutting them into the film, also ensuring that composer Ernest Troost was available to rescore the new ending. "I knew I had a piece of music at the very end where Val walks up to Rhonda at the car and that music had to segue into a song, but I didn't know what song it was so I didn't know what key it was in," said Troost. "At the last minute they said it was Reba's "Why Not Tonight", so I made it a recapitulation of the theme you heard on the pole vaulting. There's a slide guitar that goes up at the end, some piano comes in and it's the same key as the one at the start of hers." The result was a smooth transition from the romantic tone of the final scene to the up-tempo end title song.

Studio instructions had been followed with the new edit, but the next preview screening revealed that the audience was not entirely receptive to the changes. "The dead rabbit sequence was screened for a test audience and the reaction was nearly violent," said Steve Wilson. "In overwhelming numbers the audience notes were, 'How *dare* you kill a rabbit for your worthless film?' Many seemed to have forgotten or ignored the movie that followed. In our defence, we pointed out that we'd procured the already-dead rabbit from a specialty food supply shop, but that didn't vindicate us, and the rabbit scene was quickly excised, never to be spoken of again."

"We thought that part of the fun of the film was not knowing where the creature was from and that nobody in that period of time would ever figure it out," added Underwood. "When the audience turned on the film because of the rabbit being eaten we were kind of happy about it. We were very happy that the studio said, 'Well that's OK let's not use that prologue.' Also, while the audience was fine with the kiss at the end of the film, they certainly had no stronger reaction than they did with the prior version. However, the studio wanted to keep this new ending."

What should have been a simple case of removing the new pre-title sequence led to more changes when Ron Underwood screened the final cut for Gale Anne Hurd. "We were all proud of the film when it was finally mixed and played back for Gale," said the director. "Everyone turned to her, expecting accolades, but she said that the score did not work. We were all deflated and Ernest was devastated. A new composer, Robert Volk, was hired and given only a week to replace many of the cues. It was a difficult time as we were racing toward completion and delivery of the movie."

"I was hired at the last minute," said Volk. "We had a fairly normal schedule when I started on my first day of working, but by my second day I got a phone call saying 'the release date's been moved up, write everything you can in one week!' We just replaced as much of the original music as we could. I did not take credit on the film because there was an odd clause in the original composer's agreement and I didn't want a shared credit. A strange set of circumstances, but a terrific film to work on."[2]

Twenty-five years on, Troost is philosophical about the treatment of his music. "This kind of thing happens in Hollywood and the executive producer had her own agenda. She felt like some of the action scenes should be punched up and brought in her own composer. They don't call you up and say, 'Could you do this again? Take another try and we want this a little bit more like this.'"

Confident they now had the film in the best possible condition, Underwood and his team prepared to unleash their film upon an unsuspecting world, hopeful they'd take the box office by storm.

RELEASING TREMORS

Though there were attempts to keep the film under Hollywood's radar by referring to it as *Dead Silence* during the Lone Pine shoot, the cast and crew were always under the impression it would be called *Beneath Perfection* on its release. The plan changed when Universal Studios chairman, Tom Pollock, took a personal interest in the name. "The studio felt that the title *Tremors* would suggest the connection to earthquakes and that would be better received in Japan," said Ron Underwood. "Jim Jacks took a crew jacket as a gift from the production to Tom, who was angry that it still had *Beneath Perfection* on it. He threw the jacket across the room at Jim. This is when the new title became official."

"I thought the title was cute but you had to know the town was called Perfection," reflected Universal's Jim Jacks. "We lost on the title, and I don't know that *Beneath Perfection* was better," added Wilson. "Little kids think that *Tremors* is the name of the monster. I didn't realise this until years later when I got letters saying, 'When the Tremor comes into the basement ... ' and I'm wondering what they're talking about before I realise that a Graboid is a Tremor."

Actor Tony Genaro was another member of the crew who knew the film under its original title. "Everybody said, 'Oh that's a great title, *Beneath Perfection*.' When it came out it was called *Tremors* and I went, 'What the ... ? *Tremors*? Oh, I'm not sure I like that!' Well, they knew what they were doing; they know how to sell the stuff and we know how to make it."

Acutely aware of sensitivities around her latest film's non-union status, producer Gale Anne Hurd had successfully managed to maintain a veil of secrecy around the project during the shoot, though this ended when journalist Jane Galbraith broke the news of Hurd's involvement with a new "sci-fier" starring Kevin Bacon and Fred Ward called *Tremors* in the 19 April 1989 issue of *Variety*. The report went on to note that "only sketchy details" were available on *Tremors* and that "Hurd preferred to keep the production quiet because it was a non-union picture that is expected to become a negative pickup by Par [Paramount]." According to Galbraith, production assistants at Hurd's office "pleaded ignorance of those involved in the film, even so far as to say they were able to reach the producer by phone but couldn't say where she was." Hurd's agent, Lou Pitt, "refused to discuss *Tremors*, saying 'it was a political thing.'"[3]

In August 1989, *The Hollywood Reporter* noted that *Tremors* would be released by Universal Pictures in "early 1990", going on to state "the studio picked up the worldwide rights to the science fiction comedy." The report also mentioned that another of Gale Anne Hurd's projects, the James Cameron-directed *The Abyss*, would be in cinemas the following week.[4] Hurd was executive producer of the underwater spectacular.

Daily Variety featured Gale Anne Hurd in a 14 August piece discussing her numerous projects, with the paper noting that they reflected "her balance between independent and studio productions." Hurd told Lawrence Cohn that the Tremors script was "walking a fine line between outright comedy and science fiction."[5]

Writing in *LA Weekly*'s 19 November edition, Anne Thompson touched upon the negative preview audience reaction to the newly shot earthquake footage (noting that shots of the San Andreas Fault had been filmed just two days before San Francisco's Loma Prieta earthquake which had taken place on 17 October) and the fact that "producers had obediently cut the sequence."[6]

Just before *Tremors* was scheduled for release, Universal carried out a market research screening to gauge audience reactions. Instead of recruiting fans of comedy or adventure films, Hurd was appalled when they brought in a horror audience to watch a film that was supposed to be funny. "They thought it was unintentionally funny and it got terrible scores, the worst in my career," said Hurd, "I think it averaged a 45, which is below low.

It shocked everyone when the reviews came out and it became one of their most liked and enjoyed films. If you ask people if they liked *Tremors*, I think 99% will say 'loved that film'. From that point on I insisted on knowing what questions the audiences were being asked before they were approached to attend screenings. It was very disheartening because we knew it was good."

"Even in those days we'd talk to the marketing people about how to get people into the theatre," explained Jim Jacks. "They asked what it was, a comedy or a horror? Well, it's both. We had the same argument on *Field of Dreams*. We said, 'It's about a guy who hears voices in a cornfield, how do you put that in a trailer?' I said, 'Don't sell it on what it is, sell it on how it makes you feel,' and ultimately that movie did business, but not as much as you'd have thought given its reputation. That happens to a lot of movies. I made *Dazed and Confused*, which is considered a classic, but it didn't do much business in theatrical; many build their reputation on video."

"The studio wanted to get the core horror audience, because with them they could make money on the film," said Ron Underwood. "But this wasn't like the films being made for the horror audience at that time, films like *Friday the 13th* or *A Nightmare on Elm Street*. They were much darker, much harder, much less comedy, and this was such a quirky film. So they wanted that audience but that audience really didn't want this film."

Universal began planning *Tremors*' marketing early on in the film's production, entrusting art director David Reneric, who had worked on the advertising campaigns of some of the biggest films of the 1970s and '80s, including the teaser poster and logo for George Lucas' *The Empire Strikes Back* (1980)[7], to oversee the development of the visuals. Reneric knew little about *Tremors* apart from the basic plot, something he explained to young Los Angeles-based illustrator, Donn Greer, who had been working on various animated series as a character designer and layout artist. Greer was hired to sketch "comps", the rough elements that would make up a final poster design.

Various sketches from Donn Greer's early work on the *Tremors* poster design © Donn Greer

Another of Donn Greer's rough sketches of
a possible poster design © Donn Greer

The ideas for the sketches came from Reneric, usually based on conversations with the marketing director at the studio who would give him a general direction. "I'd meet David at his studio in Hollywood, we'd go over the ideas, then I'd take his thumbnails home, often just doodles with copious notes, and spend all night working on them," explained Greer of his process. "David was very much a perfectionist and we'd sometimes hire models, often my sister who he had the hots for, and rent props for photo shoots. When we first started working on *Tremors*, David had almost no information on the film and no stills, all we knew was that it was going to star Kevin Bacon and he'd be battling the creatures."

In the days before the internet, if Greer needed photos of an actor he had to drive to a store that specialised in movie memorabilia, thumbing through stills to find something suitable. "On *Tremors* I only worked on "first stage" black and white comps, though some of them did get fairly detailed. After a couple of weeks David finally got stills from the film, though at that point we'd already sketched up a number of completely inappropriate comps," noted Greer, with reference to one image featuring a close-up on the face of a young woman being pulled under the ground and another of a muscle-bound Kevin Bacon firing a machine gun at a mass of tentacles attacking him from the air, while a blonde girl in shorts looks on. "I remember in one instance we rented a prop mini gun which was made out of rubber and weighed a ton."

Another of Greer's sketches showed three of the main cast standing atop what could be an early design of Chang's General Market, beside the iconic Perfection water tower. As the trio stare at the ground, giant cracks are visible in the dirt. "We tried one version with mounds instead of cracks, but it looked like they were being attacked by a gang of tough moles," mused Greer.

"The idea for the final poster came partly from a sketch I'd come up with which was a crack or fissure rising up through the earth towards the principal actors," Greer continued. "I only suggested the idea as it would be easy to sketch; whether a comp took an hour to draw, or five hours each paid the same. David liked the idea and thought it could be expanded upon, whereby each side of the fissure would open revealing one of the Graboids. I seem to recall a few of these opening cardboard posters may have been built for the premiere in Hollywood."

Despite the time and money spent on Greer's contributions, Universal decided to move away from a painted version and replace it with a photo based design. Perhaps owing to the "creature under the ground" premise of *Tremors* having similarities to the central "shark under the water" conceit of Spielberg's *Jaws*, the studio capitalised on audience recognition of the latter by substituting the sea with desert, the shark with a toothy creature and the swimmer with Kevin Bacon, Fred Ward and Finn Carter. "I remember the first time I saw the final poster thinking it was clearly a *Jaws* take off," said Greer. "Of course I was a little disappointed it was done using photos rather than artwork, but at that time there was a major shift in the industry from using illustrators with paint brushes to using art directors and Photoshop."

Angry at the finished poster design, Brent Maddock announced his displeasure to Universal, only for them to ignore him. "The billboards in LA used that same graphic and I had a friend ask when my movie is coming out," said Maddock. "I said, 'There's a billboard on Pico Boulevard, you've driven by it every day,' and he said 'That's your movie? Wow.' It misrepresented the film and I think that hurt it theatrically."

"I remember it not staying out very long, it was in and out [of cinemas]," Robert Jayne said. "Everybody thought it was this really scary horror movie and I think that might've been the mistake in the marketing of it. They really went after this "*Jaws* in the desert" type of thing and I think it should've been promoted as a kind of family action movie that's a little scary."

The film's cast and crew screening took place at 8pm on 6 January 1990 at the Lorimar Cary Grant Theater in Culver City, though its youngest star had some issues with the Graboids. "Even though in person the worms were not very frightening, I was sitting with my mom in front of my sister, she was right in the row just behind us," said Ariana Richards. "There are some parts in the movie that are kind of scary and when those creatures would hit, I would shut my eyes or turn around towards my sister, who was four years younger than me, brave as can be, eyes wide open. When it got to a place where somebody might be sucked under the ground or eaten alive, she would say to me 'OK, Ariana, you better turn this way, it's coming!"'

Robert Jayne attended a screening at Hollywood's Mann's Chinese Theatre. "I remember sitting down in the front and I heard these two girls behind me. Every time I came on screen they were saying, 'Gosh, I hope they eat him, I hope he dies.' After an hour I remember turning around and saying 'Hey!' and they were like, 'Oh, we're just kidding!'"

"When we went to the Hollywood premiere of the film we were blown away, I mean the film was fantastic," said Hilbert Hakim, who had attended the original friends' preview screening on Gale Anne Hurd's invitation. "It was a very entertaining, really well-directed film and Ron had done a great job. Hollywood audiences are very critical and they don't like to applaud or laugh at a competitor's film and this had everything going for it."

TROUBLE AT THE BOX OFFICE

Tremors received a PG-13 rating from the Motion Picture Association of America (MPAA) and opened in 1,472 North American theatres on 19 January 1990, grossing $3,731,520 on its opening weekend ($4,817,760 in its opening week) and entering the box office charts at fifth place behind *Born on the Fourth of July*, *Tango & Cash*, *Internal Affairs* and *The War of the Roses*.[8] "The studio really wanted the film to make a minimum of $5m dollars on the opening weekend and it didn't reach that benchmark," explained Ron Underwood.

"It did not do a lot of business up front because it was a hard movie to market," admitted Jim Jacks. "I think if it was opening today it would do a lot better in domestic theatrical box office because we would have built a lot of word of mouth on the internet with the fanboys. If you get good openings, word of mouth is strong. I forget what it took on opening weekend but it wasn't much. But not for a moment [did the studio regret] they made it. From the opening weekend they were proud of it."

"Tom [Pollock] and Casey [Silver] were disappointed because they really liked it and Tom called me and said, 'We blew the ad campaign,'" said Wilson. "They thought it was going to be a really big hit. They sold it more as a comedy than they should have. At the time they said they were selling it as a horror film.

The ad department worked hard trying to get the word out, and it wasn't a monster flop, but it wasn't the success they want every film to be."

As the box office numbers came in, members of the cast and crew watched its progress from their various vantage points.

"It wasn't [in cinemas] more than a week and it was gone," sighed Michael Gross. "My friends would say to me, 'Oh Michael, I don't see those kind of movies.' I said, 'No, no, you don't understand, this is not just a monster movie,' and they'd say, 'That's what I see in the trailers.' The quirkiness of it was something that I don't think they knew what to do with. They have nice little neat categories in which they place films. For me, this was to science fiction movies what *The Naked Gun* was to the crime genre. I saw it once or twice because I was curious to see an audience's reaction, and I heard them howl. But I guess there just weren't enough howls or enough press, and I'm not sure to this day what happened, but it was disappointing."

"I remember when I first saw it I was in Seattle," recalled Tony Genaro. "I saw a sign with *Tremors* in huge letters and it showed three people, Fred Ward, Finn Carter and Kevin Bacon, with a big toothy creature behind them. It looked like it could devour the world. I had a bunch of nephews that were all in the same age range, they were like eight, and my sister called me up and said, 'You're going to have to explain to these kids that you're still alive and that nothing bad happened to you.' I had to tell them, 'Uncle Tony's fine, I'll be over to see you next week.' They just loved playing *Tremors*, it became a game with them."

Ivo Cristante kept an eye on the trade papers to see how *Tremors* was faring. "I was very disappointed it didn't do well, but by that time I'd done about a dozen low-budget films and if they got a week of distribution that was good. Most of them were direct-to-video. The other film I did with Gale Anne Hurd was *Bad Dreams*, which also crashed at the box office."

"A lot of people were reluctant to see it," recalled Robert Skotak. "I know people who wound up seeing it because somebody called them and said, 'I saw this movie, and you need to see it.' It was word of mouth because the advertising could not convey what it was or what its special qualities were. The one thing about the comedy is that it comes out of the natural behaviour of the characters and their attitudes. There's a sweetness to it, it's charming. If I hadn't worked on it I would still be saying this."

IN THE PRESS

It wasn't long before reviews started appearing in US newspapers, magazines and trade periodicals, with *Variety*'s unnamed reviewer remarkably prescient when it came to predicting the film's box office success: "*Tremors* has a few clever twists but ultimately can't decide what it wants to be – flat-out funny, which it's not, or a scarefest. Confusedly marketed, pic has *Aliens* producer Gale Anne Hurd's stamp on it but should unearth only limited box office before crawling off to homevid."

The paper acknowledged that the script had drawn inspiration from films such as 1959's *The Killer Shrews*, noted the genre conventions, baulked at the "low-brow" opening sequences and was cautious in its praise of the "fine if bland" performances. On the plus side, the film's sound, creature effects and Ernest Troost's score (with no mention of the uncredited Robert Volk) were deemed "first rate".[9]

The *LA Times*' Michael Wilmington wrote enthusiastically of the "jocular good-time monster film with surprises up its sleeve", commenting on its B movie heritage before suggesting the moral of the story: "If we all pull together, we can survive any catastrophe." Wilmington also gave Maddock and Wilson a backhanded compliment by stating that they were imitating hack writers ("but at least they're trying to be clever hacks") before neatly summing the film up: "It's a zippy melodrama for small-town America and small-towners at heart: well-executed kitsch for audiences that will still be amused at the notion that the bugs are getting so big, they'll drag us all down."[10]

LA Weekly's Ron Stringer questioned the PG-13 rating ("I mean you didn't hear Fred [Ward] say 'pecker' back in reel two?") and summarised the plot as "an engagingly cornball story of a little kid, a teenage kid, and six or a dozen big dumb grown-up kids getting chased around the desert by giant smelly pumpkin-pulp-oozing worms." Ultimately, Stringer felt *Tremors* was "*Hee-Haw*larious enough to qualify it as some kind of family entertainment hit."[11]

Cindy Fuchs in the *Philadelphia City Paper* suggested *Tremors* was "one of those "coulda been" flicks: it coulda been smarter, coulda been nastier, coulda been funnier, if only it had pushed its own idea a little harder." Fuchs' main bone of contention with Wilson and Maddock's script was the absence of "off-the-wall metaphor" with relation to the Graboids: "What allusions exist are vague and underdeveloped; to birth (mama earth spews forth deadly gaping mouths); to the loss of the western frontier and "personal freedom"; and to an inexplicably warped Nature not unlike that presented in *The Birds*."[12]

Michael Musto was also searching for those elusive metaphors in *The Village Voice*, stating: "The large, voracious creatures that are the stars of *Tremors* may well be the ultimate image of '80s yuppie greed", before admonishing the script for not addressing this or any other metaphor. Acknowledging that the film "settles for a sort of good-natured, slam bang dopiness that's enjoyable enough if not exactly challenging", Musto went on to mistake Melvin as the teenage son of the Gummers and to recommend the film "for anyone looking for an excuse not to move to a warmer climate."[13]

The *New York Times*' Vincent Canby didn't find much to praise, feeling: "*Tremors* wants to be funny, but it spends too much time winking at the audience ... more than anything else, it looks like the sort of movie that might have been put together so that tourists visiting Universal Studios could see a movie being made."[14]

At *The Washington Post*, Richard Harrington exclaimed that *Tremors* was "a delightful throwback" to fifties and sixties creature features that was "less focused on its oversized monsters ... than on their potential victims, and how these people react". Harrington concluded that director Ron Underwood "also throws in some funny allusions to *Jaws* and *Moby Dick* and comes up with a horror film that's rare in its appropriateness for family audiences."[15]

By the end of its four-week stint in North American cinemas, *Tremors* had grossed $16,667,084, ending up the 71st highest grossing film of 1990. It subsequently rolled out into cinemas around the world, reaching Australia first on 12 April while the Philippines had to wait until 16 October.

THE AFTERMATH

Though *Tremors* had failed to become a hit at the box office, those associated with the film remained proud of their work, aware that the quirkiness of the script and the mishandled advertising campaign had led to confusion amongst the target audience.

"I have some regrets because it certainly would have raised my profile as an actor on the big screen, not that it hasn't done marvellously well in the after market," said Michael Gross. "I think no one was more chagrined than Kevin Bacon, who was really taking the lead in this thing and whom I thought was brilliant. He and Fred Ward were just dynamite, I mean the chemistry was just marvellous. Thank God for the after market response."

Kevin Bacon remained tight-lipped on the subject of *Tremors* for many years, though one story has repeatedly been quoted in interviews. Suffering from anxiety around the time of filming in 1989, Bacon told how one afternoon in New York, on the corner of 86th and Broadway, he "broke down and fell to the sidewalk, screaming to my pregnant wife, 'I can't believe I'm doing a movie about underground worms!'"[16] A 2011 interview shed more light on this event and Bacon's reticence to discuss the role of Valentine McKee. "When I think of *Tremors*, in a very short amount of time I've gotten engaged, gotten married, my mother's gotten cancer, my career is in the shitter, my wife is nine months pregnant with our first child, and I am terrified. That's *Tremors*."[17]

"Kevin complained to a friend of mine that after all these incredible films he's done, like *A Few Good Men*, people would always bring up *Tremors*," said Ron Underwood. "I think it was just like 'Oh my God, will they just stop talking about this?' But he had a great time doing it. I think he has since accepted *Tremors* as part of his past."

Today, Bacon feels far more comfortable with the role he crafted more than two decades ago in Lone Pine. "I liked it," said the actor in 2015 about his initial reaction to the completed film back in 1990. "It's always hard for me when something is just done, I look at it with a super-critical eye, saying, 'I wish I'd done this or that [differently]' and I have to get a little perspective on it. In retrospect, it does hold up and it really is a good film. It's subtle in its humour at times, not always subtle with its monsters, but there are things that are handled deftly. I think Ron did a really great job and it was a good script."

Someone else who remains happy to be associated with *Tremors* is Reba McEntire, who added the film's closing song to the set list of her live shows. "I'm totally proud of *Tremors*," said the singer. "I've done 11 movies and [it's the one] people mention the most."

"Reba was so just great, she was so high energy and fun and we've been friends ever since," said Ariana Richards. "In fact, Reba is the reason that I like country music. I would always attend her concerts and she'd give me the special backstage pass and we could hang out. I'm happy to have that friendship, we still stay in touch quite a bit."

Alexander Gruszynski, the cinematographer who had found the 1989 shoot to be one of the toughest of his career, later discovered a new appreciation for the film. "Thousands of horror films are made and very few of them survive in the history of cinema. This is one of them because it's hard to categorise, it stands out on its own. A few months ago I was on location in

Atlanta and I couldn't sleep, so I turned on the TV and *Tremors* was on. It was kind of like the old acquaintance you haven't seen that you're curious what happened to. I got totally sucked in and could watch it with a distance, as if I wasn't part of it. I thought, 'Oh my God, this is really incredibly good.' It was almost like an epiphany."

Cristen Carr Strubbe also views her time on the film with affection. "I have three kids and the youngest is the 10-year-old, the movie means something different to each one of them. It's such an iconic horror film, almost on that list of films you have to see sometime in your youth to scare you."

"I look back on it and think if you tried to make it now it wouldn't happen," said Gale Anne Hurd. "It took a great script, terrific producers and directors, a great cast and very much for the studio, Jim Jacks to fight for it. Even though $10m doesn't seem like a lot, [that was money] they had to give out to a film so there were others that didn't get made. Not only did they make their money back, but I remember that when it aired on network TV, I think it was NBC, it got incredibly high ratings and it would be repeated year-after-year. A lot of films weren't back then, but every time it aired on TV it turns out there were more fans than anyone expected."

One of the reasons *Tremors* has continued to grow its audience through the years is thanks to its regular airings on TV and the subsequent release on domestic home video, something that wouldn't have been possible just a few years earlier. "We had this big audience that came to the film later, after the film was initially released," said Ron Underwood. "I hear from people all the time who are introducing their kids to it because they want them to have the experience they had when they were young. It's kind of weird that it's lived on so long but I just feel lucky that it's still hanging in there."

The success of *Tremors* on home video was the first sign that this was a film that could exceed the expectations of even its biggest supporters.

CHAPTER SIX
TREMORS 2: AFTERSHOCKS

The years that followed the release of *Tremors* saw Ron Underwood's feature film career take off, leading him to helm 1991's Oscar-winning comedy western, *City Slickers*, while Steve Wilson and Brent Maddock continued to write scripts. Nancy Roberts converted her talent agency into a management company in 1992 and now counted Wilson and Maddock among her clients.

In the same year, Roberts, Wilson, Maddock and Underwood co-founded their own production partnership, Stampede Entertainment. With *Tremors* a distant memory, the team were keen to find new success in original features. Said Wilson, "Tom Pollock was disappointed at the response [to *Tremors*] and said, 'Good try, move on', so we started writing screenplays back-to-back."

Stampede's first project in 1992 was another film for Universal, fantasy comedy *Heart and Souls*, which starred Robert Downey Jr. as a man reunited with his four guardian angels. Released in 1993, the film involved various *Tremors* alumni both behind and in front of the camera; not only did Wilson and Maddock co-write the screenplay with Underwood directing, but Roberts produced alongside Jim Jacks, Pam Dixon was casting director, Tony Genaro made a cameo and O. Nicholas Brown was its editor.

While the creators of *Tremors* may not have been considering a return to the town of Perfection, sequels to successful horror films were being welcomed by audiences, if not necessarily by critics. On 13 August 1993, the same day as *Heart and Souls* entered American cinemas, so did *Jason Goes to Hell: The Final Friday*, the ninth film in the long-running *Friday the 13*th series, while the sixth *A Nightmare on Elm Street* sequel, *Wes Craven's New Nightmare*, was in development for a 1994 release. Elsewhere, Don Coscarelli was directing *Phantasm III: Lord of the Dead for Universal* (the film was ultimately given a limited theatrical release in 1994 before going to VHS) and the *Halloween* franchise was bubbling under; *Halloween 5: The Revenge of Michael Myers* had arrived in 1989 and numerous attempts had been made by 1993 to finalise a script for what would become 1995's *Halloween: The Curse of Michael Myers*.

Soon after *Heart and Souls*' release, the Stampede team was surprised to learn from Universal Studios that they were keen to discuss the possibility of a sequel to *Tremors*, for release in 1994. Universal's only stipulation was that they needed Kevin Bacon and Reba McEntire back to guarantee a theatrical release. With two major names in the title the marketing department could justify the budget required. Without them there would be no film.

"We were a few years beyond the release of *Tremors* and there was some question whether or not we could do the sequel," said Nancy Roberts. "Generally the rule is that you do a sequel for two thirds of the original budget, so if we did the original at $10m, albeit we spent more, the rule would be that we wanted the principal stars back but at two thirds of our original budget."

Wilson and Maddock began discussing ideas for the new script, taking as a starting point the fact they already had a monster and that evolution could play a part in the story. The pair had received letters from fans asking if they would ever see a "Queen Graboid", something bigger than the first film's creatures, but this suggestion led the writers to consider whether a sequel would work where the creatures were actually smaller.

"It was very important to both of us to be consistent with the rules, that the monsters are blind and indestructible," said Wilson. "We thought about the characters and wanted to be true to Val and Earl leaving the town and going on to do something else with the notoriety they had. It grew from there and we refined the idea of the Shriekers, coming up with the idea that it would be a surprise to our characters. They knew what they were up against in the Graboids then the game changes on them."

The first *Tremors 2* script re-introduced viewers to Val and Earl a few years down the line from their success defeating the Graboids. Still living in Perfection Valley, the pair now ran an ostrich farm, having failed to capitalise on the financial opportunities that came with TV and magazine appearances; Rhonda had left Val when she realised she was earning more than him. News of a Graboid attack in Australia led the men to travel to the continent with Burt and Heather Gummer, while a new stage in Graboid evolution, the Shriekers, ensured complications for their plans to defeat the creatures.

In an attempt to fulfil Universal's request that Kevin Bacon return for the sequel, Wilson, Maddock and Underwood met the actor to discuss the role of Valentine McKee. "We had wonderful CGI animation of the Shriekers and we went to New York on Universal's dime and sat with Kevin to show him the footage," said Maddock. "We talked to him about the movie and [he] was impressed, but he'd done his monster movie and there was no way he was going to come back and do another."

The team were stunned to hear that Bacon wasn't a fan of *Tremors* and considered it a low point in his career. "I don't think he gets how good he is in the movie," said Steve Wilson. "He said, 'When people speak to me about it they never say how great you were, they say how cool the worms were.' The audience doesn't get that because Kevin is being so genuine, that's what makes the monsters work. I'm hoping he's made his peace with it."

"He said, 'I really would like to not carry films right now, I want to go back and do interesting character work,'" added Underwood. "It was a conscious decision of his not to be the lead in movies at that time and to just do some incredible roles, which he did in *JFK* and so many more. It continued to make him an amazing actor whose work was so broad."

"We're now at a time when we're just about on the frontier of the idea that you can make a film, have it live on video on demand and be successful and appreciated," explained Kevin

Bacon in 2015. "[Bong Joon-Ho's] *Snowpiercer* is a perfect example; it didn't do that much in the theatre but it had a massive following on video on demand, is thought of as a great film and is well respected. [In the 1990s], if something went right to VHS it was a disaster, so my feeling was why would I make a sequel to an unsuccessful film? It just didn't make sense to me from a career point of view."

Bacon may not have been keen on continuing with the *Tremors* franchise, but his son Travis, who had been a presence on the set of the first film thanks to his heavily pregnant mother, Kyra Sedgwick, was a fan. When asked in 2003 whether any of his children watched his films, Bacon replied: "When my son was eight, I let him see *Tremors*, because at that age he could appreciate it. When I spoke to him on the phone, I asked, 'Travis, did you see *Tremors*?' And he said, 'Yeah, I saw it. Dad, have you seen *Tremors 2*? It's really great.' I said, 'Son, I'm not in *Tremors 2*.' And he said, 'No, but it's cool.'"[1]

Reba McEntire's absence from the film wasn't a case of the actress wanting to distance herself from the character of Heather Gummer, but purely one of logistics. "Our tour schedule was getting really filled up and it was hard to schedule anything else," said McEntire, who admitted, "I've seen *Tremors 2* and loved it."

Without Bacon and McEntire in the cast list, Universal's features department passed on a theatrical version of *Tremors 2*, and the project went into limbo. However, and unknown to Stampede, developments in a newly formed division of Universal Studios that had been keeping an eye on the continuing success of the first film soon led to the idea of *Tremors 2* being resurrected.

A WHOLE NEW BALL GAME

The US home video market was established in 1975 with the arrival of Sony's Betamax video recording system. Following the unveiling of the VHS (Video Home System) a year later, the resultant VHS vs Betamax format war asked the public to decide between the two, the former winning after a protracted battle in video rental stores around the globe.[2]

Many consumers were reluctant to spend over $1000 for a VCR, while film studios were still uncertain about the format and concerned that by selling their titles on cassette they'd reduce their income from cinema releases. It took the burgeoning home exercise industry to kick-start the VHS buying craze with the release of the first *Jane Fonda Workout Video* in 1981, a title that encouraged home-based fitness fanatics to rewind and replay routines each day.[3] 17m units were sold and by 1987 the sales of VCRs alone were worth around $5.25bn in the US.[4]

Although fitness videos were a large part of the VHS market, the 1980s had seen the rise of a new trend in filmmaking, that of the made-for-video sequel to a film series that had originated on the big screen. Whereas *Ghoulies* (1984), *The Howling* (1981) and *Bloodfist* (1989) all had cinema releases, follow-ups *Ghoulies 2* (1987), *Howling IV: The Original Nightmare* (1988) and *Bloodfist IV: Die Trying* (1990) debuted on VHS. Films such as 1989's *Puppet Master* bypassed theatres completely and premiered on home video, spawning six sequels on VHS and DVD. By the late 1990s, films that originated on video were viewed as the natural successor to the 1950s B movie, with horror and sci-fi finding a home on the shelves of VHS retailers across the globe.[5]

Arriving at Universal Studios in 1978 as a sales representative, Louis Feola rose through the ranks to reach the position of President at Universal Studios Home Video by October 1992, designing the initial strategy for Universal to enter the direct-to-video (DTV) movie business. In 1992, Feola sat down with the team at Universal and made a proposal to allow him to make six follow-ups to successful theatrical releases: three sequels to 1988's *The Land Before Time*, two sequels to *Darkman* and a sequel to *Tremors*, which the studio approved.

Feola was certain a sequel to *Tremors* would be a perfect DTV title because he had been closely monitoring a number of financial barometers relating to the first film. These included *Tremors*' domestic and international box office takings, VHS performance across the top 20 markets and ratings from TV screenings around the globe. "We knew it could work," said Feola, "it was just getting a chance to prove it. We were armed with knowledge and knew how well the movies had performed in every aspect of distribution. We did a rigorous analysis and could tell it was out-performing the curve."

Feola's small team grew in 1993 with the arrival of Patti Jackson as director of programming. "Our films are always based on something you think you know and the idea is we don't need to spend the kind of marketing to get a movie out there because the original already did that," Jackson said. "The first movie our department did was *Darkman II: The Return of Durant* in 1994, and it was my job to figure out what to do next. I wasn't in the business when *Tremors* came out, but it was one of my favourite movies. We were searching for a title that would fit the directive and the demographic and couldn't find a title better than *Tremors*."

By late 1994, the team had started to explore the best way to move *Tremors 2* into production, determined to work with as many of the original creative team as possible. As head of Universal's Home Entertainment division, Louis Feola had on-going relationships with a number of producers and already knew Nancy Roberts, Steve Wilson and Brent Maddock at Stampede Entertainment. "It was a conversation with Nancy to start with, explaining what we were undertaking and where we saw a business opportunity," said Feola. "I explained why their movie fit and that we looked at things not as doing one-offs. We were assessing things thinking we could do a minimum of two because we believed in the franchises and the marketing extensions."

"This was before you automatically did this on video," said Wilson of Feola's decision to push ahead with a sequel. "Now if you have a modest hit in theatres you automatically spend $5m and put out some ghastly thing with the same title. The video division came to us to say they had their own money and would we like to make *Tremors 2*? We got a backhanded compliment from them when they said, 'We could sell an empty video box called *Tremors*, we have to have it.'"

Realising that once again they'd be left alone by the studio to make the film, the team at Stampede accepted the proposal to bring *Tremors 2* to video. Although the budget for a theatrical version had come in around the $13m mark, the DTV budget suggested to Roberts was less than $3m. "That's when we got Fred Ward to come back and it went into combination casting, we at least had to get Fred to anchor it. The possibility to do the sequel came at a particular time when the technology was shifting to be able to do it. It was almost an impossible assignment in which everybody did very well and it kept the franchise alive."

"We knew we needed to make our films for a price and my staff had experience in doing lower budgeted products," said Feola. "We associated with producers we knew could complement our skills. We didn't behave like studio executives; we behaved more like producers alongside a producer like Nancy. Nancy knew when she got in a relationship with us that we were a partner, not just a studio writing a cheque."

Tremors 2 was unusual for a DTV title, in that the original filmmakers returned for the production, with Wilson, Maddock and Roberts keen to make it a success. "Many times people move on; we own the franchise and pay them some sort of asset payment, they put their names on the credits but they never see a script or the movie," said Patti Jackson. "[The Stampede] guys love *Tremors* and wouldn't dream of not seeing it through."

"Universal had just started getting into that business so they had a new division and I think *Tremors 2* might've been one of the first that ran through there," said the film's line producer, Chris DeFaria. "We enjoyed some autonomy from a production standpoint because I don't think they knew who at the time was really supposed to be in charge of it."

Not everybody would return for a second round of Graboid hunting, with Ron Underwood passing the directorial reins to Steve Wilson. "Ron was doing gigantic movies like *City Slickers* and he had neither the time nor the inclination to do direct-to-video movies," said Wilson. "I had directed second unit on *Tremors* and had enjoyed it."

"I like that they went in different directions," said Underwood of the sequel. "Brent and Steve are always pushing for something more; it delivered what fans wanted to see with a sequel but took it in a whole new direction."

Although he'd been a vital part of the development and production of *Tremors*, Universal Studios' Jim Jacks stepped back from developing the sequel, with Gale Anne Hurd also bowing out at an early stage. "You need the studio behind you to support a film with marketing and I think the perception was they didn't have a lot to lose," said Hurd. "I think they felt maybe it would be better direct-to-VHS."

DEVELOPING TREMORS 2

The revised script, now entitled *Tremors 2: Aftershocks*, was altered from the version shown to Kevin Bacon, with the action relocated from Australia to Sonora, Mexico. Newcomer Grady Hoover replaced Valentine McKee, with the latter said to be happily married to Rhonda. The majority of Val's lines were now attributed to Grady and Heather Gummer's lines passed to Burt.

The film now opened at a Mexican oil field under attack from Graboids, leading the owners to call for the assistance of Val McKee and Earl Bassett, the renowned Graboid hunters. When oil company executive, Señor Ortega, arrives at Earl's Perfection Valley ostrich farm by taxi, his eager driver, Grady Hoover, soon assumes the vacant position of assistant to Earl, before the pair are set loose on the oil field's underground foes. The script goes on to introduce a love interest for Earl in the shape of geologist Kate Reilly, before the newly-separated Burt Gummer is called upon to help destroy the Graboids. When they encounter a new stage in the evolution of the Graboid, two-legged creatures (dubbed Shriekers in *Tremors 3*) that "see" their enemy via infra-red glands on their heads, the team destroy them for good when the refinery is blown up using Gummer's high explosives.

"We had all this stuff written for Heather, so Burt's part expanded and we started the running gag of Burt trying desperately to come up with the right equipment, then being thwarted when the monsters change into something else," noted Wilson. "We had Fred back; his only request was that he got to keep his hair long."

Michael Gross had been convinced *Tremors* was a one-off, until word got back to him that the film had taken off on VHS. When Stampede approached him about reprising the role of Burt Gummer, he jumped at the opportunity. "From an actor's point-of-view, there's nothing better than having a writer fall in love with your character. Our writers fell in love with Burt, it's that simple. They loved making him outrageous. I just sat there and basked in the adulation they had for this character and I thought, 'How could I not be there?' I was disappointed that Reba and Kevin weren't part of it because I thought they were essential. I was thrilled that Fred Ward came back on that piece."

The lack of Kevin Bacon had been a stumbling block for the feature version of *Tremors 2*, but according to line producer, Chris DeFaria, there wasn't a great sense of disappointment in his absence. "The key characters that Brent and Steve connected with were Michael Gross and Fred Ward's. When Michael signed on I think that was a tremendous wind in the sails for the project, creatively."

Gross was sent an early draft of the script, allowing him to feed back his thoughts to Stampede. "A lot of my notes were: 'Keep the stakes high, where are the women and children? Who gives a crap about an oil company?' That was my big note about the first one, 'Why is this in an oil field? People hate oil people.' I wanted to have something really worth fighting for."

"[The oil company] was only a ruse to get him into the desert somewhere," explained Maddock. "Once you're there you're still fighting for your life, it's just people trying not to get eaten, which is everyone's problem in life in one way or another."

With a smaller budget came a shorter shoot for *Tremors 2: Aftershocks*. "The irony of being a filmmaker and directing low-budget or direct-to-video movies is that you have a lot less status than a guy directing a $15m film," said Maddock. "In reality, it's much harder when you only have 27 days to shoot; it's much easier if you have 75 or 100 days. You really have to know what you're doing, move fast and make sure you can get everything shot to cut the scene together."

"We probably had the shortest prep I've had on any film," said Hilbert Hakim, who had responded to Gale Anne Hurd's request for help during the edit of the first film and now came to *Tremors 2: Aftershocks* as second assistant director. "Usually on a feature film you have anywhere from four to six weeks of preparation and during that time you schedule the film, breaking down every scene. We had two weeks prep on this film and during that time Steve and the rest of us formed the schedule, such as what scenes to do and what order to do them in."

With Fred Ward and Michael Gross in place, the producers could now cast the film's other roles. With no Kevin Bacon, the role of Earl's sidekick was replaced by cab driver, Grady Hoover. One of the actors who auditioned was *Friends*' Matthew Perry, but the role was eventually awarded to New York-born Christopher Gartin. "I went through a series of auditions with the two writers and the producers," recalled Gartin. "I had not seen the first *Tremors* but watched it to get the tone of it and became one degree from Kevin Bacon."

"We spent a lot of time trying to find the sidekick," admitted Brent Maddock. "Chris Gartin was great fun. As producers you're there looking at actor after actor, we saw a lot of people. The two most important things in making a movie are a good screenplay and good casting."

The role of scientist (and former *Playboy* Playmate Miss October 1974) Kate Reilly went to Canadian actress, Helen Shaver (*Hill Street Blues*, 1981–87, *Poltergeist: The Legacy* 1996–99). "I got a call from my agent asking if I was interested in going in and meeting the producer and director for this role. I'd read the script and we had a conversation, we went in and met, I don't remember auditioning for it. I was very excited to work with Fred Ward." 'Casting' for the part of Kate's photo double led the Stampede team to trawl the *Playboy* archives to find a Playmate who looked similar to Shaver, with the coveted role going to Miss September 1970, Debbie Ellison, when it was discovered the real October 1974 looked nothing like the actress.

Actor Marcelo Tubert won the role of oil company representative, Señor Ortega, who arrived in Perfection Valley to recruit Earl Bassett. "I loved the first movie and was thrilled when I had an audition for the second one," said Tubert. "I did *Miss Congeniality 2, Leprechaun 3, Tremors 2* ... I'm always one step behind the original. For some reason I couldn't make the first audition time, so I was there the day they were reading the leading women, it was all these beautiful girls and me. Then they took me shopping for the $850 Hugo Boss suit I wore in the film, just amazing threads."

A number of crew returned from *Tremors* to be a part of the sequel, including director of photography, Virgil Harper, who had worked with Steve Wilson on the second unit of the first film, and production designer, Ivo Cristante. Cristen Carr Strubbe, who had left *Tremors* early to work on another production, returned as production manager alongside producer, Chris DeFaria. "My job was about carving up the financial pie," said Strubbe, "ensuring the director had all the tools he needed to create the picture that he envisions and that the studio is paying for."

The team at Amalgamated Dynamics, Inc (ADI), Tom Woodruff, Jr and Alec Gillis, once again carried out practical creature effects. "They came to us and said that there was going to be a *Tremors 2* and they were very excited because Phil Tippett had come on board and had done a little test of a CG creature," said Woodruff. Tippett was something of a legend in the effects community, having created the stop-motion chess sequence in *Star Wars* before going on to teach himself how to do computer animation and becoming a key part of Steven Spielberg's plans for *Jurassic Park*. "Steve Wilson was moving into directing and he was very comfortable having been on the set with us on the first movie. He knew what we could do and what we could carry off well with practical creature effects."

Part of the reason for ADI's return was their pride of ownership over the Graboid design and the fact they were wary of it being ruined by a new effects team. "We were going to work on it regardless of budget," Gillis confirmed. "Steve, Ron, Brent and Nancy were great to work with because they understood that we would give them everything we possibly could for whatever budget they had. They weren't just necessarily out there looking for the cheapest people, they knew that we were going to deliver much more than anybody else would creatively."

The sequel may have had a greatly reduced budget, but Chris DeFaria discovered that the goodwill generated by the Stampede team on *Tremors* ensured that those returning went above and beyond what was expected of them. "There was so much love for the first film from the people associated with it that I had tremendous resources available to me that I don't think anybody would normally have had. Phil Tippett stepped up to do visual effects at a price point I don't think we would've ever been able to otherwise achieve, while Alec and Tom lent far more support than could be laid out in a contract. It's fun to be making a movie that when you make a phone call [everybody would] love to work on it."

This extra commitment proved to be vital to the production, as Stampede Entertainment attempted to make a worthy sequel to their original film, albeit with a fraction of the resources available to a theatrical release.

FILMING CLOSE TO HOME

With its sprawling mountain ranges and stunning rock formations, Lone Pine had been the perfect location for filmmakers wanting to create a claustrophobic horror film that took place in broad daylight. Despite its rich filmmaking history, the Owens Valley area was problematic for crews requiring easy access to electricity, storage and accommodation, all of which ate into budgets.

For *Tremors 2: Aftershocks*, a production with a budget of less than a third of the first film, a return to Lone Pine was out of the question. "None of the *Tremors* films have been shot in the same place," said director, Steve Wilson. "When I watch the original I get pangs of pain because it's so beautiful out in the desert. The direct-to-video versions had to be shot closer to Los Angeles because we couldn't afford to put the crew up in motels for weeks at a time."

Tremors 2 was shot north of LA behind the Magic Mountain amusement park, a location that could be made to look like the desert if the right camera angles were used. Filming began in April 1995, a few months after initial location scouting.

"When we were prepping *Tremors 2*, an area in western Santa Clarita Valley was wide open and owned by the Newhall Land Trust Company," noted line producer, Chris DeFaria. "At the time we were scouting it looked like Northern Mexico, so we wrote the story to take place there. You make your decision to do something like that in the fall, but what we didn't realise was there were big rains that year and by the time we showed up to shoot in early spring it was the most lush green countryside you'd ever seen. We were joking and saying, 'We're going to have to set this thing to be somewhere in the Irish countryside', but that gave us all kinds of problems because the characters were named Pedro and Jose. But we went with this idea that we were in this hilly part of Northern Mexico and in the end it's a much more colourful and green movie than we'd ever imagined."

"It was really rustic; we ordered construction trailers and moved our offices, I had a set of four of them," said production manager, Cristen Carr Strubbe. "One was for the art department and the construction building mill was in an old barn. My production trailer and the producer's production trailer were next to each other. Every morning the first one in turned on the generators and would get the pump going for the water in the porta-potties."

The change in the landscape, from arid desert to lush countryside, had encouraged some local ranchers to rent their property to cattle owners who were keen to graze their animals. As a result, the *Tremors 2* crew had to be vigilant for stray cows during the shoot. "You'd pan across the desolate landscape and just outside of frame was a whole huge herd of cows," laughed second assistant director, Hilbert Hakim. "We were always careful not to shoot off any explosives or do any special effects near them because they would freak out. There were no studios or sound stages, it was all one location. That became our studio for 30 days."

Production designer, Ivo Cristante, also had problems with the four-legged locals, discovering that cows liked to eat the DayGlo surveyor's ribbon used around the set. "We staked out the compound twice and came back and it was all gone. We figured some teenagers were harassing us, but then we found bits and pieces in the cow droppings so we had to ask the farmer to keep them away."

Cristante was wary of repeating some of the issues he'd faced on another recent low-budget production, *Hellraiser: Bloodline*, which was released in 1996. "*Bloodline* went over budget, the union struck it, we were a week into shooting and two weeks behind schedule. We were so far behind we went into another dimension." The designer was determined that the same situation wouldn't occur with the art department on *Tremors 2*, ensuring costs were pushed down by keeping close guard of the small budget available to him. "We got to the point where we finished all the sets and they were shooting away merrily and the construction coordinator, Roger Kelton, said, 'Fire the construction crew – we don't have any more money. The sets are made, if they want them changed they pay for it and they can hire them back.' So it worked out fine."

Unlike the cast and crew of the first film who had relocated to Lone Pine for the duration of the shoot, Magic Mountain was situated less than 30 miles outside the city. For the sequel, the cast drove themselves to and from the location each day, settling down behind the cameras to wait for their scenes rather than travelling back to the trailers that had to be stored a few miles away in case they were caught on camera. "The cameras would pan almost 360° and there was a very small portion of the area that we could put everything in," said Hakim. "Our lunch tables, parking lot and trailers were there."

"It was a genius location that looked like Mexico, it was a big key to the movie," said Christopher Gartin. "We shot long hours and it was one of those movies where there's always something happening. I was always covered in goo."

Co-writer and producer, Brent Maddock, ensured he was on set during the shoot. "I was whispering in the director's ear, 'This scene is supposed to be funny.' You have 48 things you have to remember and it's so easy to forget why you're there when you're working with lenses and camera angles and the wind is blowing and somebody doesn't know their blocking."

Although she had turned down a production credit on *Tremors*, Nancy Roberts officially became a producer on *Tremors 2: Aftershocks*. "Nancy was really supportive and was on the set every day," said Hakim. "We'd finish on schedule and I believe we even finished under budget. Usually the producer is there to kind of keep the director functioning but at the same time keeping the studio happy, but we didn't really have much studio interference. My hat's off to her because she had huge shoes to fill with Gale [Anne Hurd] not being there."

PRACTICAL EFFECTS VS CG

The build of *Tremors*' Graboids had been 100% practical in 1989, combining full size props and models to bring the creatures to life. In the intervening six years, technology had progressed to a point that saw computer-generated imagery fast becoming an industry standard.

"*Jurassic Park* started out as a stop-motion project but the CG people slowly convinced Spielberg they could do it better," explained Steve Wilson. "There was no CG in *Tremors*, but by the time of *Tremors 2* we were fortunate to link up with Phil

Tippett. He did a test for us of a Shrieker walking through a doorway and Tom Woodruff and Alec Gillis refined the design."

"We had more physical effects than CG, only because the latter were so expensive," said Hilbert Hakim. "In *The Abyss* we had a total of 150 visual shots and that was at least 40% of the budget. They take so long to generate. Today that's not the case and a comedy can have 150 visual effects shots and it's nothing."

"We were working on *Alien*[3] when *Jurassic Park* was [the film everyone wanted to pitch for]," said Alec Gillis. "Spielberg had said he wanted *Jurassic Park* to be a breakthrough in animatronic dinosaurs. One of the *Jurassic Park* producers told us that they were hiring Stan Winston because he had done the Queen Alien and that was the closest thing anybody had done to the kind of life and personality that Spielberg wanted from his T-Rex. We thought it was going to be a big development of the next phase of animatronics, which it was, but when the movie came out they were switching over from the idea of stop-motion to digital on *Jurassic Park*."

After being shown top-secret *Jurassic Park* footage of the Tyrannosaurus Rex, Woodruff and Gillis became aware of a reaction against the new technology from their peers, many of whom decided to abandon the business thinking they would otherwise be forced out. "All we saw was a benefit to us because people started making more effect movies and they realised that the digital stuff was so expensive that they couldn't afford to do more," Gillis said. "We're fans of digital when it's done right and used judiciously, and we understood that the digital stuff Phil Tippett did for *Tremors 2* made them very excited about the movie because it was going to be applied to a low-budget. But we had to do a lot of practical stuff because they couldn't afford all the digital that they might have used in *Tremors 2*."

The decision to continue with a mixture of CG and practical effects was something that appealed to Michael Gross, who was willing to pretend a creature was in front of him but preferred to act alongside a puppet. "That was great for the sci-fi fans and for practical monster makers and it was fun to be gooed up and have monster guts all over you."

Woodruff and Gillis were working in Canada on the 1995 Robin Williams film, *Jumanji*, when the call came through to work on *Tremors 2*. The pair shot *Jumanji* during the day, before heading back to their hotel rooms in the evening to work on a small-scale model, or maquette, of the Shrieker. Weekends found them placing their creations in wooden boxes and flying down to LA for meetings, showing the producers what they envisioned for the sequel.

Two types of Shrieker puppets were created for the shoot, both a cable controlled standing puppet mounted to a wooden base that required two puppeteers, and a suit worn by a puppeteer for close-ups. One of the puppeteers for the suit version was Yancy Calzada, a member of the ADI team who had also worked on *Jumanji*. "After getting back from Vancouver I was sent to where *Tremors 2* was shooting and when I arrived on set I was taken over to see a Shrieker suit. I was told to suit up and start milling around for a shot coming out of the barn. That was my primary job and it was an awkward, sometimes painful contraption to use."

The Shrieker puppets were built over a lightweight backpack frame and the operators forced to walk on their knees with the weight of the head hanging forward. "It was difficult to remain balanced while trying to walk and shake the head around," said Calzada. "Imagine trying to walk on your knees with a six-year-old kid on your neck, that's what it felt like. We didn't have any clear way to see out and could barely hear instructions. I remember one time where the aluminium frame of the backpack snapped during a shot. It felt like a 50lb weight was dropped on my back. The frame was supporting most of the head weight and it was all I could do to keep from falling on my (or its) face."

While the puppeteers were struggling inside the Shrieker costumes, Cristen Carr Strubbe ensured the camera crew could easily film them. While on the first film the main issue was transporting the three-quarter size Graboid from the mechanical effects house in LA up to Lone Pine, for *Tremors 2* the focus was the Shriekers, dubbed "the turkeys" on set. "The most difficult part was getting our turkeys where they needed to go," said Strubbe. "I ended up creating additional units and had a four-man crew that would just follow us to shoot the movements of those things."

"We had a lot of animatronics scenes, a lot of heads and tails," said Hakim. "Some of them would have puppeteers operating them and they actually looked really creepy in person. We had a lot of people manipulating gears and pulleys."

The sense of collaboration that had been so prevalent on the original *Tremors* carried over to the sequel for Ivo Cristante, particularly in his work with ADI. Budget restrictions on *Aftershocks* meant the crew couldn't afford to dig the pits and build the elevators required to explode the Graboids out of the ground. "I was able to find a small rise, build a platform off the rise and fuzz out the horizon line with bushes and pretend it was flat," Cristante explained. "They were under the platform and they burst the creature through with sheer manpower and without hydraulics."

A Shrieker prepares for its close-up © Ivo Cristante

As a low-budget film with a restricted number of crew, even the producers were called upon to help with some sequences featuring the Shriekers, which required 16 people to operate each puppet. "Once, Tom and Alec needed more people to run all of the articulation on what I called their prehistoric chickens and so everybody had to come and get a lever," said Cristante. "Each lever moved something, so they put me on a lever and when they yelled I was told to move it. We even had Chris DeFaria moving these levers. I went back to my lever after filming to try and work out what I was moving and I saw one of the chickens waving its rump – if you ever see the movie again, that was me!"

"Working with the CG was funny," Christopher Gartin said. "Sometimes there were these animatronic things, like when he was in the cage and we were feeding him. A lot of times, like when I'm screaming down at him from the water tower, they're not really there so it's like a tennis ball or nothing and you have to pretend. It makes it fun and exciting to watch it, you feel like you're going over the top when you're doing it but you never are."

ON SET

With Steve Wilson and Brent Maddock having altered the script to accommodate the reduced budget and shooting schedule now available to them, the job of preparing for filming at Magic Mountain fell to the production team.

"The fact that we only had two weeks of prep is usually a recipe for disaster because a lot of things fall through the cracks, especially if you're doing an effects movie," said Hilbert Hakim. "We had a lot of props and special effects; visual effects would sometimes be dangerous and have to be planned out just perfectly. We got lucky as we only had one location, maybe 100 square acres and you had to drive to it, but [we could get there] in a day."

According to Hakim, the level-headedness and preparation of director Steve Wilson was one of the key reasons the production moved ahead at full speed. "The first assistant director would sometimes leave the set to me and say, 'I have to go and work on the schedule,' because he had to pull scenes from the following day into the present day due to us being so far ahead of ourselves. The only things that weren't shot in sequence were visual effects shots or close-ups that we had to come back and get."

"What you're trying to do in my job is to create an environment where the reality of what you're achieving [one] day is informing the choices [you're making] the next," explained Chris DeFaria. "You're learning to get rid of things that you don't need, or suddenly emphasising things that really are playing well or feel very important, and you're doing it in real time. Filmmakers like Brent, Steve and Nancy have the production understanding, the incredibly intimate knowledge of the project and the patience and understanding to go through it on a daily basis. You're often sitting next to the director going, 'We have to be done with this scene or this shot, you're gonna have to work with what you've got.' Steve and I had a very trusting relationship, and he has a very trusting relationship with his partners, so when that conversation would come up, he would go, 'Okay, I've got it.'"

Contributing to the film finishing on schedule and under budget was the fact that most scenes were filmed in just three or four takes. "They were moving very, very quickly," confirmed actor Marcelo Tubert. "I was there around a week to 10 days and it moved a lot faster than some features I've worked on."

One of the earliest sequences to be filmed featured Earl and Grady's initial attack on the Graboids using remote controlled trucks loaded with dynamite. Under the supervision of special effects coordinator, Peter Chesney, the resulting montage of explosions proved memorable for a number of reasons. "Peter's a wonderful mad scientist and he had to shoot elements for the montage of [Earl and Grady] blowing up the big worms," said DeFaria. "He would shoot these explosions under very safe conditions, but each one he wanted to make bigger than the next, stuffing each one with gunk so that it would blow up and land bloody pieces of creature all around. He kept saying it wasn't reading on camera and he was stuffing 400 pounds of methyl cellulose into plastic latex body parts. He blew one so high it became almost comical and of course the long pause and what rained down afterwards was just the most disgusting stuff. It felt like life was imitating art at that point."

Cristen Carr Strubbe was also part of the team involved in creating the insides of the Graboids and Shriekers. "I was dealing with Peter Chesney, helping to get the right consistency of the pumpkin guts. This pumpkin was what we used for all the explosions out of the ground and that was really fun. For wrap gifts at the end of the shoot we gave everybody a can of pumpkin. We had cases and cases of it."

"I remember we'd have cases of Libby's Pumpkin Pie filling and we opened up the cans and literally emptied them out," said Hakim. "We'd be standing right outside the frame and we'd just throw them up in the air. By the end of the day, being in that sun with that pumpkin all over you, it was a horrible smell. To this day when I see pumpkin pie I think of that film because we emptied a ton of these things on actors."

Unfortunately for the crew, they were in close proximity to a number of beehives during bee breeding season, which caused problems for the pumpkin-strewn set. "We had to hire a guy to move all these bees," noted Strubbe. "We were digging all the mortars to put the pumpkin in and for some reason we had to move this little 30-feet square village of hives because they were going for the pumpkin. At each of the mortars we'd get these clumps of bees. We all got used to walking around with umbrellas because as they were testing the pumpkin, the pumpkin guts would come flying down all over the place."

Practical effects were used wherever possible, including the scene featuring Earl and Grady taking a break for lunch while listening to music on a portable stereo. After the camera tilts up to the men, a sound is heard and the camera tilts back down again, suggesting that a Graboid has eaten the stereo off-camera and left a hole in the ground, minus the equipment. "That was done entirely in camera," noted DeFaria. "The stunt crew had to suddenly create this huge hole with the steam all in real time, all off-camera and all very quietly. We would roll on that shot and it would pan over and then when it was away from it everybody jumped in quietly and the camera had to pan back. We nailed it the first time out of the gate and I thought that was really fun because it could've been a very complicated visual effect but we did it in real time."

While the cast and crew of the original *Tremors* had an opportunity to get to know each other both on and off set during their lengthy shoot in Lone Pine, a combination of *Tremors 2*'s close proximity to Los Angeles and the rapid shooting schedule meant those involved with the sequel had less time to bond. Thankfully, the actors found themselves working as a tight unit, with the returning Fred Ward a welcoming presence for his new co-stars.

"Fred Ward was incredibly charming, very pleasant with the crew," said Hilbert Hakim. "When you're a star of a film and doing a sequel you've already proven yourself and Fred had a track record of very successful films. You never know what you're going to get when they walk on the set the first day. He was just a regular crew guy. If the grips were moving C-stands and flags and so forth he'd say, 'You guys need a hand with anything?' Fred was as regular as you can get."

"Fred Ward had done a lot of travelling and I've always had a sort of wanderlust," Helen Shaver said. "There'd be days where we'd be sitting outside in the beautiful weather waiting for them to call us to do a shot. I can remember him describing Morocco, where I'd never been, and me thinking 'Boy I'd better not bring my passport to work because it all sounds so good I could just go hop on a plane and away I'd go.'"

"There's no cooler guy on the planet," said Christopher Gartin on the subject of Ward. "He's well-read and he turned me onto some good books. He's really thoughtful, what you'd imagine working with Robert De Niro would be like."

If Fred Ward was a calming influence on set, 27-year-old Christopher Gartin was the opposite, described as "the new kid on the block" by Hakim. "He was the new puppy dog you get that was so hyper and running around all over the set in a panic, you had to keep an eye on him," continued Hakim. "You could tell he was having a great time and he had a great rapport with Fred. Fred isn't a very overpowering actor, he definitely shares the camera with his co-workers, but he was like the older brother with Christopher."

"I think [Christopher Gartin's eagerness] was probably a positive," nodded Virgil Harper. "He was enthusiastic and he was sort of new at it, it's sort of like putting a wet nosed young man up against an old pro, so that dynamic helped it work. When I was on the set Fred never said, 'Hurry up, get this done, I gotta leave'; he was there 100% of the time."

One of Virgil Harper's responsibilities as director of photography was ensuring his cast looked their best during filming, something that wasn't always easy on a hot and dusty set. He was particularly nervous about capturing *Tremors 2*'s leading lady, Helen Shaver, on camera. "When you take a role you've got to look at what it is and ask, 'Can I look bad in this and still make it work?'" said Harper. "I don't know who it was that said, '[Helen's] nervous about the way she's going to look', but I thought 'Boy am I gonna have trouble.' When I shot her outside I used a white gauzy net material that I floated overhead just to take a hint of a kiss of that nasty sun off her. She was anxiously waiting to see the dailies and I was thinking 'Well I may not be on this movie tomorrow', but she saw the dailies and she was happy."

"Helen was a real pro," added Hakim. "They'd have to climb scaffoldings, go on top of the roof and wear these heavy suits; she was the first one on set ready to go. It's been my experience every time I've worked on a sequel that if the actors know that they're playing a character on a film where the first one's already a success, they come into the set with a lot of confidence."

The introduction of an older, though perhaps not much wiser, Burt Gummer was achieved with visual references to the first film, as the survivalist is first seen in his rebuilt basement. As the camera pans across the room, it reveals the wall where the Graboid broke through, before resting on a full size Graboid head mounted on the wall. "I said to Steve, 'Wouldn't it be funny if the wall where the creature broke through was just cinder block but not painted and it kind of ties you in?'" said Strubbe.

Though Gummer was a vital part of the film, Michael Gross was only on set for a few days of the shoot. "He did practically all his own stunts, the bloodier he got the more fun he had," Hakim said. "He was very proud of the fact that he was in the first one, that he had created a pretty interesting character. In-between takes he had great stories about his other films that he had worked on and his TV show; he was a walking *Hollywood Reporter*."

Said Gross, "[The Stampede team] were having fun mutating the monsters into different forms. I love everything and anything that has a heart to it; I'm not interested in monster movies per se, I was interested because I thought *Tremors*, and to a degree the rest of them, had a heart. People we cared about were in jeopardy."

"Michael is a fabulous guy, not unlike the character except for the crazy part," revealed Gartin. "Having Fred and Michael to work with was a dream at my age. It was fun, there were no bad apples and the writers had the control, which never happens. When the creators and writers are at the helm it's a pure creative experience, there are no conflicts and less friction."

"I don't remember a single moment or a day that we had to deal with any actor issues," said Hakim. "We had more issues with the monsters than we did with the actors, let's put it that way. No one ever showed up late, complaining or not knowing their lines. They came to work prepared every day and they drove themselves. They just became part of the crew, they were like a travelling circus act. It was a very well-oiled machine and the actors were a big part of it."

In Hakim's memory, the only on-set controversy revolved around a crew member's white labrador. "Dogs weren't allowed on the compound but we'd see this white dog running around, sometimes he'd get in the shot and the owner would be told not to bring him the next day. And he would bring him. If it wasn't some kind of a weather issue, it was his dog. One day we all pulled up for lunch, which was always in this tent in the parking lot, and all we could see was a little tail wagging underneath the tent. We got into the tent and the dog had his face in this big fat cheesecake. When I see that movie, I still think 'Oh my God, I remember that day. White dog running around ruining the shot.'"

Although the script had been broken down for the benefit of the various effects crews, allowing them to plan early on whether a scene would involve practical or CG effects, late changes were sometimes implemented.

"There's a shot when they're on a rock with the truck and behind them is a big moon," Ivo Cristante explained. "It took a while to talk the director of photography into that, as he wanted to do it as a process shot in post-production. I said I had the backdrop and that we could put it up and backlight it, which we did and it looks marvellous, you can't tell it's a backdrop out in the middle of nowhere. We took those chances and there's something about those productions where you end up having a bit more good luck than bad."

Other sequences required a mixture of high and low-tech solutions, including that of Earl and Grady discovering a Graboid seemingly in pain just before the first Shrieker is "born". "When Fred and Christopher come up over the rocks and see the Graboid laying there and his whole side is blown out, that was a full size creature," said Virgil Harper. "When they cut to the creature flopping around out there in the night, that was a quarter-scale model that they had to set up on a special set and they'd shoot that at a high-frame rate to try to get it more in reality. By over cranking it they help bring that back into normal movement."

"What's most important to us is how the creatures are going to work and look," noted Alec Gillis. "What's important to the director of photography is that the thing is shot well and that it all cuts together. The difficulty of digital work is that it's out of the hands of the primary people who are controlling continuity and the look. You just have to hope that the people who are following you are given the amount of time and money they need and that they care as much as we do on the live action."

"I remember the set being very busy," said Shrieker puppeteer Yancy Calzada. "Unless the puppeteers are interacting directly with actors we don't usually get much time to mingle. On this show in particular, if you weren't shooting a scene you were involved in setting up a scene somewhere else. I remember one shot where I played the Shrieker in the cage for the shot over the puppet's shoulder. It was the closest thing to doing a scene with the actors for me, but I couldn't see them or really hear them. By the time I was out of the creature, the actors were off blocking another scene, so I never personally interacted with any of them."

Burt Gummer's survival expertise was put to the test in an infamous sequence involving a Shrieker, a wall and an LAR Grizzly Big Boar single-shot .50 BMG rifle. As Burt, Earl, Grady and Kate attempt to escape by truck, Burt's bullet pierces the creature before destroying the engine of the vehicle set to take the foursome to safety. "That was a real gun and those were real bullets that Michael was shooting," said Hakim. "Not only did it sound like a cannon was going off every time we shot it, but it would fire a bullet that was eight inches long and about an inch thick. It can go through anything, so when we used it we had to be extra cautious. We cleared the set of all the crew members that weren't necessary and the actors were put into the lock down because they always think that they're the exception to the rule."

The film's final major sequence saw the Shriekers trapped in a warehouse before Earl enters covered in CO2 foam in order to arm the explosives that will destroy the building. "We took his wardrobe and covered it in fire retardant foam because we figured that would save us money on having to do it [with CG]," Hakim continued. "They shot it through lenses that would show you the body temperature, so it looks like a visual effect but it really was a trickery that we created in the camera."

Christopher Gartin, attempting to do as many of his own stunts as possible, found the final sequence – which saw him being flung through the air from the force of the blast caused by Earl – physically gruelling. "I got so beat up. I think I had a stunt double but I don't remember not doing anything. I remember jumping onto mats after the explosion, everything was so physical. I'm an athlete and have played sports all my life; I could easily have been a stuntman. It was a really nice ending and it came together well, it made the movie work. It's so hard to create good endings."

Note the miniature versions of buildings in the foreground before they were blown up © Ivo Cristante

RELEASE AND RESPONSE

Unlike the first film, which had been awarded extra money when studio executives saw the potential to improve the final cut, *Tremors 2: Aftershocks* was a more straightforward release for Universal Studios Home Entertainment. "We didn't do focus groups because we didn't have a budget to reshoot," said Louis Feola. "We knew who our fanbase was and we were very confident we knew how to reach them."

For the production team at Stampede Entertainment, the task of bringing a feature film to market under strict time and financial restrictions was both a difficult and rewarding one.

"I'm proud that I was part of the solution of how to take something like that and pour it into its second life on direct-to-video, which is a lesser budget but equally if not more challenging," mused Chris DeFaria, who later worked as an executive producer on films such as *Happy Feet Two* (2011) and *Gravity* (2013). "What can get lost on that transition is the spirit, tone and culture of a show when you make such a radical transition in budget and I'm hugely proud that wasn't the case here. The second film shares with the first film all of the sensibility, humour and humanity in the midst of a monster movie. That became a lesson for me going forward in all the films I'm doing today."

The film's upbeat soundtrack was provided by musician, Jay Ferguson, a founder member of the US rock band, Spirit. "My agent, Vasi Vangelos, submitted me for the film, and I was asked to put together a reel of music for the producers. This being a plum little project I can guarantee there were several other composers with their hat in the ring. I ended up on the short list and was asked to a meeting, which went well. They were a great bunch and I think there was a feeling we could work well together, which proved to be the case."

Ferguson's abiding memory of working with the Stampede team was the feeling of "working on a giant home movie; Steve, Ron, Brent and Nancy were definitely un-Hollywood types and the *Tremors* saga was their baby. It was family and it was literally handmade. They used puppets, for God's sake! The series always had a solid Southwest flavour, and I think they liked the fact that I could integrate a guitar driven texture into the score along with the more traditional dramatic and horror elements. As a composer you feed off of performances and Fred Ward's in *Tremors 2* was comic gold."

Tremors 2: Aftershocks was destined for VHS, but it did have an early theatrical outing one month before its release thanks to Brent Maddock. The Los Angeles Times announced that Saturday 9 March, 1996 saw a special screening of the film at Laemmle's Monica 4-Plex as a fundraiser for Grant Elementary School in Santa Monica, which Maddock's two children attended. Though the film contained a few scary moments and the occasional death, Maddock made it clear it was suitable for younger viewers: "We did the first *Tremors* before we were all parents ... but we cleaned up the language in this one. My son liked it and he's in first grade."[6]

Tremors 2 was released on VHS on 9 April 1996 (rated PG-13 by the MPAA) and a special premiere screening was held at the Alfred Hitchcock Theater on the Universal lot the same day, attended by Fred Ward, Christopher Gartin, Helen Shaver and the producers. The film arrived on LaserDisc one week later. A poster was created for video rental stores, a new take on that created for the first film, featuring Earl, Grady and Burt in the back of a truck while three creatures, vaguely resembling Graboids with teeth, roared at them from beneath the ground.

Noting that "Bacon has better things to do these days" than star in a sequel to the "witty little horror-comedy flick" that was *Tremors*, there was little evidence that the reviewer at *Entertainment Today* had done any more than read the press notes for the film, with their sole comment being: "This little sequel might be better than you expect – the original certainly was."[7]

It took weekly trade newspaper *The Hollywood Drama-Logue* until June to review the film, but they liked what they saw, commenting that the original film's "gleeful mixture of humor and hang-by-your-fingernails drama" was still intact. Admiring the "playful zest" of Wilson's direction, the review also appreciated the film's "keen self-awareness, as opposed to self-consciousness" and reckoned that *Tremors 2* was perfect for anyone wanting "to go monster-hunting at home with the VCR."[8]

The response from the critics wasn't overwhelmingly positive, but Universal had little doubt that the project would prove to be a success with *Tremors* fans around the globe. Thanks to their spreadsheets of data and the title's high brand awareness with consumers, they knew that the rental market was about to welcome *Tremors 2: Aftershocks* with open arms and, more importantly, wallets.

At the time of the film's release, the video sell through business was valued at $6bn, up 15% on 1995, with blockbuster DTV animation titles such as Disney's *Aladdin* (1992) sequel, 1994's *The Return of Jafar*, having sold over 10m copies and Universal's own *The Land Before Time II: The Great Valley Adventure* (1994) racking up over 3m sales. According to the *Los Angeles Times*, keys to DTV success included a recognisable title, a name actor and a film in the action-adventure or horror genres, all things present and correct for *Tremors 2*.[9]

"*Tremors 2* was a perfect rental title as evidenced by the fact that if it hadn't done really well, there wouldn't have been a three or a four," said Universal Studios Home Entertainment's Patti Jackson. "I was excited about its release, but unlike theatrical you don't know about the success of one of our movies for a month or so and our movies have legs that go off into years."

With *Tremors 2* on VHS, Universal saw value in releasing *Tremors* onto LaserDisc at the same time, giving fans who could afford the equipment and disc the opportunity to view the original feature in a superior format.

The success of the film had a lasting impact on its cast, including Christopher Gartin who said in 2013: "I was shooting a hard-core drama in Boston called *Sins of the Preacher*, and every guy on the set in their 20s came up to me and they all grew up on *Tremors 2*. All I could think about was that I should probably have got more cheques. It's one of those culty things, no matter what good work you do after, it's the one people are most passionate about as fans. Anything that people love and recognise and that added some joy to their life in any tiny way is rewarding."

For the time being the franchise was in good shape, with all involved satisfied they'd created a worthy successor to the original, albeit on the small screen rather than cinemas around the globe. The likelihood of *Tremors 3* depended on fans' willingness to embrace the sequel and the creators' interest in taking their characters in yet another new direction.

CHAPTER SEVEN
TREMORS 3: BACK TO PERFECTION

The six years that had lapsed between the release of *Tremors* and *Tremors 2: Aftershocks* on VHS had seen relatively few changes in the home video market. Traditionally, a theatrically released feature film would take six months to arrive on video for the rental market before becoming available for purchase a further six months later. With Universal Studios Home Entertainment busy on other projects, it would take at least 12 months for the team to start considering the success of the first *Tremors* sequel.

"Back then we did one or two movies a year and it was still a new business for us," explained Universal's Patti Jackson. "It was a one-person department and while *Tremors 2* was finishing I had to oversee the other movies and then try to get another *Tremors* greenlit. It probably took a year before I could get anyone's attention to say we ought to do another one. I had to convince the head of the video distribution division, Louis Feola, and he had a head of production that oversaw live action and animation, Susie Peterson. It was all based on how many we sold, how many were renting and did it have legs. We hadn't entertained the idea of making a sequel of a sequel."

Tremors 2: Aftershock's production manager, Cristen Carr Strubbe, explained that the film was a "cash cow" at a time when VHS was still a big money maker for Universal. "I could see where they were really excited because you'd be able to move those videos so quickly just on the word "Tremors"."

As the financials were being calculated at Universal through 1996 and 1998, Steve Wilson and Brent Maddock were busy working on their screenplay for Barry Sonnenfeld's troubled 1999 film adaptation of 1960s TV series, *Wild Wild West.* Although the pair wrote the original script, it was heavily rewritten before it went before the cameras. "That was the heartbreaker because we spent a lot of time on a screenplay that I think was probably our best one and it was turned into an incomprehensible mess," said Maddock. "Our names are on the movie, along with some other writers we never met, and that didn't help our careers at all."

Wilson and Maddock's disappointment with *Wild Wild West* was tempered with the news that sales of *Tremors 2: Aftershocks* had met Universal's original forecasts. "We were incredibly pleased with *Tremors 2*," said Universal Studios Home Entertainment's president, Louis Feola. "We waited a little while to get some results in, but we knew we wanted to move forward with Steve, Nancy and Brent. [We had] to find out their availability and give them time to write the screenplay."

In the minds of all involved, a third *Tremors* was to be the final instalment in a trilogy. "They said that would be it and that the market would be saturated so we aimed to wrap it up and end the life cycle of the creatures," said Steve Wilson. *Variety*'s Scott Hettrick announced the new sequel on 11 August 2000, explaining that Universal had given the greenlight to Stampede Entertainment to begin production on the film on 16 October for a 2001 release.[1]

Stampede Entertainment's Wilson, Maddock and Nancy Roberts collaborated on a plot that would see a return to the location of the first film and welcome another new foe. *Tremors 3: Back to Perfection* introduced viewers to a gun-for-hire Burt Gummer (a returning Michael Gross), with Earl and Grady absent after opening a theme park with their earnings accrued following the events of the previous film. As Burt heads home to the town of Perfection following an assignment for the government of Argentina involving dozens of Shriekers, he discovers that

"Desert" Jack Sawyer has started a Graboid safari service while life continues as normal for storeowner Jodi Chang (the niece of Walter Chang from the first film), Miguel, Nancy and Mindy. Melvin Plug is also back, now trying to buy up land in the valley for a new housing development.

When the town comes under attack from Graboids, government agents and a palaeontologist arrive to prevent the residents killing the creatures, which are now deemed to be an endangered species. Burt, Jack, Jodi and Miguel track Shriekers into a canyon, where they discover a new stage in Graboid evolution in the shape of the Ass Blasters, creatures who can fly. Following the death of Miguel in an Ass Blaster attack, Burt, Jack and Jodi lead the remaining creatures to their death in a junkyard, while Nancy and Mindy capture one and sell it to Siegfried and Roy in Las Vegas. At the end of the film, Perfection is left with its own government-protected Graboid in the shape of the albino (and sterile) El Blanco.

Universal's desire to move quickly on development caused headaches for Wilson and Maddock, whose work away from the dormant *Tremors* franchise had kept them busy on other screenwriting projects. Their solution was to pass their story outline to another writer. "Once the studio decided to greenlight a movie, a start date and a release date would be set and things would roll forward quickly," noted Wilson. "John Whelpley was a seasoned TV writer we'd known for some time and he was an easy choice for *Tremors 3*. He gave us lots of snappy dialogue in addition to building the screenplay from our story." Following Whelpley's first few drafts, Wilson and Maddock rewrote the script to give it their unique tone and dialogue.

Best known for his contributions to US TV drama series such as *MacGyver* (1985–98) and *Trapper John, MD* (1979–86), John Whelpley was also a client of talent agent Nancy Roberts while she was producing at Stampede. "I was in the middle of creatively producing and writing *Earth: Final Conflict*'s fifth and final season when I got the call to write the screenplay for *Tremors 3* from Nancy and Patti Jackson at Universal," noted Whelpley. "I took on the project because (a) they asked me to; (b) I loved the original *Tremors* and this one was going back to Perfection, its historical roots; and (c) they had a great story worked out that lit a fire under my imagination."

Whelpley was provided with a bare bones outline of the *Tremors 3* screenplay structure by Wilson, Maddock and Roberts, with characters including the conservative Burt Gummer and the Zen cowboy, Jack Sawyer. "They were also looking for the next evolutionary stage in the Graboid-Shrieker chain and the Ass Blasters came out of that," said Whelpley. "I remember Nancy having to rein me in on the tone, making sure it was irreverent in a family way and true to the original. My most comfortable style has always been character-driven plot with some fatalistic Irish humour thrown in."

The screenwriter relished the opportunity to mine some of the story's subtexts for his script. "The idea that people move on from rural settings like Perfection and newcomers come in and try to make a go of it, and how others see the land as a goldmine while people like Burt see it as the only semblance of peace they will ever find, these are the contrasting character elements that appealed to me about this particular sequel."

Thanks to pressing duties on *Earth: Final Conflict*, Whelpley ran out of time on the *Tremors 3* script. "Suddenly I had about five days where I did not sleep and wrote in a blind fury, constantly calling the guys on plot points. It was very stressful, by my own doing, and I really don't know what I turned in when all was said and done. I was relieved when it got a great reaction from Patti Jackson and the gang. I don't think they needed too big a revision from me, mostly cutting some things down for budget reasons and being a little more simple and inventive in the final act's run-and-jump sequences."

Just as they had on *Tremors 2: Aftershocks*, Stampede looked to their own for a director, this time proposing to Universal that Brent Maddock take on duties with the support of a trusted behind the scenes crew. "It was about convincing the studio that Brent would be surrounded, just as Steve Wilson and Ron

Underwood had been, that he would make his day and that we could deliver the film," said Nancy Roberts. "If they don't have the confidence in you, you don't do it."

"I think *Tremors 3* is the greatest movie about giant underground monsters that turn into flying creatures I've ever seen," joked Brent Maddock. "That was a very challenging movie. We shot it in 22 days which is way, way too fast, but I had a really great crew and there's a lot of stuff I'm really proud of, especially doing it under duress with as little time and money as we did."

One of the crew set to return for *Tremors 3* was Cristen Carr Strubbe, who was hired as a co-producer. Strubbe ultimately had to decline the role when she was offered a chance to become unit production manager on Michael Mann's Muhammad Ali biopic, *Ali*. "It was heartbreaking because I'd had an offer to do the biggest movie of my career and I just couldn't stay with a $2m film. I left and my friend, Anthony Santa Croce, took it over for me. The art director from the previous film took over as the production designer and it was a good way to get people to move up, but it was so limited financially that it was really going to be difficult to make."

Like *Tremors 2* before it, the new film's budgetary restrictions meant a return to Lone Pine was impossible for the shoot, with Perfection now due to be rebuilt closer to Los Angeles. The decision was taken to shoot the sequel in a valley close to the area used for the previous film, with a small portion of the town, most noticeably Chang's Market and the water tower, recreated to give the impression that this was the same Perfection from the original film. Sadly, the expansive backdrop from *Tremors* was now gone.

"The land had been sold as a housing development, which was very good for us because we could do anything we wanted," said unit production manager, Tom Keniston. "Sometimes you get all these restrictions but they didn't give a damn what we were doing. The biggest problem with that land, which we didn't realise until later, was that although we weren't super close to a freeway we were close enough that it created a constant hum in the sound recording. We ended up having to loop quite a bit of the film to correct the sound, so that was a bit of a problem. We built the interiors at Santa Clarita Studios."

As with many science fiction and fantasy franchises, *Tremors* fans played a major part in the success of the various films. Sales figures of *Tremors* and *Tremors 2* videos had been good indicators that there was an appetite for the modern creature features, but it was thanks to the burgeoning internet that fans were able to congregate to discuss the films on message boards. By the time filming of *Tremors 3* commenced in 2000, the production team were aware that aficionados wanted to do more than just consume the films; they wanted to help create a mythos surrounding them.

"When I started on *Tremors 3* I was looking at some websites [to find out] about what Graboids ate," said Keniston. "I went in to Brent and Steve and said, 'Wow, you've created all this stuff about this?' They said, 'No, that's all made up by other people." It [was becoming] a phenomenon."

REVISITING PERFECTION

The third film's return to the town of Perfection was a homecoming in more ways than one for actor Michael Gross, who had always felt the townsfolk made Burt a stronger character. "To me, the standard was the first film where you had men, women and children. You had an ersatz community, a family of sorts, whether they were related by blood or not, it was a family and that was, I felt, the chemistry that always worked best for Burt."

Although Kevin Bacon had declined an offer to return for the first sequel, *Tremors 3: Back to Perfection* was developed without an approach to Fred Ward to reprise his role of Earl Bassett. "We wanted to be true to our characters," said Wilson. "We'd said that Earl and Grady had made a lot of money at the end of *Tremors 2* and we felt that Earl wouldn't come back to Perfection as they had no need to do so." Though he continues to work in films and TV movies, Ward rarely conducts interviews and his feelings towards the *Tremors* films remain unknown.

Michael Gross prepares to be swallowed by a Graboid
© Susan Chuang

With Michael Gross replacing Ward as the franchise's lead actor, the casting of the film's ancillary roles could begin. Craig Campobasso, whose career had kicked off in 1984 with work on David Lynch's *Dune*, came aboard as casting director. "You always read the script first, so that you can go in and talk about it intelligently," explained Campobasso. "The next process is seeing the film's budget, the budgetary allotments for the lead actors and the timeframe, so we know what calibre of actor we can aim for. I then talk to agents and managers and start to see who's available and who might be interested in doing it within the price range. Then I start auditioning actors to see who fits it the best and I bring in the cream of the crop for Nancy, Steve and Brent."

Luckily for Campobasso, it was common knowledge within the industry that Stampede Entertainment was producing films that were both profitable and professional. "They set a great tone, where work got done but everybody enjoyed it. It was hard for them to choose with the embarrassment of riches of actors that were willing to come and be a part of *Tremors 3* even though, back then, sequels were looked at as 'the naughty children' of the originals."

In the casting director's experience, the stigma attached to direct-to-video sequels often ensured that he was limited in his choices for such films. "Nowadays a sequel is gigantic when a studio does it, but if they're straight-to-video all the larger actors or the ones that are up-and-coming won't go near them. They're holding out for the TV series or the part in a big studio picture. Then there are the actors who just like to work and in this town work begets work. The more people you meet, the more people that enjoy working with you that want you to come on board the next one."

Of the film's returning Perfectionites, actor Tony Genaro, was surprised to be asked to reprise the role of cattle rancher, Miguel, from the 1990 original. "Because I wasn't in *Tremors 2* I thought 'Well, guess they've just done away with that guy.' They called me up and told me what they were planning and they were going to make a movie for DVD. *Tremors 3* wasn't too bad, I thought they could have called it a theatrical release."

Also making a comeback was Charlotte Stewart as *Tremors*' Nancy Sterngood. "We couldn't go back up to the desert but they were out in the San Fernando Valley and they matched the original town perfectly. With the exception of the few places that got knocked down in the first movie, it was like being there again. The first time we did the movie in six weeks, the second time we did it in a week. Then we did some work on a sound stage. We also got Ariana again, it was just so much fun to have the two of us together again on that, a real mother and daughter."

Stampede's ambitious plan to reunite the original cast of Perfection looked to be in jeopardy when the time came to approach Ariana Richards. "I remember Nancy Roberts saying, 'Craig, we can't find Ariana. She has no agent, all her numbers are gone and we're extremely worried,'" said Campobasso. "I just smiled and said, 'I know exactly where she is, she's in college', because I had cast her in a film called *Prancer*. I called her and said, 'We really need you in this movie.' She talked to her teachers and they let her take class work home while she shot the film. If they had said no, she would not have been in the movie."

"The producers asked me to do it so I did it as a favour to them, to jump right out of college and do this part," said Richards. "It was just a cameo. I recently lined up some of the films I had been in on my entertainment area and saw all these teeth on the *Jurassic Park* and *Tremors* DVD covers."

Robert Jayne returned as Melvin Plug, a character once again designed to be hated by viewers as he attempted to buy up land in Perfection Valley for new homes. "When you're under the gun with your budget it's hard to make a good-quality movie and they didn't give Brent much to work with. It was a low-budget movie when we shot the first one, so we were probably doing *Tremors 3* for around $2m."

Alongside the returning cast, *Back to Perfection* saw some new characters taking up residency in Perfection, including good-looking cowboy, Jack Sawyer, played by Shawn Christian. "Some of the other guys I read for [the role] were Nick Stabile and Brian Krause, but when Shawn got into that little accent thing he just had a charisma about him that we all fell in love with," recalled Campobasso.

Said Shawn Christian, "At that point in my career it was standard that agents called [and said], 'Here's the third installment of a really good franchise, would you go in and read?' I think I was on a short list of actors that they had in mind and I went in, auditioned, earned the role, and had the good fortune of reading with around 15 women to play the Jodi Chang part."

For the role of Walter Chang's enterprising niece, Jodi, the producers set about looking for some of the most prominent Asian actresses available to them, inviting them in to carry out a chemistry read with Shawn Christian. "In the chemistry reads there were certain actresses who would lean away from him, others that would almost be on his lap," said Campobasso. "With his outgoing personality, if somebody is leaning away from Shawn that's not a good sign. We fell in love with Susan Chuang after seeing outtakes from her episode of *Dharma & Greg* where she had the two lead actors constantly breaking character and bursting out laughing."

"It was pretty early in my career, I just remember going to audition several times," admitted Chuang. "You're always elated when you get the news that you got a job and it's shot locally. I've worked in television more so than films and it's harder to get science fiction and action films. I hate to say it, but I think if you're Asian your best chances of an action project would be something with martial arts and I'm not a martial artist, so I'm kind of out of that category."

He may have been the new boy in Perfection, but Shawn Christian was aware of the significance behind the returning cast and crew from the original *Tremors*. "I felt like I was being welcomed into an old tribe, you saw the faces light up when they saw each other again and the history came to life when they all got together. Years passed between each film, but you wouldn't have known it with the way they collaborated together and with regard to their creative process and also the friendships that have been cultivated over the years."

INTRODUCING THE ASS BLASTERS

In their quest to offer fans a new twist in their latest sequel, Wilson, Maddock and Roberts decided to bring back the Graboids and Shriekers while adding yet another new creature, the Ass Blasters.

Tom Woodruff Jr. and Alec Gillis, who had designed the creatures for the first two films, based the Ass Blasters on a real insect called a Bombardier Beetle, infamous for being able to mix chemicals in its abdomen that create a firecracker sound to scare predators. "They like to design from the real world, even though they design these horrific and bizarre things," said Steve Wilson. "It's important to them for the skin textures and movement to not go too far away from the real world object. We added the ability to launch themselves into the air."

Unfortunately for Universal's Patti Jackson, the army of creatures put a strain on the film's limited budget. "It's way more expensive having three monsters instead of one. The Graboids didn't last very long, they disintegrate, and we had to do a lot more building. There was also some CG."

Computer effects had been used sparingly on *Tremors 2*, partly due to the high costs of the relatively new process. By the time *Tremors 3* entered production, technology had moved on to a point that the costs had been lowered significantly. "We designed the creatures and built them, but because they flew and walked it meant that there was little else for us to actually execute," said Alec Gillis. "Once you're into a walking or flying creature you're into a certain amount of digital work. We pitched them the idea of doing more rod puppetry and compositing rather than digital. But they were of a mind that they just wanted to go digital."

Two of the visual effects team recruited to bring the film's creatures to digital life were Linda Drake and Kevin Kutchaver. Drake had known Steve Wilson long before the making of the first *Tremors*, and had worked on films such as *Blade* (1998) and *Stuart Little* (1999). Kutchaver was one of the three partners in Flat Earth Productions, the visual effects team responsible for the 1990s fantasy TV series *Hercules: The Legendary Journeys*

(1995–99) and *Xena: Warrior Princess* (1995–2001). When Flat Earth disbanded, Kutchaver started his own company, HimAni Productions.

"It seemed like a good opportunity because I loved the first two movies," said Kutchaver. "*Tremors 2* was Phil Tippett's foray into computer animation and I thought it would be nice to jump into the third one and show off with the new company."

Linda Drake was supplied with the new script, from which she began to break down each scene to work out how many visual effects would be required and how much they would cost. "There were 12 CG shots in *Tremors 2* and I think we ended up doing maybe 40 for *Tremors 3*. I told Nancy Roberts and Patti Jackson that there were 80 shots with the CG creatures and they said, 'We don't have that kind of budget, we have to have it capped.' Then of course the editor starts putting it together and it turned out we need those kind of shots."

The knock-on effect on Drake and Kutchaver's workload wouldn't be felt until shooting had ended and post-production had begun, but in the meantime they travelled to the set with the rest of the effects crew to begin filming.

SHOOTING

The opening moments of *Tremors 3* quickly establish the tone for the next 90 minutes, introducing viewers to a still-active Burt Gummer on a mission for the Argentine government. Whereas *Tremors 2* began with a Graboid attack, this time it was an army of Shriekers who took their chances with America's best-known survivalist. Rather than travelling to Argentina, filming took place at three in the morning close to Magic Mountain, with Michael Gross firing 50-calibre blanks at a non-existent army of Shriekers that were inserted digitally in post-production.

"That was the night that Steve Wilson had the best time," Kevin Kutchaver stated. "I can't even begin to tell you how loud those blanks were. Steve looked like a kid in a candy shop, he was just sitting there and they'd let him blow some rounds off. I had a friend that lived in a residential area half a mile away and he said, 'What the hell was going on?' I said, 'That was us! That was your *Tremors* alarm.' For at least an hour they were blasting that thing. I don't know how you get a permit for that, maybe you don't."

To ensure continuity with the Shriekers seen in the previous film, Linda Drake and Kevin Kutchaver visited Tom Woodruff and Alec Gillis' Associated Dynamics, Inc workshop to photograph full-size display models of the Shriekers, before building their own computer generated versions.

Due to the location's close proximity to Los Angeles, the cast and crew made their own way to set each day. "I live in Hollywood, so I drove probably about an hour and 45 minutes each way," said Shawn Christian. "I was so excited to go to work, I was all hands up, jammin' in my car; great music got me in the right frame of mind. It was such a joy to work with these people, these talented and gifted writers and certainly Michael Gross."

As might be expected with a 22-day shoot, the pace of filming was hectic; while many films shoot between five and eight pages a day, for *Tremors 3* it was in the region of 15 to 20. "We were never really rushed but we knew we had to get it in under budget and certainly in a timeframe," said Shawn Christian. "By comparison, I've worked in primetime TV dramas where they do 10 pages a day and I also do a soap opera, I'm doing *Days of Our Lives* now, and we do eight episodes a week, probably 150 pages a day. It was pretty fast for a film but compared to a daytime show, it's nothing."

Director Brent Maddock also found the pace challenging. "It's one of those things when you're in the middle of it saying, 'This script is just too elaborate, what were we thinking? Today we're shooting a scene where the flying creatures land on this thing and this thing blows up and they're rolling down a mountain ... who wrote this?' You begin to hate yourself."

"A feature runs at a different pace than television," said director of photography, Virgil Harper, returning from *Tremors* and

Tremors 2: Aftershocks. "Television used to be a lot of 'just grab stuff quick, gotta get a lot of page count'. I like to think about stuff and I'm very strict about when I shoot, or the angles I shoot, in regard to sun and light."

Just as *Tremors 3* had seen the replacement of the Shriekers with Ass Blasters as the humans' central foe, the new film found Earl Bassett replaced by Burt Gummer as the main protagonist. In addition, while Earl had acquired Grady Hoover as his new sidekick, Burt gained his own helper in the shape of Desert Jack. "I thought we had an interesting dynamic, Burt's wry sense of humour and Jack's fly-by-the-seat-of-his-pants sort of character," said Christian.

For the third time in the franchise's history, it was time for a new set of actors to learn the intricacies of the "*Tremors* tone", the unique mix of comedy and drama that had set the original film apart from so many other creature features. "Quite honestly, you're not sure what tone you're going to take when you approach these kinds of action fantasy horror flicks," admitted Christian. "[The writers] set a great tone and gave me an enormous amount of freedom. I got to find this cowboy and as we started building the character, they were giving me these great Zen zingers."

According to Craig Campobasso, one of the most memorable actors from Universal's point of view was Billy Rieck, who played Jack's soon-to-be-eaten assistant, Buford. "I got a call from Universal and they said, 'Is this Craig Campobasso, you cast *Tremors 3*?' and I'm like, 'Oh man, I'm in trouble.' They said, 'Did you cast Billy Rieck?' I said, 'Yes' and they said, 'That guy is awesome! We just watched his screening, we love him!' I thought that was pretty funny, that they had picked him out of the haystack of actors and just loved Billy Rieck."

The character of Jodi Chang was a nod to the franchise's roots, the business school-educated niece of Walter Chang giving everything up to reside in the desert as she tried to make a living from the Graboid-obsessed tourist trade. "My character's whole thing was making money and profiting from the monsters coming to the area with the merchandise," noted Susan Chuang. "Jodi's got all her projections and profit margins."

Perhaps reflecting growing real-world concerns regarding the environment and endangered species, the moral question of whether ferocious underground monsters should be killed was raised in the script, as a team of government agents arrived in Perfection determined to protect the Graboids. Such a twist was something usually ignored by genre pictures, where the protagonists are too busy trying to stay alive to debate the issues surrounding the extinction of a species.

Taking on the role of palaeontologist, Dr. Andrew Merliss, was actor Barry Livingston, known to US audiences for his role in TV comedy, *My Three Sons* (1960–72). "I read for Dr. Merliss because Brent Maddock was a personal friend and was going to direct the film," said Livingston. "I was on the set a couple of weeks to film my role and it never felt rushed, even though I knew of the time constraints. I loved working with both Michael and Shawn, who were both very committed to making the film in the spirit of the original. I also loved getting slimed for my death scene, those are the fun parts of acting."

In another link to the first film, one of the Department of the Interior agents, Charlie Rusk, was played by actor John Pappas; Pappas had portrayed one of the road workers, Carmine, in *Tremors*.

As in all of the *Tremors* films, the majority of the shoot took place outdoors, offering few luxuries for the cast as they worked in the sun and heat for much of the day. "We were out in a desert, beautiful mountains, beautiful big sky, it felt like we were a travelling circus on a camping adventure," noted Shawn Christian.

For Christian, the sequence in which Burt, Jack, Jodi and Miguel were trapped overnight in a box canyon was one of his character's defining moments. "We were in a dilemma; you're stuck on this rock, the Graboid's got you locked in overnight and Jack's taking in a Zen-like quality, the beauty of the moment, the clouds, the sky, the stars. That frustrates everybody and if you juxtapose that with the drama of the moment then you have comedy. They did a really nice job of setting that up and creating Desert Jack that way."

Though much of screenwriter John Whelpley's dialogue remained following Brent Maddock and Steve Wilson's edit, he was aware that some things would change during the shoot. "Brent and Steve had to rewrite on location, mostly because of the physical variables that presented themselves in the here-and-now. I understood why some of the dialogue cuts were made; I tend to be an Irish-American rambler with my dialogue and the bottom line is that pacing is very important in a franchise like *Tremors*. The core characters are ordinary people in an extraordinary situation, and they never quite have time to breathe until the last monster is slain. I learned a lot about writing for a film budget."

Filming of the rock sequence also introduced Susan Chuang to Michael Gross' sense of humour. "The first time I met him we were shooting out in the desert and he handed me a cow pie, which is basically dried up manure from out in the field. I took it because I was new and didn't know what it was. He was a very kind man and he helped me a lot, because all the parts I had played up until that point were so small and there were technical things that he was kind enough to help me out with, like finding your light. He would position me, saying, 'If you feel that, that's where you need to be.'"

Shawn Christian also enjoyed his time working with Gross. "I was proud to work with Michael. For an actor to be in the business that long, quite honestly sometimes I've worked with people who are just jaded, they're done, they don't do their homework anymore. He cares very passionately about every moment, none of it is self-indulgent, he truly cares about what's going to be put up on the screen. You just take notes and learn, you go along for the ride. I approach the work very much with the same kind of discipline."

TAMING THE MONSTERS

Tremors 3's dependence upon digital creatures required those behind and in front of the camera to alternate between physical props and green screen, often in the same scene and with variable results.

"We were a little less in the middle of the decisions, so as a result there's things like digital worms in there that don't really match the look [of the physical creatures], even their shape is not quite the same," said Alec Gillis. "I thought they did a pretty good job on some of the walking little Ass Blasters. We would like to have been more involved in it, but by that point the team had changed to become a little bit more visual effects-heavy than practical creature effects-heavy."

Gillis and Woodruff had built a mock-up of the Ass Blaster before creating a small maquette that was moved to a stand. "Back then we were still taking the maquettes, drawing grids on them, then using a digitiser pen to put them into the computer," said Kevin Kutchaver, who was creating the CG versions. "Then we would massage all of the data after that point blank. They were manually just digitised in."

An Ass Blaster is helped to fly using the Lydecker Technique
© Linda Drake

"*Tremors 3* was one of the first times I'd dealt with puppeteers," said production manager Tom Keniston, who wasn't overly impressed with his first experience of the Ass Blasters. "When they arrived they had the puppets with 20,000 tubes and air pressure hoses coming out of their butts and they'd say, 'OK, now it's going to move' and it would take three steps. Brent and his assistant director, Carl Ludwig, just looked at it like 'That's it? The thing moved three-feet?' It had a lot of limitations, as puppets always do."

The effects team of Linda Drake and Kevin Kutchaver encountered a recurring issue while shooting the Ass Blasters' introduction. While it was their responsibility to make the CG creatures look as similar to the practical creatures as possible, the need to shoot scenes quickly often led to key steps in the process being skipped. "We had a shot with the puppet Ass Blaster behind a fence, then we cut to the people and we cut back and they'd cut in the CG one where it actually comes around the fence, in full-body, which the puppet couldn't do," explained Drake.

"They shot the puppet at 10am and I said to Virgil Harper, 'While you're set-up with the camera you need to shoot the plate without the puppet so we can put the CG one in later.' I got told, 'We don't have time,' and I said, 'You need to do it now, the sun is leaving.' By the time they got back and shot that plate it was three in the afternoon. So you have the sun on the puppet and then the CG one comes around the corner with no sun. Later, Patti Jackson said, 'How come the CG doesn't look right?' and I had to say, 'Well, it's because you didn't shoot it at the same time.' That's why I think people criticise that it doesn't match."

The team also had to deal with flying Ass Blasters, something that added new complexities to the shoot. Director Brent Maddock requested that he be allowed to use a mini helicopter with a camera attached to film the Ass Blasters' point of view. "There are three or four of those shots that help explain what's going on and add another dimension to the film. If you look you'll see we flipped the same shot a few times and used the mirror image."

Remote control helicopters had previously been used by Drake and Kutchaver on *Starship Troopers* (1997) to great success. "We also had some shots of the Ass Blasters that was a full-scale model," explained Drake. "I suggested we use a technique referred to as the Lydecker Technique. Theodore and Howard Lydecker did a lot of the stunts on 1930s serials like *Rocketman* and *Lost In Space* in the sixties. They would take full-sized models and fly them from one side of the camera to the other. The Ass Blaster must've been five-feet long and we ran a rod through the centre so we could put it on a wire, so that sometimes when you see it flying in the distance, it's a full-size one. So we were able to do some of the shots in practical and that worked really well."

Miguel survived Graboid attacks in *Tremors*, but his story came to an end in the second sequel after being forced off a cliff in an Ass Blaster attack. Unfortunately for actor Tony Genaro, a further *Tremors* sequel and a spin-off TV series were not in the pipeline in 2000. "I never imagined that this thing was going to go on, so I actually didn't feel too badly about it. It's kind of dramatic to get killed and then everybody crying about you saying, 'Ooh, Miguel!' I thought it was pretty cool. Had I known [about future sequels] I would have professed that I was just badly wounded."

Genaro had mixed feelings about his time on the sequel, unlike his fond memories of shooting the original in Lone Pine. "The first one did feel very special, I can't explain why that is. On *Tremors 3* it wasn't really Perfection. The mountains weren't in the background and it just didn't have that same feeling. You had to drive 50 miles a day each way yourself, and it just didn't seem like there was the cohesiveness that there should've been. It was a good company, they're all real nice, but the budget was probably very difficult for them. It was more of an acting job."

Elsewhere, Charlotte Stewart was relishing her fight with the Ass Blasters alongside screen daughter, Ariana Richards. "We had fun up on the roof. They had us in a box that was tied to a cable. They pulled this cable so fast we came flying toward the camera. There's a scene at the end where Ariana and I are fighting the creature and it comes popping through the door, and that was a combination of mechanical and digital. When you see it flopping around in the room by itself, that's digital. When it was close up they had a practical head that came at us."

THE FINAL SHOWDOWN

The film's most complex sequence, the final junkyard showdown in which Burt, Jack and Jodi came face-to-face with the four remaining Ass Blasters, proved to be a challenge for all of those involved. "The junkyard dealer actually gave us permission to shoot there and then we found out that he didn't really quite own it," Tom Keniston said. "I think he owned the junkyard but he didn't own the land and legally you have to kind of rent both, but we sorted it between him and the land owner."

As with desert locations on the previous films, another issue to contend with was the local wildlife in the shape of snakes. "That was the bane of our assistant director's existence; every time we went to any of these locations we had to bring in snake wranglers to clear out the rattlesnakes," added Keniston. "Because they work in these areas the crew are used to it, but some of the actors were like, 'What do you mean?' I was constantly itching Carl's ankle and he'd freak out, because junkyards are heaven for rattlesnakes."

The sequence required the Perfectionites to dodge attacking Ass Blasters by coming up with increasingly extreme methods to mask their body heat from the creatures. For the shot of Michael Gross, Shawn Christian and Susan Chuang hiding in a portable toilet, Virgil Harper suggested an unusual camera angle to Brent Maddock. "When they go in the outhouse for safety I said, 'What if I shoot up through the toilet lid?' It's just something I saw when we took the back off of the toilet. A lot of people would probably find that gross, but I think it actually worked because of the expression on her face when she looks through the toilet hole."

Shawn Christian was happy with the heroics required of Desert Jack in the junkyard, taking on as many of the stunts as possible. "It was like an obstacle course, they had set up on top of these old abandoned buses and I had to go from one car to the next. I was well padded up and there were stunt people there of course, so I was really safe, but I'm like, 'Nah, I wanna do this, pad me up, let's go for it!' It was awesome, it's exactly what I felt like as a kid, in my backyard, playing make believe with me chasing the monsters or playing cowboys and Indians."

During filming the actors were required to react to practical Ass Blasters while imagining others that would later be inserted in post-production. "I got to wrestle with the Ass Blaster puppet and I remember moving and shaking it," said Christian. "The Graboid was a tennis ball on a stick, so that was a little more difficult. Firing at Ass Blasters in the sky was a little more challenging, but wrestling the puppet was pretty badass."

"It's a lot of screaming and expressing fear at something that isn't there," added Susan Chuang. "At that point you trust that the director's watching and seeing if it's what he wants and if he gets what he needs then you move on."

"What we did in *Tremors 2* and *3* is that if there was a problem with a practical effect you could, to an extent, solve it with CG," said Brent Maddock. "We had some creature shots where if you held on it for more than a second you were aware you were looking at something that wasn't alive, so we had to lay CG over them. But the pre-CG stuff was the most fun to do. As we always said on *Tremors*, whatever's going on, make sure somebody's just out of the frame with a shovel throwing dirt which will obscure everything and it won't look so phoney."

Solving problems with CG was the responsibility of Linda Drake and Kevin Kutchaver, who had been told before shooting commenced that the effects budget had to be capped due to rising costs. By the time *Tremors 3* entered post-production, the pair faced a major headache when they realised they required almost 80 effects shots compared to the 40 allowed by the budget, meaning they'd have to complete the work in their own time.

"It got to the point where Brent was saying, 'If we can't get these shots then there's no movie,' because the whole last act of that movie was [effects-heavy]," said Kutchaver. "I said, 'How much can you cut? If it's no good there won't be a film.' We wanted to show what we could do, so as the shots started to pile up, Linda and I started to dig in and do them. The other problem was that we were still finishing on 35mm film back then and that was coming out of my budget as well."

"Even though work was being done at the computer, you had to have a film recorder to put it back out to 35mm film and sometimes we were having problems with the lab being able to time shots," said Drake.

"We went through a lot of colour correction issues in just trying to get the stuff out," continued Kutchaver. "At that time for film output you were paid by the frame, so it was expensive. I think the 40 original shots that we broke down are really great and most of the free ones are OK, I can still watch them. Brent was very happy, he said, 'We wouldn't have a movie if we didn't have all of this.'"

RELEASE AND PROMOTION

Following post-production and editing, *Tremors 3: Back to Perfection* was on track for a US DVD and VHS release on 1 October 2001. The film was a major production for Universal Studios Home Entertainment, but the promotional activity that had accompanied *Tremors 2: Aftershocks* in 1996 was now conspicuous by its absence.

"We got to a point with *Tremors 3* when there was no promotion at all," said director Brent Maddock. "I remember saying to Universal, 'There's not even a poster to put up in a video store.' What some stores were doing was putting up their own posters to notify customers there was a thing called *Tremors 3* available. That was part of Universal's austerity; they wanted to spend as little money as possible on these films. I'm not sure saving money on promotion is the smartest way. Rabid fans would find out about it, but as far as the general public knowing there's another one of these movies available, that wasn't the case."

"Universal made a lot of money off that product, it always sold well, especially in the Asian world," remarked Tom Keniston. "I was the unit production manager on *Tremors 3* and the TV series and I still get residuals off them. [*Tremors* director] Ron Underwood told me a story about the premiere of his second film, *City Slickers*, in Japan. They sat in the theatre and nobody laughed the whole time. He was really depressed and when he came out the publicity people came up and they said, 'There's a lot of people that want to talk to you'. There was a line around the block and all they wanted to talk about was *Tremors*."

"I travel to some of these small cities across the country for appearances for other shows, but there's always some sort of *Tremors* fan out in the audience that I end up signing DVD covers for," said Shawn Christian. "They can tell you every line, every action sequence, because they really have a deep passion for the franchise."

Susan Chuang also discovered that her time in Perfection was popular with viewers. "When we first moved into my neighbourhood I went to a local Thai restaurant and I think I'd just come from the gym. I was eating by myself and one of the servers kept staring at me when she walked by and I thought it was because I wasn't dressed appropriately. She came by to fill my water glass and was very sweet, asking if I was an actor. I said, 'Yes' and she said, 'Oh, I saw you recently' and at that time I think I was in the film *Bewitched* but had literally one line. I said to her, 'It's a really small part' and she said, 'No, you're all over it' and she was referring to *Tremors*. She was a fan, this Thai waitress, she was really sweet."

With a career spanning TV series and films from *Little House* on the *Prairie to Twin Peaks* (1990–91) and *Eraserhead* (1977), Charlotte Stewart is regularly stopped for autographs from fans, but *Tremors* holds a special place in her heart. "There's a box boy called Aaron at my local supermarket here in Napa. He has a disability and watches *Tremors* every single day in the break room. I arranged to meet him and gave him a picture of me with Kevin Bacon that I had autographed to him. When Kevin came to Napa with his band, The Bacon Brothers, Aaron took that picture and had Kevin autograph it. Then Aaron brought me a picture of him with Kevin and autographed it to me. It was very sweet."

Despite Universal's almost non-existent promotion, the fans managed to track the film down, making it yet another success for the Home Entertainment division. "*Tremors 3* has been wildly successful in the US, it immediately surpassed all sales predictions for VHS and DVD units," explained Steve Wilson in 2002. "When it aired on the Sci-Fi cable network it got the second highest ratings in the network's entire 10 year history, second only to the made-for-cable *Dune*."[2]

The 2001 Video Premiere Awards found Michael Gross nominated in the "Best Actor for DVD and VHS film release" category for his role of Burt Gummer. Also up for the award were Adam Baldwin for *Dr. Jekyll and Mr. Hyde*, Jean-Claude Van Damme for *Replicant*, Christopher Lloyd for *When Good Ghouls Go Bad* and Gross' old *Tremors* co-star, Fred Ward, nominated for his role in the thriller, *Full Disclosure*. Both Gross and Ward attended the ceremony on 23 October 2001, with Gross taking home the award. The actor thanked the film's cast and crew while singling out producer Nancy Roberts for special thanks.[3]

Far from VHS and DVD being the key indicator of *Tremors 3: Back to Perfection*'s success, the film's popularity on cable television would prove to be the platform for the next entry in the saga. While the film continued to sell well on disc, the potential for spinning the *Tremors* brand off into yet another new direction soon presented itself to Stampede Entertainment.

CHAPTER EIGHT

TREMORS: THE SERIES

The television hall of fame is lined with successful spin-offs from theatrical feature films, with series such as *M*A*S*H* (1972–83) *Highlander* (1992–98) and *Buffy the Vampire Slayer* (1997–2003) finding appreciative audiences willing to tune into small screen stories once the big screen tale had been told. Less successful transitions, including *Planet of the Apes* (1974), *Ferris Bueller* (1990–91) and *Blade: The Series* (2006), came and went with little fanfare, lasting a handful of episodes before descending into interesting footnotes in the history of their progenitor.

By the time of *Tremors 3: Back to Perfection*'s release in October 2001, the franchise had gained a loyal following, keen to see what new adventures were in store for Burt Gummer and the townsfolk. With the team at Universal Studios Home Entertainment restricted from developing further films until sales figures had been calculated, the success of the third film on the Universal-owned Sci-Fi channel led to discussions in 2002 about the viability of a *Tremors* TV series.

Originally envisioned as a natural home for classic film and TV series owned by Paramount Pictures and Universal Studios, The Sci-Fi Channel launched in 1992 before dropping the word "Channel" in March 1999 (the network would rebrand again in 2009, finally settling on the name Syfy). By 2002, Sci-Fi was owned by Universal and known for its low-budget original series and made-for-cable movies. "We went to the Sci-Fi guys and said *Tremors* should be a TV series, but we weren't part of the development process," said Universal Studios Home Entertainment's Louis Feola.

"Sci-Fi came and said, 'What about a *Tremors* series?' and we told them we'd been trying to pitch one for years, with story ideas, artwork, a map of Perfection and new monsters," recalled Steve Wilson, referring to an idea for a spin-off TV series that had first been mooted in 1995 during pre-production on *Tremors 2: Aftershocks*.

With *The X-Files* (1993–2002) riding high in the ratings, the 1995 *Tremors* series would have seen Val McKee and Earl Bassett taking on new cases each week from various sources, including tabloid newspaper readers and people who believed in UFOs. As Kevin Bacon and Fred Ward would have been unlikely to commit to a TV show, the roles of Val and Earl would almost certainly have been recast, though Michael Gross may have reprised the role of Burt Gummer.

Wilson and Brent Maddock's pitch included monsters such as Bigfoot (a fan approaches Val and Earl to investigate ghostly goings-on, only for them to discover it's Bigfoot wearing a sheet to scare people away); The Thing in the Trees (when people mysteriously disappear in the woods, Val and Earl discover an arboreal octopus lurking above); Killer Toaster Ovens (Perfection is invaded by rectangular robots that begin systematically tearing the place apart and the boys discover they're the US Military's latest hi-tech weapon); The Great White Graboid (Val and Earl discover there is one surviving albino Graboid who torments them throughout the series); a Vampire (Val, Earl and Burt discover a mountain man with odd vampiric qualities); and The Awful Wing-ed Thing (a mysterious creature swoops down on sheep and people, Val and Earl try to trap it by dressing as sheep, Burt tries to bring it down with a homemade heat-seeking rocket).[1]

Now that Sci-Fi was keen for a television version of *Tremors*, Stampede began discussing the logistics of bringing it to the small screen. "They agreed to let us be the executive producers, which in that instance means they had writers, because in television an executive producer is a writer rather than an ancillary person," Wilson said. Alongside Wilson, Brent Maddock and Nancy Roberts, David Israel (*Midnight Caller*, 1988–91) was appointed as the series showrunner, the person responsible for the day-to-day operation of the project, by Sci-Fi.

Tremors: The Series' premise followed on from the events of *Tremors 3: Back to Perfection*, with Burt Gummer still living in Perfection alongside Nancy Sterngood and Jodi Chang. New residents included Miguel's niece, Rosalita Sanchez, and ex-NASCAR racer, Tyler Reed, who now owned the town's Graboid Adventure Tours, having been sold the business by Desert Jack in Las Vegas. Perfection was under constant federal government monitoring by local agent, W.D. Twitchell, while Melvin Plug also returned, once again attempting to set up a profitable business selling ranchettes in the valley. Also returning from the third film was El Blanco, the albino Graboid who could not develop into a Shrieker thanks to being sterile. Now an endangered species under Twitchell's protection, it was in the best interests of the townsfolk to ensure El Blanco's safety or risk the full force of the law.

With a 13-episode order from Sci-Fi to be produced by USA Cable Entertainment, the team at Stampede Entertainment was excited at the opportunity of bringing *Tremors* to a wider audience. In late 2002, work began assembling a team to write the scripts, while consideration was given to where the series should be filmed.

STAFFING THE SERIES

Just as many crew members had returned from the original *Tremors* to work on the direct-to-video sequels, the TV series welcomed back *Tremors 3*'s production manager, Tom Keniston, to carry out the same role. His first task was to find a location to rebuild the latest version of Perfection. "I'd been in Lithuania filming *Attila* with Gerard Butler and when I returned to the USA they asked me if I wanted to do the series," said Keniston. "We couldn't return to the set used in *Tremors 3* because at the end we sold it to someone who owned a western town on another piece of land. Also, when we were doing the series, [Sci-Fi] wanted to reach a certain price and it was much cheaper to work in Mexico."

It soon became obvious that Sci-Fi's apparent enthusiasm for the TV series was at odds with their approach to funding the production. "It was a rough start and there were a couple of really bad decisions made," said Wilson. "We wanted to shoot in New Mexico, but Sci-Fi put their foot down and said, 'You will shoot in Mexico in six days and you will only get this much per episode.' Sci-Fi is notoriously low-budget and their shows show it; our show showed it."

Tom Keniston's search for a production crew led him to recruit many of his staff from San Diego, a city adjacent to the Mexican border. "We were based at Fox's Baja Studios and we supplemented [the San Diego crew] with people from Mexico City. The Tijuana crew don't like the people from Mexico City because they think they're snobs. The Mexico City crews are super good filmmakers and they worked for a reasonable amount of money, so that's how we made the whole film. I brought the stuntmen in from Slovakia because they had worked on *Attila*, Lubomir Misak and those guys."

Keniston next hired a helicopter and began scouting locations with the head of Fox Studios and the series' Mexican production manager, Iram Collantes. "We scouted from the sky to find a space where we could put the town and made a deal with a guy who owned a farm with acres of land," said Keniston. "The problem was it was about three miles down a dirt road and we had to redo it by packing it down and oiling it so that it was much more passable for our trucks. It was still intense because you had to drive down what was basically a dirt road and after a couple months that wears out with 50 or 60 cars going down there every day. We built the town ourselves and rarely went on location out of there."

* * *

By June 2002, as production was being set up in Mexico, the writing staff assembled at Universal Studios' Abbott & Costello

Building in Los Angeles, primarily under the supervision of Brent Maddock. Maddock and Steve Wilson took on the job of scripting the series' first few episodes along with producer Nancy Roberts, hoping they could use the template for new-to-the-franchise writers Babs Greyhosky, John Schulian and Christopher Silber.

Although Maddock and Wilson had been producers on the *Tremors* films, this was their first time as executive producers on a TV series and the first time they had been put in a position where they weren't writing every script themselves. *Tremors 3* had brought John Whelpley into the fold to write a script based on Wilson, Maddock and Roberts' outline, but the series would bring different sensibilities and ideas from various new writers. "It was difficult to figure out who was right for this material and who wasn't," said Maddock. "That became one of the big challenges on the series. Every writer was very talented and wanting to do good work, but you don't realise what you do until you see other people try and imitate it."

"We plunged into it and that's where we discovered how hard it is to get the humour right," admitted Wilson. "We didn't realise, having worked so long with just me, Brent, Ron [Underwood] and Nancy [Roberts], how internalised our style of humour had become."

One of the series' behind the scenes staff was Steven Binder, a young screenwriter whose work on Sci-Fi's *The Invisible Man* (2000) had led him to consider a career change. "After *The Invisible Man* it was just sort of hard to get arrested and I decided, 'Fuck this, I'm gonna go to medical school.' I didn't really have my head in the game and I just happened to go to a pitch meeting for a show called *Dead Zone* and then my agent called me and said, 'We sent a package of scripts over to *Tremors* and the only person they want to meet is you.' The next day I bought the movies, got popcorn and watched them all."

After a successful meeting with the producers, Binder was hired as a staff writer, responsible for working with more experienced screenwriters to discuss possible story ideas and write outlines for scripts. "It was an office of nine people and we were on the first floor, the other six floors above us were used as parking garages. The walls would creak like a Graboid was going by all the time. The process is you come up with an idea and you write a paragraph or one-page describing the idea, the showrunner will take a look and then you send that over to the network for approval, so they can get a sense of what you're doing before you do it."

Once approved by the network, the next stage was to write an outline of the story, breaking the elements down into brief scenes. "It might be: Burt Gummer's sitting down on the steps, there's a noise, he looks out the window, he sees a new alien, cut to title; it literally could be as short as that," said Binder. "Once you do that, in the confines of the writers' office, everyone can add notes and you send that to the network. The network has notes on that and once you get approval from that you write the script."

"You'd get something that was like a soap opera or that was just bizarrely silly and it was exhausting," said Maddock. "As executive producer you have to make sure the scripts are right and a lot of it ended up explaining to the writers what you wanted, and sometimes having to rewrite the writer, which you don't want to do. You don't want to take their credit away because they get paid and get residuals according to having a credit, so we never took anyone's credit away or shared them, which some executive producers love to do."

One of the series writers was Christopher Silber, who, like Steven Binder, was new to writing for television and had recently completed a writers' programme through Warner Bros. "I got a call from my agent saying she'd submitted me for a show at Sci-Fi and that the showrunner wanted to sit down and meet with me. I met with Brent, Steve, Nancy and David Israel and the next day they hired me. I'd never done anything at all, I'd never even spent any time around other writers or been in a writers' room, so I had no idea what to expect."

Silber discovered that in their haste to commission a series, Sci-Fi had bypassed the need for a pilot episode, requiring the writing team to quickly get to grips with the concept. "The trial was that we had to figure out what the show was while we sat there, figure out what the first episode was. We didn't have any money, so you're trying to do a giant worm show when you can't show the giant worm all the time. You also have a show that takes place in a town of five people, which means you can't have lots of monsters and you don't have a lot of characters to interact with. There were a lot of growing pains that I think lasted the entire season; what is this series, how can we make stories, how can we make it exciting and how can we make it different?"

CASTING

With the scripts in development, work could begin on casting. The first actor secured for the series was Michael Gross, reprising his role of Burt Gummer while also assuming the role of producer. "I saw this as an ensemble of people who live together and who were facing difficult times and challenges together," said Gross. "I began to get very excited about the possibilities, as did Brent and Steve, of a character-driven piece where there are monsters just as there were bad guys in *Gunsmoke* with James Arness. You got to know Miss Kitty, Doc and Chester; these people became very real. Sometimes it became about them and who they were as individuals. So we started pitching ideas like Burt trying to find love online, great character-driven stuff."

Though she had returned for *Tremors 3* as Nancy Sterngood, a contract problem meant actress Charlotte Stewart had to miss out on a third stay in Perfection. "I'm a cancer survivor and I had a national commercial on TV for a cancer drug; they had an exclusive on me and I couldn't do anything else for two years. I really wanted to go to Mexico and had started making arrangements. Finally, Nancy Roberts called and said, 'We can't take a chance, they could sue us, and Universal would not enjoy that at all.'"

With the original Nancy unable to return, the search was on for a replacement. Enter Marcia Strassman, an actress used to the pressures of TV thanks to roles on series including *Welcome*

Back, Kotter (1975–79) and *Booker* (1989–90). "I hadn't gone to any of the preliminary auditions when I got a call saying, 'You should go in and see them.' I went in with these other four actresses who had auditioned 14 times and I got it. I was in Mexico two days later. At Michael's age and my age, you don't usually get the opportunity to run around and chase monsters."

Another character originally expected to return for *Tremors: The Series* was Desert Jack Sawyer, though once again the actor responsible for originating the role was unavailable at short notice. "I was already on a show called *Summerlane* at the time, so there was no possibility of me doing it," Shawn Christian said. "It would've been fun to do."

After a hasty revision to the series premise, Sawyer was replaced by Tyler Reed, played by *One Life to Live*'s (1968–2013) Victor Browne. "I was a big Kevin Bacon fan and had been told many times growing up that I looked like him. I was very familiar with the first movie and a couple of the other ones; Shawn Christian [was a friend of mine], so I was very excited to get the role. I was newly married and we had a young toddler, so the most challenging part was trying to figure out how to coordinate my family being there with me and my wife's work schedule in LA. We travelled back-and-forth."

Originally portrayed by Susan Chuang in *Tremors 3*, Jodi Chang was played by actress Lela Lee (*Friends*, 1994–2004) in the series. "My agent thought it would be a good role for me. Jodi runs the general shop and is business-minded. In my real life I was entrepreneurial, running an online shop for my comic strip merchandise. I auditioned the first time and had another call back within the week and then we had to get to Mexico by the end of the same month. I watched *Tremors 3* when I learned I got the part so I could be familiar with the franchise and the world of *Tremors*."

The role of the mysterious Rosalita Sanchez went to actress Gladise Jimenez, who had spent time on soap operas such as *The Young and the Restless* (1973–) and *The Bold and the Beautiful* (1987–). "There was an audition that came through and I love science fiction, so I was like, 'Oh, yes, let's do it!' I went in there and I nailed it. I'm a very physical person and every day I was riding a horse, running away from a monster, jumping in water, jumping on the roof, off the roof, in a car followed by giant insects ... I loved working on the show."

Continuity with the third film was increased by the decision to bring back Perfection's resident entrepreneur, Melvin Plug. "I don't think I was originally part of the TV show at all and I was really disappointed," stated Robert Jayne. "I remember calling them saying, 'Hey, I heard you're making a show', they're like, 'Yeah but the network didn't want anybody from the movie.' It was Brent and Nancy who put me in the show because they didn't really need the network approval, they just wrote me a part."

For the part of W.D. Twitchell, the permanently harassed government agent, the producers selected character actor Dean Norris, known in 2002 for guest roles in dozens of films and TV series including *Lethal Weapon 2* (1989) and *Millennium* (1996–99). Norris' name would become better known in 2008 when he won the role of Hank Schrader in AMC's hit drama, *Breaking Bad* (2008–13).

It's possible that had the team at Stampede Entertainment known a TV series would follow *Tremors 3*, Tony Genaro would have returned as cattle rancher, Miguel. "I wouldn't have let them kill me if I'd have known they were going to do that," joked Genaro. "I never did watch that series. I don't pay a whole lot of attention to television, other than sports, but by the time I knew it was on, it was over. A lot of big actors wanted to be in it because they'd grown up on *Tremors*."

Some of the names attracted to the series as members of the guest cast included Christopher Lloyd, Michael Rooker, Armin Shimerman, Richard Biggs, Nicholas Turturro, Vivica A. Fox, Branscombe Richmond and Sarah Rafferty.

LOSING CONTROL

As the cast made their way to Mexico to shoot the first episode and the writers in Los Angeles attempted to come to terms with the series they were creating, developments at Universal Studios Home Entertainment meant that the dormant idea for a fourth *Tremors* film suddenly became a reality. "While we were in the throes of doing the TV series the opportunity came up to do *Tremors 4*, and of course they wouldn't wait, they needed it right now," said Maddock. "That's when we decided Steve and Nancy would look after the fourth film and I was left attempting to run the TV series."

Perfection is once more rebuilt, this time in Mexico © Al Burstein

As well as losing Wilson and Roberts, later episodes of the series had to do without the character of Burt Gummer, as Michael Gross was needed on the set of the film back in the USA while shooting was still taking place on the series in Mexico.

"If Universal had been willing to delay the start of *Tremors 4* by two weeks, or if Sci-Fi had been willing to wait until the end of T-4's shoot to start the series production, Michael Gross could have been in all 13 episodes," stated Wilson on the Stampede Entertainment website. "Both sides absolutely refused to compromise, even though they're both owned by the same parent company. After all that, Universal Home Video then delayed the release of the finished T-4 several months. Go figure."[2]

Walter Chang's Market continues to serve the Perfectionites
© Al Burstein

"We tried to stay abreast of what we were working on and tried to coordinate, but there were dividers up, 'You stay on your side, I'll stay on mine', that happens in studios and companies," noted Louis Feola, whose team was busy developing what would become *Tremors 4: The Legend Begins*.

For Brent Maddock, it had become clear that the premise of a small town beleaguered by bizarre monsters week after week had major issues. "Someone once said that movies are about endings. If you're writing a movie you need to know from page one how you're going to end it. TV shows are all about beginnings, how to get everything going and getting all the balls in the air and juggling them for five, six or seven seasons. We took a movie idea and tried to turn it into a TV series and it never worked. It got more and more broken as it went on, more and more things to explain why people weren't leaving town, and that wasn't a good way to go. It was the only way we could go, but it wasn't satisfying as storytellers."

In the writers' room, much of the discussion was about how to keep the show fresh each week, ensuring that storylines revolved around more than just returning Graboids and Ass Blasters by drawing inspiration from the other writers, including Christopher Silber. "One writer wanted to do their version of *The Thing*. I did one that was about people protecting Graboid rights and we were constantly trying to come up with new takes on how we could exploit this, or try to get a new kind of monster or a new kind of scientist trying to exploit the worm to keep it entertaining and fun."

One idea generated within the writers' room was Mixmaster, a compound that conveniently altered the genetic make-up of anything it touched, thereby providing a regular stream of new creatures. "Mixmaster [was] a way of explaining why things were happening so quickly and changing so rapidly," explained Wilson. "I remember pitching Mixmaster to the head guy at Sci-Fi and convincing him it would allow us some freedom with the stories."

While the writing team on *Tremors* was keen to progress with scripts, delays both in-house and with the network meant precious time was wasted. "There was a lot of waiting for stuff," admitted Steven Binder. "I could write a one-pager or an outline and wait two weeks for feedback. Chris Silber and I took many walks around the Universal back lot, we went on the *E.T.* ride a couple times; it wasn't the most efficient use of time. With a show like *Tremors*, which was in its first season and no one really had a handle on what the show was, you could hand in a one-pager that ended up being a concept and then you could write a whole outline and find out that there's nothing about it they want to do."

Ironically for a franchise that had begun as a way for its creators to maintain some degree of control over their work, *Tremors: The Series* marked the point where control finally slipped away from them. "With any show that has a showrunner that's been hired and he's not the creator, and the creators are there and have been with this particular franchise for a long time and knew it better than anyone but they had no TV experience, there's going to be some growing pains and miscommunications," said Silber.

Events came to a head for the production in November 2002 when a management change took place in the boardroom of Sci-Fi. "As we were coming up with story ideas and the first scripts, the people who took over decided they wanted the brand to be something completely different," said Silber. "The tone of *Tremors*, at least from my point of view, is a little bit campy, fun, a little tongue-in-cheek. Sci-Fi wanted to be hip and cool; the other project they were developing at the time was *Battlestar Galactica*, which was completely different. So suddenly we had a new vice president come in and not like what we were working on. We had to pause production for a little while and try to serve a new master."

According to Binder, a show shutting down mid-production is the TV equivalent of a nuclear bomb going off. "When you shut down the shooting of your show you've got a schedule, everything's lined up, you've rented the packages, you've got the crew, you've got the cast, you've got an office and the ball is rolling. Two hundred people stop getting paid and if a network does it to you, it's them saying they've lost all confidence. Our showrunner said, 'I don't know why but they're keeping me' and that was when things were really off the rails. They were getting scripts and they just weren't happy with what was being shot and what was being written at that point."

Production resumed on the series after a few weeks, but delays in Los Angeles inevitably had a knock-on effect on the Mexico shoot, with Tom Keniston and his crew unable to begin work on sets and props without completed scripts, which were still being faxed between locations. Unlike many hour-long dramas, *Tremors* had the added complication of elaborate scientific equipment being needed on a regular basis. "You'd be waiting for a script and [it would say], 'There's a phone, it's planted in the ground and when you press the buttons it lights up'" said

Keniston. "That's great, but if I get a script on Friday at 9pm and I have to shoot this on Monday, how am I going to get these contraptions built?"

Compounding the issue was the fact that the writers would send short descriptions of equipment rather than drawings, while Sci-Fi were opposed to staff working overtime. "My prop and special effects people would be out there saying, 'What the fuck is this?' We had to suggest how they might modify something because you're working at a fast pace and sometimes we were like, 'You know, we can't build that.'"

The writers' lack of familiarity with the Mexican locations meant scripts occasionally lacked the sort of detail required by the production team. "You'd try to describe what you had in terms of location as they wouldn't always know how to write to where you were standing," said Keniston. "They'd write, 'He runs down three blocks' and it was like, 'If you're running down three blocks we're at the mall' and we can't do that."

"There were times I was on the phone with someone on some bad cell phone on set and we would have to rewrite a scene as they were shooting; we'd be calling in the dialogue," said Christopher Silber. "The great thing about other shows I've worked on is that the writer produces his episode. I don't know that there was the money to send writers down to Mexico for two weeks, but also I don't know that our boss valued it as much as some people do. He had a producer/director down in Mexico to oversee things and he wanted us working on our scripts. I went down to Mexico to visit our set for a day and it was run and gun. There was no money to be had, it was more like an independent movie than a classic TV show."

Silber was aware that without proper communication between the Los Angeles and Mexico teams, the flow of ideas that could have led to a stronger production was also absent. "They built the town for us and that was wonderful. In my recollection it was two blocks and that was that. It meant a lot of creative thinking to try and make it interesting and I don't know we always succeeded as well as we wanted to."

While it proved to be less than satisfying behind the scenes, the actors weren't aware of the full extent of the issues as they filmed the series in Mexico.

"There was some miscommunication," admitted Lela Lee. "Probably because there was a relaying of information that took longer than if it were all done in the same place. But that's to be expected. There's always logistics behind the scenes that is stressed due to time, cost and creativity. I think the producers, writers and creators made a great first season."

"We were stuck in Rosarito Beach, which is not the nicest place in the world and we had each other and that was it," said Marcia Strassman. "Most of the crew were Mexican and we couldn't really talk to them, so we just hung together. We ate dinner together every night, we went out together every night and got drunk. They do make great margaritas there."

"You become a family when you're working with your cast and crew and you're close quarters so many hours a day," said Victor Browne of the experience. "It was a lot of fun and there's all sorts of toys and guns and 4x4 vehicles. I'm all about off-road vehicles so I was in hog heaven driving the tour jeep and Burt Gummer's vehicle. Everything about the series was just a lot of fun, it was an adventure, you got to play around, explore, and I can't really say anything negative about it."

One of the original *Tremors* cast who did notice a difference between the pace of the films and the series was Robert Jayne. "TV is very fast. I remember one of the episodes I did, getting to set and being told, 'Alright, let's walk the rehearsal!' and we'd just walk through it, we didn't even rehearse. The director said, 'Actually, let's film the rehearsal.' I'm like, 'Huh?' They filmed it and said, 'Okay that's good, let's get on!' Where's the creative integrity? It's hard to create high-quality content when you're in a hurry, the scripts are rushed and you're in another country. All your money's going towards monsters looking good and I don't even know if that was really working."

As on *Tremors 2, 3* and *4*, creature effects were a vital part of *Tremors: The Series*, though this time around CG played a greater part in the production. Los Angeles-based post-production house Encore Hollywood was selected to provide the small army of monsters seen in each episode. "We had Encore create ghost clouds of bacteria, ravenous hordes of mutant insects, hybrid killing machines with X-ray vision, and even a version of El Blanco, our hero Graboid, and all of them turned out great," explained executive producer David Israel to CGchannel.com's Chuck Boston in 2003. "We asked them to do a lot of work in too little time without the biggest budget in the world, and they always did a terrific job."[3]

For the series' initial six episodes, it was estimated that around 60% of the creatures were traditional puppets created by KNB EFX Group (*Scream* (1996), *Looney Tunes: Back in Action*, 2003), with the percentage swinging the other way for the remainder of the run. "We loaned KNB our Graboid moulds and that was the extent of our involvement," said original Graboid co-creator, Alec Gillis. "We're friends with the guys so we said, 'Here, we'll save everybody some headache and money and you can borrow these moulds to make worms.'

Receiving scripts at an early stage, Encore broke down the number of effects required and decided whether CG or puppets worked best for sequences. Animator Matt Von Brock explained to CGchannel.com how the effect of El Blanco moving underground was achieved. "We will generally start with an empty background plate where the camera may or may not be moving. We then replace a section of the shot with a CG furrow. In blending the two elements together, we often have to replicate elements in the background plate in CG. We also have a library of practical dust and particle elements that we can draw on to make it all look seamless."[4]

PREPARING FOR LAUNCH

Production on the 13-episode season finished in early 2003, with a March launch set by Sci-Fi. Steve Wilson and Nancy Roberts had left Brent Maddock to oversee the day-to-day production of the series while they focused on *Tremors 4*, but the trio was still determined to be involved with delivery of *Tremors: The Series* by contributing to the post-production process.

Those in charge at Sci-Fi and USA Cable Entertainment apparently had different ideas, with Wilson, Maddock and Roberts barred from the Los Angeles editing room in early 2003, with just months before the series was due to air. "There was turmoil, factions that didn't like Nancy, Brent and Steve and other factions that loved Nancy, Brent and Steve," said Tom Keniston of the behind the scenes situation. "We lost control of our own material, but we hung in there and fought to finish all 13 scripts," said Wilson.

Publicly it seemed Sci-Fi was behind their latest project, with network president, Bonnie Hammer, telling the *LA Times* in March 2003 that she believed *Tremors: The Series* would "beat the curse" of failed movie to TV transitions. "Oftentimes ... you buy the idea, you buy the franchise and then you bring in a whole new creative team and copy the tone or sensibility. We decided to see if the franchise could work as is. Where we expanded it is that the characters have a little bit more story." Showrunner David Israel explained to the paper that the series was effectively "*Jaws* meets *The X-Files* at the intersection of *Northern Exposure* and *Little Shop of Horrors*."[5]

A few months earlier the Sci-Fi marketing division, under the supervision of Hammer, had taken the decision to film original trailers on the Mexico set for broadcast ahead of the series premiere. "*Tremors* was a big priority for the network; it was an original series and a well-known and loved franchise," explained Al Burstein, a writer and producer at Sci-Fi who developed scripts for the trailers. "We shot two sets of promos plus still photography for the key art, the main advertising image that is used in the ads and billboards and PR, the photos released to magazines, newspapers and blogs for editorial use."

The first set of promos was shot on film and depicted Perfection's residents going about their daily routine. "We made a series of vignettes showing life in Perfection, including the proprietor of the store hanging up a shirt, Burt Gummer loading weapons into his bunker and a pair of tourists taking a picture," said Burstein. "The voiceover was folksy, kind of like those old Country Time lemonade commercials, and talked about life in Perfection."

A second series of promos was filmed on digital video using a handheld camera and showed Burt Gummer giving a survival lesson to a student. "I played the clueless student and we even had a girl dressed in a cheesy Graboid costume who would run up behind us," recalled Burstein, whose team created rough edits of their promotional films back in Los Angeles, though the reaction wasn't as positive as they'd hoped. "If I remember correctly, Bonnie Hammer didn't like the spots we shot so they were never 100% finished and never aired."

Rather than giving up on the idea of filming new material, Burstein and his team were next commissioned to shoot promotional spots featuring Burt Gummer talking to camera. By this time, Michael Gross had left the set of the series and was back in Los Angeles filming *Tremors 4*. "It was a simple shoot, basically Michael Gross just standing there addressing the camera, but we shot on film and used a crew so it had to cost a decent amount. I remember them giving us a tour of the western set, they were filming that day so it was pretty cool. We shot the promos down the hill and off to the side."

The 30-second spots began with captions that read "AN IMPORTANT MESSAGE FROM BURT GUMMER" and spoofed the hit US reality game show, *Survivor*, as Burt scoffed at "Average folks eager to hang off buildings and choke down huge helpings of earthworms", noting that in Perfection, "You don't eat the worm, the worm eats you."

Burstein also helped build buzz for the upcoming series by writing the copy for more promotional material that was placed around the US. "We commissioned a cover story in *Weekly World News*, a trashy tabloid with stories about alien invasions, with street teams giving out copies in New York; gave out Perfection

Smoothies at a smoothie shop; designed billboards, including a 3-D billboard in New York's Times Square; and ran print ads in magazines."

As the series edged closer to transmission, it became clear to the team at Stampede Entertainment that the turmoil in the editing room was going to have an impact on the series' running order. Production issues on the planned second episode, "Shriek and Destroy", led to Sci-Fi facing a dilemma. "The director had difficulty with the full size Shriekers, I don't think he was prepared for working with those kind of props when you've only got days to shoot things," said Wilson. "The episode was having problems and you have two choices; you fix the problems and move forward or you change the episode order. We were fixing the problems and the studio said they'd just show them out of order."

True to their word, March 28 2003 at 9pm saw Sci-Fi air both "Feeding Frenzy" (the original episode one) and "Ghost Dance" (the original episode six) back-to-back, followed a week later by what should have been episode seven, "Night of the Shriekers". "Shriek and Destroy" was shunted down the schedule and aired as the 12th episode. "We said [to Sci-Fi], 'The first three episodes are very carefully constructed to be shown in a certain order' and they said, 'We don't care'," recalled Wilson. "That's what we were up against."

Sci-Fi's confusing scheduling had repercussions for the programme's internal logic, resulting in the introduction of Cletus Poffenberger (Christopher Lloyd) being aired in episode eight rather than episode five, while his second episode aired as episode two rather than six. Despite the confusion, *Tremors* fans showed their appreciation for the series by making it Sci-Fi's highest rated show during its run. "I actually think the show did really well," mused Tom Keniston. "Originally it did OK in the ratings and then they showed it again in the summer and it did fantastic."

Following a two-month break in transmission between episodes six and seven, the series completed its run on 8 August 2003 with the delayed "Shriek and Destroy". Just two days later the Stampede Entertainment website broke the news they knew their fans didn't want to read:

> To our loyal *Tremors* Fans – GOOD NEWS/BAD NEWS. Well, fans, the numbers are in and *Tremors: The Series* didn't quite hit the demographics and market share Sci-Fi was looking for (it was SO close!). We're sorry to report that the rumors are true, the show will not be back for a second season. But the Good News is that *Tremors 4* will be coming soon. It's all new, all different, and Universal is extremely happy with it (as are we at Stampede, of course). They like it so much they moved its release to near Christmas, so you all know what's going to be in your stocking this year.

"You hold your breath at the end of the season and wait for word to come down and they told us we'd missed it by a tenth of a point," said Wilson. "It was really a shame we didn't get to do another season as I think it would have been a lot better, it would have been all about the fun of *Tremors* and less about the struggle of writers and directors trying to find out what *Tremors* was. We had a lot of plans of what we would do with the character of Rosalita. We'd have found out she wasn't related to Miguel; we had a whole long complicated thing about how she'd come to America and co-opted his little farm. It was a fun reveal."

Other ideas left unexplored due to the series' cancellation included the arrival of two new residents in the shape of Jodi's niece, Natalie, and Rosalita's brother, Roberto, while Burt would have started looking for romance online and found himself unexpectedly communicating with Nancy through an internet dating site. The writers would have explored Twitchell's personal life, with viewers discovering more about his family and what led to his posting in Perfection. "You always get mixed messages; I was told it would be coming back for a second season," admitted Christopher Silber. "At the end, some of us were shocked and disappointed that there wasn't one."

"There was a little bit of animosity that some of the upper level executives had not done their homework correctly," said Tom Keniston of the series' abrupt end. "I think people at the network were a little pissed because they realised that, had they been a little more organised about what they were doing, they could've had a bigger hit on their hands."

"I remember after we shot the final episode and it came out we had a big pilot party in Hollywood and it turned out to be a huge success," recalled Victor Browne, who was positive about the future of the show following its high ratings. "I think there was fighting between NBC Universal and the French company that bought it at the time; it wasn't down to the show or the ratings, it was all corporate stuff. It would have been nice to get a few years out of that one. I think it deserved it, that's for sure, and the producers deserved that. There was nothing else out there like it."

For actor Dean Norris, the cancellation was unfortunate at the time but it's likely his career would have gone in a very different direction had *Tremors: The Series* run for longer. "I had probably done seven or eight pilots, something like that ... and I had done one called *Tremors* and they cancelled it after a year, but they regretted it because the numbers on it were really good," said Norris. "What if that thing had gone? I'd be the guy from *Tremors*! And I never would have had *Breaking Bad*."[6]

LEAVING PERFECTION

To better understand the climate into which *Tremors: The Series* entered at Sci-Fi, it's worth pausing to look at some of the other programmes being aired by the network at the time. For many years the channel had been a depository for repeats of older series such as *Star Trek* (1966–69) and *The Twilight Zone* (1959–64), with ex-Sci-Fi staff member Al Burstein noting that until the late 1990s "their brand was kitschy and kind of cheesy."

Burstein joined Sci-Fi in 2000, coinciding with a rebrand for the network. "We did a whole new on-air look and they started making original series, including *First Wave, The Invisible Man* and *Farscape*. We got a lot of credibility and buzz in the industry for our rebrand. It elevated the channel from what it was and took us in a more mainstream direction." By the time of *Tremors: The Series*' debut in March 2003, things were already starting to change at Sci-Fi, with *First Wave* ending in 2001, *The Invisible Man* in 2002 and *Farscape*'s final episode airing just one week before the first episode of *Tremors* was broadcast.

Plans were also underway to shoot a four-hour mini-series based on a fondly remembered 1970s science-fiction series, *Battlestar Galactica*. Though the mini-series wasn't aired until December 2003, it was clear to those working at the channel that the words "kitschy" and "cheesy" weren't part of the new lexicon. "*Battlestar Galactica* was a definite turning point," said Burstein. "The show was really great and got a lot of mainstream buzz. Around that time we did another rebrand. A guy named Dave Howe came in and took over our department. They wanted to make the channel more human and warm; the previous rebrand was super cool but kind of techy."

Though ratings and demographics were a key factor in the decision not to renew *Tremors: The Series* for a second season, it's tempting to speculate that the imminent arrival of *Battlestar Galactica* and a new direction for Sci-Fi were also factors in the programme's demise. "I wonder if *Tremors* was thought of as 'old Sci-Fi Channel' because of the production values and monsters?" mused Al Burstein. "They were trying to go in a more human direction and away from monsters/creatures."

Whatever the reasons for the non-renewal of the series, the abruptness of the decision-making took everyone by surprise. It had been a difficult process for the writers to understand the opportunities and limitations offered to them by the series, and now it was at an end. "There were varying degrees of feeling among the writers, but I was super enthusiastic and I wanted it to keep going because you work so hard to get this kind of job," said Christopher Silber.

Universal Studios Home Entertainment's Louis Feola had been one of those responsible for manoeuvring the TV series into production, though he had no say over the finished product. "We had a different vision of the series, that it should have been Michael Gross and the worms [at its] core. The series got a little distracted by love relationships and other things typical of TV. I remember talking to Michael about moving to different locations and that would have been *Burt Gummer: Monster Hunter*, which is a pretty good idea."

Gross recalled that the relationship between Sci-Fi and the creators of the franchise was never an easy one. "While Steve, Brent and myself wanted more emphasis on character development along with the monsters, all the network ever seemed to want was a "Monster of the Week" series, which became uncomfortably formulaic to me. Though I was sorry to put Burt to rest after just 13 episodes, I did not miss the mismatch of ideas that characterised the relationship. This happens all the time in this business, and I'm still surprised how a network can hire a great creative team and tell them, 'We've hired you because of the wonderful things you've done – don't do them anymore!' It was very frustrating."

"I was frustrated by the TV series only from the point of view that the core group of Nancy, Brent and Steve were not allowed to be as hands on as they should have been," said Feola. "Putting my ego to one side, I did feel that my team were better equipped to oversee development because we understood *Tremors* and the brand, but that was secondary to the fact that the Stampede team should have been the primary team working on the series. It was one of those internal conversations you have at a studio and somebody makes a decision and that's what it is. You need to understand the worms and the Stampede guys get the worms."

For Brent Maddock, a symbolic gesture gave him closure on his time on the series. "As the executive producer they give you videos, I don't think it was DVDs, of each episode and the dailies. I remember coming home and throwing them all in the recycling bin. I have no record of that series, none of the episodes. It was important for me to throw all that away and move on. That's how hard it was to do that."

Another chapter in the *Tremors* saga had come to an end for the Stampede team and their collaborators. Their foray into television had left them emotionally bruised and wary of their original concept being taken in the wrong direction by executives with little understanding of the franchise. At the same time, their lack of experience with the rigours of running a weekly TV show led to fundamental problems with the series' basic premise that hampered its development almost from day one. "When that was over, and we were so relieved it was over, at that point I think we were ready to make a TV series," said Maddock. "We knew what mistakes we had made, things we had agreed to that we shouldn't have. The TV series was the low point, but it was incredibly educational."

Just as viewers were mourning the loss of further adventures in present-day Perfection, production was underway on *Tremors 4: The Legend Begins*, a film that would take them back to the earliest days of the town, when Burt Gummer was but a glint in the eye of his great-grandfather in the town of Rejection, Nevada.

CHAPTER NINE

TREMORS: THE SERIES – EPISODE GUIDE

Note: The following guide lists episodes in the order they were originally intended to be broadcast, though Sci-Fi's broadcast order has also been noted. Each episode is given a brief plot summary, minus spoilers, with commentary supplied by the relevant cast and crew.

REGULAR CAST

Michael Gross (Burt Gummer), Victor Browne (Tyler Reed), Gladise Jimenez (Rosalita Sanchez), Marcia Strassman (Nancy Sterngood), Lela Lee (Jodi Chang), Dean Norris (W.D. Twitchell)

EPISODE ONE
FEEDING FRENZY

Written by: S.S. Wilson, Brent Maddock & Nancy Roberts
Director: Bradford May

Original Air Date: 28 March 2003
Original Order: 1 Aired by Sci-Fi: 1

GUEST CAST

Robert Jayne (Melvin Plug), Branscombe Richmond (Harlowe Winnemucca), Zack Grakal (Hiker), William Cowart (Biker)

SYNOPSIS

Tyler Reed arrives in the small town of Perfection to take over Desert Jack's Graboid Adventure tour, only to find himself under attack from resident Graboid, El Blanco. Along with Burt Gummer, Tyler discovers that something or someone is antagonising El Blanco, while an old "friend" returns in the shape of Melvin Plug.

COMMENTARY

Opening to the strains of Stillwater's 1978 single "I Reserve the Right", the first four minutes of *Tremors: The Series* act as a concise introduction to life in Perfection Valley. New arrival Tyler Reed stops to take his photo beside a sign warning of "extreme wildlife danger", before a hiker is killed by El Blanco. There's a nod to the first movie when Tyler's Dodge Charger is pulled under the ground, in a similar manner to Dr. Jim Wallace's car in *Tremors*. Burt Gummer also makes his first appearance ahead of the title sequence, firing a concussion grenade near the Graboid rather than killing him due to the latter's government-protected status introduced in *Tremors 3: Back to Perfection*.

"I had a great time shooting the pilot," said Victor Browne. "It was around eight days per episode and 13 hour days; early mornings, late nights and lots of waiting. It was very physical but I loved every part of it. It was always exciting to get a new script every week to see what the next one was going to be like."

The episode updates viewers on events in Perfection, revealing that Burt was profiled on the US TV news magazine, *60 Minutes* ("Made me look like I was some kind of anti-social, paramilitary paranoid," growls Gummer to Tyler), before focusing on Melvin Plug's plans to redevelop Perfection as "Melville", with Chang's Discount Market at its centre. Jodi and Nancy reject his vision, with the former explaining that the town is becoming a viable tourist destination.

For Robert Jayne, returning for the TV series was a chance to catch-up with old friends behind the scenes while continuing the story of Melvin. "It was great to go down to Mexico and shoot the

TV show a little bit. I really enjoyed going down to Baja and spending some time there, seeing everybody again. I think it was hard to shoot a show in Mexico, let alone on a tight budget with monsters."

Unlike the *Tremors* films, which had no recognisable theme tune running through the franchise, the weekly series had its own supplied by Steve Dorff to accompany the short title sequence. As with many other elements on the show, the music led to problems between the creators and the network. "I went to the composer who did the music for *Tremors 2* [Jay Ferguson] and he wrote these sample themes for the series and I thought they were fantastic," said Steve Wilson. "I brought them in to the powers that be and they didn't like them. I couldn't believe what they came up with. All the music [Jay] used in his sample reel I used in *Tremors 4*."

References to the first three films continued in the script with Burt's mention of Graboids, Shriekers and Ass Blasters. Looking at the series' original running order it's clear the writers had planned to gradually ease viewers in with nods to the franchise's past. The appearance of a Graboid in "Feeding Frenzy", Shriekers in "Shriek and Destroy" (episode two) and Ass Blasters in "Blast from the Past" (episode three) suggests they were designed to reassure long-term fans that this was still their *Tremors*, while new viewers could quickly swot up on their *Tremors* history.

EPISODE TWO
SHRIEK AND DESTROY

Written by: S.S. Wilson & Brent Maddock
Director: Jack Sholder

Original Air Date: 8 August 2003
Original Order: 2 Aired by Sci-Fi: 13

GUEST CAST

Pat Skipper (Bill McClane), William O'Leary (George Meadows), Tom Hanson (Mayor Tom Dillon), Stephen Walters (Officer Jerry Rinks),

Alison MacInnis (Courtney), Jeff Kelly (Pick-up Driver), Clayton Blocker (Boyfriend), Toni Cafaro (Farmer's wife), Matthew Reidy (Rancher), Hosea Simmons (Watchman)

SYNOPSIS

Burt and Tyler are called upon by Twitchell to help rid the town of Juniper, Arizona of Shriekers, with the boys arriving during the annual Pioneer Days Festival.

COMMENTARY

The director chosen to helm "Shriek and Destroy" was Jack Sholder, veteran of genre films such as 1985's *A Nightmare on Elm Street 2: Freddy's Revenge* and 1999's *Wishmaster 2: Evil Never Dies*. "I believe my agent got me the job, I don't recall that I had much input; I met with Wilson and Maddock before I went down to Mexico and we had a friendly chat," said Sholder. "The big issue was doing the special effects sequences. They were complicated and there wasn't much time scheduled to shoot them, so there was extensive storyboarding and pre-planning."

Though most episodes of *Tremors: The Series* clocked in at around 43 minutes in length, "Shriek and Destroy" came in at just over 38 minutes, a result of the behind the scenes turmoil that typified the programme's production. Problems with the episode resulted in it being rescheduled during the original Sci-Fi run, from episode two to thirteen.

Steve Wilson addressed some of the behind the scenes issues that affected "Shriek and Destroy" on the Stampede Entertainment website: "The *Tremors* creators (Wilson, Maddock and Roberts) were barred from the editing rooms at the end of series production. Sci-Fi and USA for some reason thought "Shriek and Destroy" was a terrible episode and almost unusable. That's why they aired it last instead of second. We saw some later edited versions and sent in suggestions for changes, but these generally were not taken."

"There's always a lot of politics on these things," said Sholder, who was aware of issues back in Los Angeles. "I sort of got the feeling Sci-Fi wasn't listening a lot to Wilson and Maddock, which is too bad. I found there was a lot of pressure on me for reasons I didn't quite understand, but perhaps it was because I was perceived as their ally? You try to do your job well and escape in one piece."

Luckily, the cast enjoyed their time on the episode. "The county fair episode was a lot of fun – I had that vehicle sideways a couple of times," said Victor Browne who, more than a decade after it ended, is still happy to be associated with the series. "We were at a little street fair last year and I was walking with my son and at least two people recognised me from *Tremors*. My son had never really experienced that before and he was like, 'Dad, that's really cool.' I'd do it again in a heartbeat, to work with those guys and Michael Gross."

Despite network negativity, "Shriek and Destroy" is regularly named one of the series' best episodes by fans, with IMDb's rating system comfortably putting it as the top-rated episode.

EPISODE THREE
BLAST FROM THE PAST

Written by: Babs Greyhosky
Director: Michael Shapiro

Original Air Date: 11 April 2003
Original Order: 3 Aired by Sci-Fi: 4

GUEST CAST

Harrison Page (Mead), Stuart Fratkin (Rosser), David Doty (Mosely), Gary Weeks (Brock)

SYNOPSIS

Burt's first survival school class becomes embroiled in the return of an old foe to Perfection, Messerschmitt the Ass Blaster from *Tremors 3*. Despite Nancy's reservations, the residents attempt to catch and return Messerschmitt to its rightful owner.

COMMENTARY

Elements of "Blast from the Past" were borrowed from John Whelpley's *Tremors 3: Back to Perfection* script, as the Ass Blaster sold to Siegfried and Roy (renamed here as Sigmund and Ray due to rights issues) makes its way to town. Although Whelpley's script had helped shape the premise of the TV series, he had no involvement in the end product.

"I was not involved with the TV series because I was producing my own show, *Body & Soul*, in Saskatoon, Canada," said Whelpley. "However, when I got cancelled (the only show to be cancelled because a network went bankrupt), I was asked by Nancy, Steve and Brent to come in and meet with executive producer, David Israel, and pitch stories. I pitched five bloody great stories and couldn't get much more than a pulse from the man. Then he had me back because he was suddenly interested in one story but the series got cancelled."

The need to recast the role of Nancy Sterngood from Charlotte Stewart to Marcia Strassman had an effect on the character's appearance and demeanour. "I played it totally differently than Charlotte," said Strassman. "The way she was described was like this Earth Mother, very plain, and I said, 'I'm not going to do that, I'm wearing tight jeans and t-shirts and I'm going to look good or I'm not doing it.' It was 10 years ago so I was in my mid-fifties and I thought if I still look good at this age I'm not making myself look bad for a part, unless it's a big movie. You have to have a sense of yourself in this business or you're screwed."

"Blast from the Past" also featured one of the series' most infamous scenes, as Rosalita is forced to hide from an Ass Blaster in an outdoor vat of water. "The scene with me in the wet t-shirt, I remember that very clearly because it was cold," laughed Gladise Jimenez. "I kept telling everybody, 'You'd better make that water hot, I'm not getting in if it's cold.' [They kept saying] 'Oh no, no, it's gonna be warm.' So I went in there and checked and it was cold and I said, 'I am not going to do it.' When it was time to actually get in they made it hot, like a jacuzzi. But being outside for five minutes you're cold again because it was winter."

Rosalita's popularity with viewers is something Jimenez is well aware of thanks to personal experience. "I recently went out on a date with a producer and we were drinking wine, having our food and chit-chatting. He said, 'I didn't check out your resume or anything like that.' When people in the industry happen to date each other we don't want to talk about work, because then it gets confusing. Then we started talking about it and I mentioned *Tremors*. He looked at me and gasped before saying, 'Oh my god, I'm on a date with Rosalita!' He explained how he and his best friend have had this on-going thing where, when they see a girl that's attractive, they look at each other and they go, 'Nah, she's no Rosalita.' He grabbed his phone and called his friend to say, 'I am on a date with the actual Rosalita!' It was hilarious."

EPISODE FOUR
HIT AND RUN

Written by: Christopher Silber
Director: P.J. Pesce

Original Air Date: 25 April 2003
Original Order: 4 Aired by Sci-Fi: 6

GUEST CAST

Michael Rooker (Kinney), Nicholas Turturro (Frank), Troy Winbush (Max), Jason D. Smith (Large Tourist), Pamela Kay Davis (Reporter)

SYNOPSIS

El Blanco attracts the unwelcome attention of two Las Vegas mobsters who get more than they bargained for when the Graboid eats one of them, leaving his friend to try and retrieve an important object.

COMMENTARY

"Hit and Run" highlights some of the tonal differences between the films and TV series, with a higher gore factor evident in scenes such as one in which a spear pierces a character before he's eaten by El Blanco.

With numerous voices trying to be heard during production, including the network, director P.J. Pesce and screenwriter Christopher Silber, it's perhaps understandable that a consistent tone was difficult to achieve across the 13 episodes. "When we were starting out and pitching ideas, I had an idea for Spring Breakers coming to town and [showrunner] David Israel hated it," said Silber. "I was devastated because I'd worked hard on it and I think he said to try and come up with a mobster idea."

While driving home one evening, Silber had the idea of two men who had made a bet to see if they'd be afraid of the Graboid. "I was pleased that we'd come up with an idea that we all agreed would be fun, a way to bring in outsiders to mess with the worm and they get messed back at." The episode's premise came to Silber before production on the series began. "We had a bunch of weeks where nothing was happening where we could try to bank episodes, which rarely happens. So I probably had a couple of weeks on the first episode then did rewrites."

According to director P.J. Pesce (*From Dusk Till Dawn 3: The Hangman's Daughter*, 1999), who helmed four episodes of the series, the secret to balancing the mix of horror and humour was to play everything as real as possible. "That brought out the absurdity of living with a murderous monster in your neighbourhood."[1]

Though it had a short run, the *Tremors* brand name was strong enough to attract a strong roster of guest actors to the TV show's Mexico location, with the "Hit and Run" cast including both Nicholas Turturro (*NYPD Blue*, 1993–2005) and character actor Michael Rooker (*Guardians of the Galaxy*, 2014).

EPISODE FIVE

PROJECT 4-12

Written by: John Schulian
Director: Chuck Bowman

Original Air Date: 27 June 2003
Original Order: 5 Aired by Sci-Fi: 8

GUEST CAST

Christopher Lloyd (Dr. Cletus Poffenberger), J.D. Walsh (Larry Norvel), Branscombe Richmond (Harlowe Winnemucca), Lorin McCraley (Roadhog)

SYNOPSIS

Tyler and Larry recall their first encounter with Cletus Poffenberger, a scientist who has long observed goings-on in Perfection and who has a very unique best friend in the shape of the ferocious Project 4-12.

COMMENTARY

With a need to remain within the confines of Perfection Valley for as many episodes as possible to reduce production costs, the writers made the decision to introduce a small scientific community to the area along with the gene-altering compound, Mixmaster. John Schulian's "Project 4-12" was the episode chosen to reveal the existence of Mixmaster, with a very special guest star welcomed to the Mexico set in the shape of *One Flew Over the Cuckoo's Nest* (1975) and *Back to the Future* trilogy actor, Christopher Lloyd, as scientist Cletus Poffenberger.

Lloyd's casting was another example of the series' ability to attract respected actors based on the *Tremors* name. "Christopher's in his 70s and he roller skates up and down Venice Beach when he's not acting," said Steve Wilson. "That's what makes a difference between a horror film working or not working, your actors committing to the crazy idea."

"Christopher was so amazing," said Marcia Strassman, who shared a number of scenes with Lloyd. "He's a very quiet man and I think everybody was surprised by that. People were afraid to talk to him, so I walked on set and immediately went and sat down next to him and we became great pals. We'd go out to dinner together and people would say, 'What do you talk about?' and I said, 'What does anybody talk about at dinner?'"

Filming on the series often ran late into the night, with Lloyd required to shoot a four-page monologue towards the end of the day. "He ended up doing it at 2am and never missed a word, he just got better with every take," said Strassman. "The nights would be freezing, the days would be sweaty and he never complained about anything."

Victor Browne also found Lloyd's presence a boost to the series. "He was amazing, he had a lot of very scientific dialogue and you really had to listen to him to understand where he was coming from."

"Christopher was kind of a low-key guy and the only thing he wanted was to stay in the corner hotel room with an outdoor balcony on the first floor overlooking the ocean and the New York Times every day," noted Tom Keniston. "He was great to work with. Those people were troopers."

The creation of Project 4-12, a beast created thanks to Mixmaster, was detailed in an interview with CGchannel.com's Chuck Boston. The team at KNB EFX prepared a small-scale model, while Encore Hollywood created a 3D version of Cletus's pet using a software tool called Boujou2, which allowed animators to extract 3D camera tracking data from ordinary production footage.

"The creature is capable of running at great speeds and one of the biggest challenges for us was determining how such a creature would move," said Encore animator, Matt Von Brock. "We studied the motion of horses and dogs, but neither was appropriate to the characteristics of the creature's body. It is broad-chested but has narrow hindquarters. Ultimately, we developed a kind of hybrid motion in which it lopes along – in a very frightening manner."[2]

As a result of Cletus's second episode, "Ghost Dance", originally being shown by Sci-Fi before his first, a new introduction was hastily shot for "Project 4-12" to turn it into a flashback episode, with Tyler explaining to Larry how the scientist met the Perfectionites.

EPISODE SIX
GHOST DANCE

Written by: S.S. Wilson & Brent Maddock
Director: Whitney Ransick

Original Air Date: 28 March 2003
Original Order: 6 Aired by Sci-Fi: 2

GUEST CAST

Christopher Lloyd (Dr. Cletus Poffenberger), Branscombe Richmond (Harlowe Winnemucca), Michael Harney (Gene Fallon), Jamie McShane (Charlie Wilhelm), Gregg Collins (Lynch), Kevin Otto (John Draper), Randy Mulkey (Captain Drake)

SYNOPSIS

When three severely dehydrated bodies are discovered in an abandoned mine, the Perfectionites suspect paranormal activity has taken place, until the arrival of government agents sends Burt off on a different trail.

COMMENTARY

"All [the network] wanted was a different creature every episode," said Michael Gross of the numerous abominations that terrorised the townsfolk of Perfection on a weekly basis.

Perhaps inspired by the fact that a different mutation of the Graboid featured in the first three films, Sci-Fi's push for increasingly elaborate monsters had led to the invention of Mixmaster for

Tremors: The Series, a solution that helped the screenwriters but irritated the show's lead actor. "[The writers] were going crazy because [Sci-Fi wanted] endless mutations and a different kind of monster every week," continued Gross. "I said, 'There will be monsters, but it's not the whole story.' We wanted to get to know the people as well, to have fun with them in a world that happens to include monsters."

"Michael was right; television as he knows, because he was on a hit show for many years, is about character, that's what keeps it going, and we couldn't resolve those two things," said Brent Maddock. "We couldn't keep the channel happy and you can't go purely about the character because it becomes a melodrama in the desert – 'I'm in love with her, she's not in love with me, I don't like that guy, what's her problem' – and that's not *Tremors* either. The blend of those two was something we were never really able to find. It becomes *Dallas* with monsters, which is OK if you're doing a comedy, but not if you're trying to believe that these are real people."

The monster at the centre of "Ghost Dance" was one of the series' more interesting creations, a gaseous entity that sucked the moisture from its victims. "Due to time/budget limitations, we needed to come up with ideas which did not require the design, construction, and puppeteering of full-fledged monsters," said Steve Wilson of the creature. "We liked the idea of something that appears to be one thing (ghost) but actually has a scientific (or at least semi-scientific) explanation. Working backward from those end-points, we came up with the glowing cloud idea."

"Ghost Dance" proved to be memorable for Gladise Jimenez, who starts the episode on horseback. "My horse got spooked and he reared up, turned around and just took off. I remember looking back, as I'm hauling ass, and saw [stunt man] Lubomir Misak jump on his horse and come after me. He finally caught up to me, jumped from his horse to mine, grabbed hold of my horse, and I was like, 'My hero!' Nobody caught it on film, but that was pretty awesome, our hearts were racing so hard."

EPISODE SEVEN
NIGHT OF THE SHRIEKERS

Written by: John Schulian, Brent Maddock & S.S. Wilson
Director: P.J. Pesce

Original Air Date: 4 April 2003
Original Order: 7 Aired by Sci-Fi: 3

GUEST CAST

Melinda Clarke (Dr. Megan Flint), Matt Malloy (Dr. Harold Baines), Patrick St. Esprit (Karl Hartung), Tom McCafferty (Otto), Karen Gordon (Irma Gold)

SYNOPSIS

Shriekers arrive in Perfection Valley under the control of a government project to train them as search and rescue animals, to the consternation of Burt. When a lightning storm hits, it's up to Burt and the locals to save the day from escaped Shriekers.

COMMENTARY

A firm fan favourite, "Night of the Shriekers" opens with Burt Gummer putting his skills to good use as he tracks a Shrieker through the desert. The episode also reveals that another Graboid was discovered, this time in the Sahara, while there's a nice nod to *Jurassic Park* in the dialogue.

Though it wasn't designed to be the first Shrieker episode to make it on air, "Night of the Shriekers" did offer fans an early glimpse of the creatures. For the crew who had to transport the various monsters to the Mexican set, the experience was a memorable one.

"We had the Graboid, Ass Blaster and Shriekers and we brought them to the border, because we made them in the US and of course they had to go through customs," said production manager, Tom Keniston. "The customs people were like, 'What's a Graboid?'

When they saw it they knew exactly what it was and it took another two hours while every single one of them came out to get their pictures taken with it. They thought it was the greatest thing ever, it was like the Chupacabra [a mythical Mexican creature] come to life for them."

Another problem for Keniston was that the number of weapons that had to be brought to Perfection caused more delays with the border authorities. "Getting guns in Mexico is quite a task; it took us almost five months to get permission," said Keniston. "I think the US delay was even worse because they were very concerned about guns going into Mexico and them not controlling them. We had to go to courts in California and get permission from Washington D.C. In order to speed up the process we then got a gunsmith in Mexico City who was able to travel with these guns. That was an incredibly involved process for us."

With over a third of Mexico's population living below the international poverty line, it was impossible for the cast and crew not to be aware of the issue. "At first I was excited because it looks like paradise," said Lela Lee of her time in Rosarito. "It's the beach, the sand, the novelty of a new location. But about two weeks in you saw that the beach was littered and there's a lot of poverty. We stayed in the tourist section and our accommodation was near a really loud bar, earplugs did not help. The days were long and the nights were late [but] it was great fun working with everyone."

"We lived right on the cliffs and one of the biggest surf spots was right below me," said Victor Browne. "I'm always exploring; I get out to see what the people and land are about as I think it's important to understand other cultures. Mexico is third world; you had shacks at the side of the road as you're driving to work so it can be very sad, but at the same time you just have to conform to your environment."

Director P.J. Pesce found it difficult to cast extras in Rosarito Beach who looked like Caucasians and who could act. "In one episode, we were trying to cast a featured extra and didn't have the money to bring someone in from San Diego," explained Pesce. "The line producer brings me over to this trailer and there's this guy there, he's around 25-years-old and he looks positively demented ... he's looking at me as if I'm his ticket out of Rosarito and onto stardom." After a dismal initial line reading, Pesce offered some direction to the wannabe actor, encouraging him to add emotion to the line reading. "They start the scene again and the guy goes nuts ... he throws himself on the ground and screams and yells, completely insane ... we were truly terrified that he was going to hit the producer!" Needless to the say, the part went to somebody else.[3]

EPISODE EIGHT

A LITTLE PARANOIA AMONG FRIENDS

Written by: Babs Greyhosky
Director: Michael Grossman

Original Air Date: 20 June 2003
Original Order: 8 Aired by Sci-Fi: 7

GUEST CAST

Armin Shimerman (Cecil Carr), Joel McKinnon Miller (Red Landers), Audrey Wasilewski (Rosie Landers), Sal Lopez (Deputy Manny Garcia), James Whitson (Kevin), James Saba (Tucker)

SYNOPSIS

Burt and Tyler are encouraged by Twitchell to leave Perfection to tackle a potential Graboid problem in New Mexico, believed by the locals to be a case of alien abduction. The pair must pose as government agents to win the trust of the townsfolk, much to Burt's disgust.

COMMENTARY

Early attempts to ensure a consistent writing style for the series had resulted in problems for co-creators Steve Wilson and Brent

Maddock, their deft mix of humour and drama developed thanks to years of collaboration. "Babs Greyhosky wrote a couple of our best episodes and yet it was a really rough start," said Wilson. "We completely rewrote her first draft and it was a shocking experience for her because the humour was all wrong. Then she got it and wrote "A Little Paranoia Between Friends", one of my favourite episodes."

"A Little Paranoia ..." was one of the few times Burt and Tyler left Perfection, something the writers were keen to see happen more regularly but which production manager Tom Keniston had to curb. "[I had to say to the writers] 'I'm glad you're thinking that way, but I've got this much money and I can't do that.' You have to stay within the budget and I think we were producing the cheapest hour of television at the time. That's why we were in Mexico, we were able to make it for significantly less than everyone else."

"There was talk of taking it to different locations, but we were a little bit tied down," recalled Christopher Silber. "For it to be *Tremors* it needs to feel like *Tremors* and all the movies feel like *Tremors*, so I don't know how far afield you could have taken it without it feeling like something else."

For Victor Browne, acting alongside Michael Gross was a memorable experience. "Michael was unbelievably gracious, a great actor and he really helped me along with the comedy. I was sitting looking at a guy I'd idolised in *Family Ties*. Sometimes after we'd wrap at a weekend he and I would drive in my truck back to LA in the wee hours of the morning. That was the only hard part, those late night drives; the border crossings could be a nightmare."

The episode featured an entertaining performance from genre-favourite, *Star Trek: Deep Space Nine*'s (1993–99) Armin Shimerman as radio host, Cecil Carr.

EPISODE NINE

FLORA OR FAUNA

Written by: S.S. Wilson & Brent Maddock
Director: Chuck Bowman

Original Air Date: 18 April 2003
Original Order: 9 Aired by Sci-Fi: 5

GUEST CAST

Christopher Lloyd (Dr. Cletus Poffenberger),
J.D. Walsh (Larry Norvel), Sarah Rafferty (Dr. Casey Matthews),
Richard Biggs (Roger Garrett), Danny Hitt (Pete),
George Woods (Carl), Mario Soto (Robert)

SYNOPSIS

The Perfectionites discover that the Mixmaster compound has created a new animal/plant hybrid, at the same time as a team of government scientists reveal they're investigating goings-on in the area.

COMMENTARY

"Flora or Fauna" introduced the not-so-Top-Secret research team headed-up by Dr. Casey Matthews (Sarah Rafferty), whose party is depleted on arrival in Perfection Valley. The scientists' Mixmaster Research Lab consisted of a large dome built to house their equipment, a set that caused problems for the production team. "The dome was a great set," recalled Tom Keniston, "but the first few times we walked onto it, it was a huge sound issue; it created a mass of echoes, although we redid the floor with cork so it absorbed some of the sound."

The dome remained at the Mexican location after filming had finished, much to the delight of the locals. "We'd left the sets there [after the season ended], not knowing if we were coming back," continued Keniston. "A few months later I remember being told people were living there, it was a now a town. They just moved right in. I was like, 'Well they weren't really built for that', but people didn't care."

As important as it was for everything to look good while the cameras were rolling on set, ensuring things were fine during breaks was of equal importance. "We'd hired a local caterer to cater the food and at first it wasn't very good because they were trying to make American food for the US crew," said Tom Keniston. "After a while Michael Gross came up to me and said, 'Why don't we just have them make Mexican food, I'm fine with that and obviously they know how to do it.' From that point on I went to them and said, 'Just make Mexican food.'"

In Keniston's opinion, the studio executives "were afraid of Mexico, afraid of getting a disease. The problem with living and working in a foreign country, especially if you're the crew, is that you can't really live there for five or six months and not drink the water. You have to acclimate yourself. Most of the water is fine, especially because we're at hotels or condos and they're filtering all their water. There were a few that didn't drink the water and those are the people that ended up getting super sick, because they hadn't slowly acclimated themselves to the biology of what they were eating and drinking."

Tremors: The Series wasn't afraid to pay homage to other science fiction films and TV shows during its run. Along with Larry's *Battlestar Galactica* t-shirt (the 1970s version of the series revived by Sci-Fi in 2003), "Flora or Fauna" featured a reference to 1990s TV series *Babylon 5* in a scene that includes actor Richard Biggs, who starred as Dr. Stephen Franklin in the space opera. The episode also makes reference to Christopher Lloyd's role as Dr. Emmett Brown in the *Back to the Future* trilogy, with Larry asking Cletus if he ever did "experiments with time travel" in his lab.

EPISODE TEN

GRABOID RIGHTS

Written by: Christopher Silber
Director: P.J. Pesce

Original Air Date: 1 July 2003
Original Order: 10 Aired by Sci-Fi: 9

GUEST CAST

Sarah Rafferty (Dr. Casey Matthews), Tinsley Grimes (Mindy Sterngood), Jeffrey Johnson (Chad Ranston), Rebecca McFarland (Dr. Ellie Bergen), David J. Wright (Ray Maguire [Garcia in credits]), Trevor David (Protester), Heather Simpson (Kelly), J.D. Walsh (Larry Norvel [uncredited])

SYNOPSIS

Tyler's business plans are jeopardised when a group of activists descend on Perfection, determined to fight for the protection of El Blanco. The situation is complicated for Nancy when she realises her daughter, Mindy, is part of the organisation, and that things aren't quite what they seem when El Blanco gets sick.

COMMENTARY

"That was the interesting one because I wrote it over Thanksgiving, handed in the draft and that was when shit was going down with the replacement of vice presidents at Sci-Fi," said writer Christopher Silber of his script for "Graboid Rights". "There were new people coming in and my episode got caught up in that. I wrote it and it sat there and nothing really happened, suddenly I got notes on it from David [Israel] and I was writing it pretty much from page one over the Christmas break."

When production restarted after Christmas, the network read Silber's script just a few days before it was due to be shot. "They came back and had a ton of notes, so I had to sit down with Brent Maddock over the course of a weekend and completely rewrite it again from page one," said Silber. "It was the worst weekend in my writing life. I've had some bad ones but it was the only time I thought, 'I don't think I want to do this anymore.' I couldn't begin to tell you what changed, for my money it was my favourite episode and I think it came out the best. All I know for me is that the senior writers felt I'd been initiated as a proper TV writer after that experience."

The idea of El Blanco's health being at risk also cropped up in an unmade episode proposed by Michael Gross. "I wrote a treatment for a script where El Blanco somehow got sick and we realised that if we lost our monster we lost our tourism and the reason for the town's existence. Burt found himself in the ironic position of playing nurse to a dying monster, sitting at El Blanco's bedside singing bedtime stories to him. It was ridiculous. We were willing to go off in weird and, I thought, fascinating directions."

"Graboid Rights" saw the return of Mindy from *Tremors* and *Tremors 3: Back to Perfection*, with actress Tinsley Grimes replacing Ariana Richards, whose career had taken a different path. "I went to college and really focused on the finer arts, which I'd already been focusing on while growing up; it runs in my family all the way back to the Italian Renaissance," said Richards, who opened her own art establishment, Gallery Ariana, in 2001. "I just got swept up in it and the gallery started asking for my paintings right after I graduated from college. That's not to say that I don't think I'll say yes to an acting project again at some point, it could happen. I will always have acting in my blood, especially when it's a compelling role and story."

EPISODE ELEVEN
WATER HAZARD

Written by: Nancy Roberts
Director: Chuck Bowman

Original Air Date: 1 August 2003
Original Order: 11 Aired by Sci-Fi: 12

GUEST CAST

Robert Jayne (Melvin Plug), Sarah Rafferty (Dr. Casey Matthews), Richard Biggs (Roger Garrett), Jim Beaver (Sheriff Sam Boggs), Don Swayze (Orville James), Bart Johnson (Deputy Mack), Duane Daniels (Dwayne), Jared Aaker (Security Guard)

SYNOPSIS

When financial problems lead Rosalita to accept a job offer from Melvin in Bixby, the discovery of a headless corpse suggests another monster is on the loose, leading to Tyler investigating the fishy goings-on.

COMMENTARY

Although it took until 2003 for *Tremors: The Series* to arrive on Sci-Fi, some elements from Stampede Entertainment's 1995 pitch for a series featuring Val McKee and Earl Bassett survived the eight-year gap. As well as featuring an albino Graboid in the shape of El Blanco, another of the creatures mentioned in the original pitch document, a killer shrimp, resurfaced in Nancy Roberts' episode, "Water Hazard". "Brine shrimp were always sort of floating around as a subject because they can be brought back to life after a dormant stage — they became a natural idea for a series episode," said Roberts.

Though Burt Gummer is present in much of "Water Hazard", he does mysteriously disappear before the episode's climactic sequence, a result of Michael Gross leaving the series to shoot *Tremors 4*. Gross looks back on his departure with mixed emotions. "I was never bored because it was always challenging keeping up the pace and thinking of ways to make it our own. But it was ultimately not as satisfying as it could have been."

Burt's absence allowed more screen time for Dean Norris as Twitchell who, despite being in the opening credits, wasn't in every episode. "You had to be on your toes with Dean," noted Victor Browne. "He was spontaneous and a great actor, a lot of fun, always had great chocolate on him, I think he and his wife owned a chocolate factory. He was very creative and brought a lot of life to the character."

"Dean is insane," added Gladise Jimenez. "I would watch him come over from the distance and I would be laughing, he didn't have to say a word, he'd just give me a look and I'd crack up."

EPISODE TWELVE
THE SOUNDS OF SILENCE

Written by: Babs Greyhosky
Director: Michael Shapiro

Original Air Date: 18 July 2003
Original Order: 12 Aired by Sci-Fi: 10

GUEST CAST

Joan McMurtrey (Dr Donna Debevic), J.D. Walsh (Larry Norvel), Scott Benefiel (Bud), Darrin Long (Darryl)

SYNOPSIS

Swarms of flesh-eating insects attack Perfection while Burt is out of town, leaving Tyler to team up with Dr Donna Debevic as they try to eradicate the deadly menace.

COMMENTARY

Thanks to the need to remove Burt Gummer from episodes of the TV series due to filming on *Tremors 4: The Legend Begins*, the writers had to come up with explanations for his absence. In Babs Greyhosky's "The Sounds of Silence", animal communication expert, Dr Donna Debevic (Joan McMurtrey), is an obvious Burt clone.

"The guest cast all came from the United States, June Lowry Johnson did the casting for us, and we would bring them down to San Diego by train then pick them up," said Tom Keniston. "They always said, 'How come we're not getting a plane ticket?' They soon realised it was much faster, in a couple hours you're there; the train is actually beautiful from LA to San Diego. The problem is that Americans don't travel that well, especially Californians, they don't go to a lot of places. So when they did go to places they'd ask, 'Can't we use American dollars?' [We'd have to say], 'No, you're not in the United States.'"

While filming the series, Victor Browne's son was only two; 10 years on, and thanks to *Tremors* marathons on US TV, he's now able to appreciate his father's work as Tyler Reed. "In the last year and a half, my son and his buddies [have started] watching the TV series and I'm in the other room hearing them laughing," said Browne. "It gives me so much joy to sit and listen to them cracking up over this show, he gets a kick out of them. They're funny, Ass Blasters, Shriekers and all these things. It was a lot of fun."

EPISODE THIRTEEN

THE KEY

Written by: John Schulian, Christopher Silber & Brent Maddock
Director: P.J. Pesce

Original Air Date: 25 July 2003
Original Order: 13 Aired by Sci-Fi: 11

GUEST CAST

Vivica A. Fox (Delores), Nicholas Turturro (Frank),
J.D. Walsh (Larry Norvel), Richard Riehle (Helmut Krause),
David Grant Wright (Dr. Towne), Michael Albala (The Accountant)

SYNOPSIS

Las Vegas mobster, Frank, returns to Perfection to retrieve the key swallowed by El Blanco in "Hit and Run", with deadly results.

COMMENTARY

The idea to continue Frank's story from "Hit and Run" wasn't originally part of the season plan. "As we kept going through the season, my boss said we should bring this character back and it was John Schulian, Brent and I who wrote the last one," said writer, Christopher Silber.

Despite the stress of filming, there were moments to savour in the rural Mexican location. "We were in a valley and we had great things happen there, like wild horses running through the middle of the shot," said Tom Keniston. "We heard this rumbling, looked around and all of a sudden they were just running right down the road, 25 or 30 horses just galloping through as fast as they could go."

Shooting of "The Key" was particularly problematic for Keniston and his crew, with bad weather conditions causing delays. "I'd been on the set and had to go back to the office to do some work. It was wet and rainy and we were trying to rush it, we thought we'd go to the store to shoot some stuff. The second assistant director called and said, 'Tom, we have a problem, there's a mud slide and the hill's coming down.' The town was just a mudslide. We'd built the road through a stream, but it was a trickle at the time so we just packed a bunch of dirt into it. Unfortunately now the stream was a river and the crew was caught on the other side."

The next step was to find boats to safely bring the cast and crew back across the river. "We discovered that we could actually bring them across in passenger vans because the motors are so high on them; they could drive through it because the water wasn't that high," continued Keniston. "As we were doing it the water was coming in the doors and everyone's feet were getting wet. Vivica Fox was on set and she shouted, 'I'm drowning!' because it was so full of water. At the end of the day she laughed it off. The next day we had to basically go out and clean out all the mud. It was a difficult location, especially as the winter started coming, it's a little miserable to be out there."

"The conditions were quite brutal," agreed director P.J. Pesce. "If it wasn't pouring rain it was hot and dry."[4]

CHAPTER TEN

TREMORS 4: THE LEGEND BEGINS

By the summer of 2002, the *Tremors* franchise had become almost as unpredictable as a Graboid in heat. The original theatrical release had come about thanks to a concerted effort from the creators and those who believed in the project, while its two direct-to-home-video sequels and recently commissioned TV series had been something of a surprise to Steve Wilson, Brent Maddock and Nancy Roberts, approached each time by eager studio executives.

Following *Tremors 3: Back to Perfection*'s release in October 2001, it had taken some months for the team at Universal Studios Home Entertainment, under the supervision of Louis Feola and Patti Jackson, to collate the figures required to convince their superiors that there was interest in a third sequel. By the time they were ready to greenlight another film, production had begun on *Tremors: The Series*, meaning both the team at Stampede and lead actor, Michael Gross, were tied up indefinitely. "In my memory, we were already prepping *Tremors 4* when the series came about, which was a bit of a nuisance to me and people were unhappy," stated Patti Jackson.

"Universal had said that *Tremors 3: Back to Perfection* was absolutely the last one and they were closing the door on *Tremors*," said Steve Wilson. "We said we'd finish the life-cycle, explain the Ass Blasters lay an egg that becomes a Graboid and we're done. Lo-and-behold it's an even bigger success than they thought it would be and they come to us saying that they really need a *Tremors 4*. We said we thought that three was the last one and they said, 'We've got to have *Tremors 4*, we're going to do it anyway, whether you guys do it or not.'"

As with most Hollywood films, once a studio has purchased a script or concept, the rights of the original creator become the property of said studio. Steve Wilson and Brent Maddock may have created the world of Graboids, Perfection and Burt Gummer, but when they sold the screenplay to Universal Studios in 1989 they gave up ownership of the concept. "When you sell a screenplay your contract says you sell "all the rights in any form of distribution now in existence or herein after invented throughout the universe" and if I did something with *Tremors* on Mars, Universal could sue me," said Wilson. "They have total control of the property."

Thanks to the huge success of *Tremors 3*'s first screening on Sci-Fi, Universal Studios Home Entertainment made the decision to premiere *Tremors 4* on the channel before releasing it on DVD. "We were trying to deliver our films for $5m and under," said Louis Feola. "We never had issues with our producers; they understood our model and we worked very hard in pre-production. I looked at what we did not as made-for-home-video but we tried to coin the expression "made for home entertainment" because we didn't really care necessarily if it premiered on DVD, VHS or TV or Pay TV. *Darkman 3* premiered on HBO. We probably could have released the movies theatrically (every film was made on 35mm) but they were not made for that purpose."

The issue for Wilson and Brent Maddock was how to keep the franchise interesting and true to their original concept. Following a discussion with Patti Jackson, in which Wilson queried what was left to do that didn't break the rules and explain there was yet another iteration of the Graboid, he hit upon the idea of a prequel. "Patti said that she loved the idea of a western *Tremors* and so I went back to Brent and Nancy with the idea and Michael was all in favour of it as he got to do a new character, the complete opposite of Burt. The fans were not as pleased with that decision."

With production on the TV series underway in Los Angeles and Mexico, the decision was made to move Wilson and Nancy

Roberts over to the new film, leaving Maddock to oversee the show alongside David Israel. With their workload growing daily, Maddock and Wilson repeated the process from *Tremors 3* whereby they commissioned a *Tremors 4* script from a new writer who would work from their extensive outline. "I don't remember as clearly how we came to Scott Buck, known for his work on *Six Feet Under*, but he brought a real flair to fleshing out our story for *Tremors 4*, in particular doing some nice work with the young boy, Fu Yien, and Michael's character, Hiram," noted Wilson.

"We never cared who came up with what idea or whose name went first on the credits," said Maddock. "It was quite a departure and not a bad idea; it's not my favourite of the sequels but I think it was pretty good."

For the new film, now entitled *Tremors 4: The Legend Begins*, Wilson and Maddock played with the franchise's basic elements by setting the action a century before the events of 1990's *Tremors*. In 1889, Perfection Valley is known as Rejection Valley and its residents are dependent on a silver mine for their income. When 17 miners are killed by newly-hatched Graboids, the mine's owner, the prissy Hiram Gummer (Burt Gummer's great-grandfather), reluctantly travels to the town of Rejection to resolve the problem.

Along with a miner named Juan (a possible ancestor of *Tremors*' Miguel), hired gunfighter (and template for Burt Gummer) Black Hand Kelly, hotel owner Christine Lord, the Chang family (Walter and Jodi Chang's ancestors) and a native American called Tecopa, Hiram decides to tackle the Graboids (including new mini-Graboids dubbed Dirt Dragons) while his frosty demeanour softens during the adventure and Rejection finally becomes Perfection.

The new film saw the return of Steve Wilson to the director's chair, following his work on *Tremors 2: Aftershocks*. "I was aware of the incredible difficulty Steve had shooting the film," said Maddock. "A monkey could direct the sort of movies where people are walking and talking and getting into cars; the hard thing is when you have action and you're adding horses and firearms. But he pulled it off, so that was pretty great in my opinion."

As with the previous sequels, the budget for *Tremors 4* was tight, with production manager, Jon Kuyper, recalling "it definitely started with a four. I think that sometimes [the studio] inflate the budget just to say, 'We did it for this and sales are whatever.' It included everything, from music to effects to all of our shoot costs and post-production and everything to deliver the movie."

Kuyper was familiar with the budget range he had to work with and knew he was dealing with filmmakers who had high aspirations and a certain quality threshold in mind for the sequel. "I'm not saying that it was in any way snobbish, they just weren't willing to do it if they couldn't do it right. We had to be very clever about how we were going to tell a period western that was shooting in Greater Los Angeles and that took place somewhere in Nevada. And do it all for a number that started with a four."

Working with the Stampede Entertainment team also ensured Kuyper quickly became familiar with the *Tremors* style. "It sounds common sense, but I didn't really understand that the comedy in this movie is that everybody takes it seriously. Funny things happen, but they happen because it's not a joke. The way they were able to tell that story and follow those rules, it was a bit of an eye-opening experience for me because they knew that quirky personality of this franchise; they knew their audience and they meant to deliver."

Someone else who understood the need to produce a quality product on a tight budget was director of photography, Virgil Harper, who returned for the fourth time to the franchise. As someone who'd grown up on cattle ranches and enjoyed classic westerns, he was excited about the possibilities offered by the period setting. "I love John Ford films because of the way they could keep your interest with simple set-ups and the talent seemed to carry the movies. I'm not a big fan of films where they've got loads of CG because they don't represent stuff in reality, they go past what's physically possible that you couldn't do normally."

As with the previous films and TV series, finding a suitable piece of land on which to build Rejection was not an easy one. "Steve really wanted to go back out to Lone Pine, and we hunted for locations that were within the studio's zone," said Harper. "They didn't want to have to put crew and everybody up [in hotels] because it was a major cost factor, so we found this place out on this plateau."

"We couldn't be in a place that would show aircraft contrails or have any telephone lines, our restrictions were pretty tight," Kuyper said. "We ended up finding a place out near Acton, close to the LA County Line. It was definitely a long drive to work but the advantage was we were shooting for the most part in one location."

According to Virgil Harper, Steve Wilson's main concern was the close proximity of the mountains to the new town set; while the Perfection of the original *Tremors* was miles from any surrounding rocks, the lower budget sequels required fans to accept without question that this was the same location. "I tried to shoot as much as I could with wider lenses and pick angles that minimised the mountains to some extent," said Harper. "I told Steve, 'You know, they could have built this town here and then moved it to a different area.'"

The task of building Rejection from the ground up was left in the hands of Jon Kuyper, who brought a new member on board in the shape of production designer, Simon Dobbin. "He had done a western called *Posse* and had made all of these tents and structures," recalled Kuyper. "Because we couldn't afford a western town and it wasn't right aesthetically to go into one of those Disney Ranch, pre-built western towns, we started researching and found that in those days there were temporary mining towns that went up very quickly. Usually they were canvas walls with timber, and if the mine worked and it stayed for a while then they would start building much more permanently."

"That was the hardest place to build as it was really cramped and we were sandwiched in the valley," said Wilson. "I had two angles where I could see any distance and sky so I used those a lot. I kept putting the camera at the end of the street so I could see the blue sky that was vaguely reminiscent of the real town."

Just as it had been a problem on *Tremors* and *Tremors 3*, one of Virgil Harper's main concerns was ensuring the production's equipment could be concealed from the camera in an area that offered very little camouflage. "We were shooting in every direction and my base camp was behind the canvas hotel with the façade. I had them put weird pole walls to hide the trucks. That was part of the design we had to come up with prior to shooting."

CASTING

For the first time since assuming the role of Burt Gummer 13 years earlier, Michael Gross was joining the cast of a *Tremors* film as a new character, Hiram, and leaving Burt (and the TV series) behind. "It felt like going home," said the actor.

Gross understood the writers' take on Hiram and set about bringing his own sensibilities to the role. "Steve and Brent had a take on this character they wanted to see, this somewhat effete, stand-offish guy who doesn't want to have anything to do with firearms or the Old West and [by the end of the film] is enjoying that Gatling gun, cranking that thing saying, 'You know something? I think this is fun.' They even let me throw in some Shakespeare. We had lost one of our own and over the gravesite I wanted to have something from this man who was well bred, well-read and educated. Steve said, 'You know what, I'll buy this, a little eulogy.' So they were just wonderful about incorporating that."

"The thing about Steve and about Brent is that they have no ego as far as 'Don't change my words' or 'I wrote this script, this is the way it's got to be,'" said Virgil Harper. "Michael would get his script and come in the next morning saying, 'What if I do this and this and this, instead of this?' It's like you can see Steve's mind work, he'll listen and if he likes it he'll say, 'Yeah'. Most of the time Michael Gross is so in tune with what they want to do and the character that he takes it and enhances it."

Working with Gross again was a bonus for Harper, who knew how to get the best from the actor on a tight schedule. "I can go to him and say, 'Michael, I need a little something from you that helps me get into the shot.' When he's first sitting in the tent listening to the townspeople, they're leaning against the bar and he's sitting in a chair tapping his finger on the top of the cane, he came up with that and he really helps you out. He'll look at you and say, 'What do you need from me?' because he's got that experience of how to help the director of photography get in and out of shot and how to look and how to react. He's got great timing."

Gross may have been happy being back on the set of a *Tremors* film, but he wasn't always convinced he should be playing the part of Burt's great-grandfather. Told that he would be playing Burt's ancestor, coming from the east to the west, the actor suggested that the idea be taken one step further. "I said to Steve, 'What if Burt's ancestor is a female, not a male?'

"There's some milquetoast guy in this little town of Rejection who sends away for a bride from the east, and what he gets is this rip-snorting steam locomotive of a woman who happens to be 6'3" and played by me. I wanted to play Burt's great-grandmother and you could see that Burt's craziness came from the female side. It's the great, lost, *Tremors* film because I so wanted to do it. I didn't want to poke fun at it and go 'wink, wink, get it folks?' I wanted to play a full-on straight female role, as Dustin Hoffman did in *Tootsie*. That was a bit too much for Steve and Brent."

"He's got great range and I remember that proposal, but not if it was a joke," said Maddock. "Perhaps that could be the fifth movie, the transgender movie."

One of the new members of the *Tremors* family was actress Lydia Look, who had auditioned for the role of storeowner, Lu Wan Chang, Walter Chang's great-grandmother. Look attended an audition with Steve Wilson and Nancy Roberts alongside nine other potential actresses. "They kept us there for a while and paired us up with different people. Usually they'll give the supporting cast the three biggest scenes that they have and then they'll test you out to see if you can do them."

Also auditioning were two actors who became Look's screen husband and son, Ming Lo (Pyong Lien Chang) and Sam Ly (Fu Yien Chang). "Ming and I have worked together scores of times, we've played husband and wife in countless other things," continued Look. "Not many people know this about him but he loves classical theatre and he does a lot of Shakespeare and Chekov. I had heard of Sammy through another stunt brother of mine in the community, he's an amazing Wushu artist and we call him Little Jet Li. He was Jaden Smith's double in *After Earth* and he's sort of become my Godson. I see him all the time and we're still very much in contact."

Cast alongside Look were August Schellenberg as Tecopa, Billy Drago as Black Hand Kelly, Sara Botsford as Christine Lord and Brent Roam as Juan Pedilla, all of whom the actress recalls fondly. "I was thrilled to work with Auggie, who passed away recently; he was a terrific actor and I learned a lot working with him. I had a great time hanging out with him every day, listening to him tell me stories. I loved working with Billy Drago, one of the all-time great American character actors. He shows up and he's always great to work with, generous, loving and so creepy, but in a beautiful way."

Look also enjoyed her time on set with Michael Gross. "Michael was absolutely terrific to work with. It really helps when the "Number One", the leading person in your film, is a terrific person. Michael is an actor's actor. He shows up, loves to play with the rest of the actors, he gets what it's about."

PRE-PRODUCTION AND EFFECTS

Budgets had always been an issue on *Tremors* productions, with the central team of Brent Maddock, Steve Wilson and Nancy Roberts constantly fighting to ensure the quality of the finished films didn't suffer as a result. With their fourth film, an expensive period piece, Maddock was aware they were taking on an even greater challenge. "If you're doing a little $5m sequel and you've got 25 days to shoot it in, the last thing you do is to say, 'It's in the Old West, everyone's in costume, we've got to get an old town and horses and wranglers.' You're fucked!"

Careful planning had gone into bringing the ambitious script to screen, with each scene broken down and costed to ensure the budget wasn't exceeded. *Tremors 4*'s budget wasn't immune from cuts, something that became apparent when producer Nancy Roberts announced to a meeting of department heads during pre-production that savings of $40,000 had to be made. One of those present was director of photography, Virgil Harper, who recalled a scene in which young Fu Yien is inside Chang's Market when the telegraph goes off, causing the Graboid to enter and chase the boy around the interior. Harper knew that it would be a major set-up requiring many of the creature effects team.

"I suggested that we change it so the kid looks out the window, he's watching the people and they're concerned and you see the Graboid coming as the telegraph key goes off. You cut back to the kid, his eyes get really big, you cut back outside to people starting to panic because they see the Graboid coming under the ground, and then you cut to the kid and then you cut back and the store collapses. Then we can just cut to them all panicked and they go to the store and they find the kid in the rubble. Steve sat there and thought it all the way through and said, 'That's doable.' I think it saved him about $60,000."

Said Jon Kuyper, "Ultimately it comes down to 'time is money and money is time' – we were so compacted in our schedule that if we tripped up, even to the extent of a couple of hours, we were either looking at changing the way that we were going to shoot something to make it simpler or changing the script. There's what I call "The Golden Triangle". On the corners you have good, fast and cheap and you can pick two. So you get "good and fast" but it's going to be expensive, or you get "good and cheap" but it's going to take a long time, and so on. So you can kind of get two, and we're always playing that equation against how we're building a set and how we're going to achieve a practical effect."

In true *Tremors* tradition, the Stampede team was committed to using practical effects as much as possible to tell their story, though they weren't averse to utilising computer effects. *Tremors 3* had used the latest visual effects technology to provide Graboids, Ass Blasters and Shriekers, with mixed results. For *Tremors 4*, the decision was made to only use CG to blend full-scale and miniature creatures, often in the same scene, leaving it up to keen-eyed viewers to determine which was which.

Returning from *Tremors 3* to help manage visual effects were Linda Drake and Kevin Kutchaver, while the team responsible for practical effects on the original *Tremors*, 4-Ward Productions' Robert and Dennis Skotak, also made a comeback. KNB EFX, the company responsible for El Blanco and other creatures on *Tremors: The Series*, provided full-size Graboids.

"It was a lot of fun, but they had even less money than on the original," said Robert Skotak. "The first *Tremors* was pretty cheap, but this one was a third of the budget. We were asked to do *Tremors 2*, but we were in the middle of a bunch of projects. We were indoors shooting *Tremors 4* and outdoors shooting *X-Men 2* and I shuttled back-and-forth, running from one movie to the other. We'd shoot a take on *Tremors*, then I'd run outside and prep the other one."

"That was great because the Skotak brothers are just awesome," enthused Kutchaver. "I think like all of us they really enjoy doing what they do; *Tremors* plus the Skotak brothers, you can't beat it."

"They did all the tabletop miniatures, but the tabletop would probably be 20-feet by 10-feet with the green screen behind it," said Linda Drake. "There was a hole in the table and at that point we had quarter-scale miniatures of the Graboids and they would burst up from underground while shooting at high speed, so that the dirt and everything was flying."

"I'm glad they didn't go completely down the CG route; for this type of movie those creatures weren't necessary," said Skotak. "I'd used practical models in the past to give creatures a little extra flex or bend, something to make them convincing and more authentic. In a way it's more satisfying because it isn't a lot of interpolation done by digital programs. There's still a lot of satisfaction in that hands-on realm."

"That was something I really had to get indoctrinated into, it wasn't just what I would do on any movie, it was what I would do on a *Tremors* movie," noted Kuyper. "We had to be careful not to go overboard on visual effects and keep it real because the first movie was almost all practical effects, even though they had a lot more time and a lot more budget. When the Graboids exploded, we would relish those times because we got to throw all the goop on the actors. Again, that's something Stampede was very specific about, 'You've gotta give the *Tremors* fans that shot.' There is a loyalty to the fans. I don't want to be cheesy and say, 'They're giving back', but they feel like they owe the fans."

ON SET

Filming didn't get off to a smooth start for the cast and crew, as heavy rain swept into Los Angeles in February 2003 and made driving to set each day a major challenge. "Ming Lo flipped his car one day and he didn't show up for work," said Lydia Look. "We had to send a van down and we found him at the side of the road. It would be sunny while we did our work and at night it poured all the way till noon. It was like that for three weeks."

Steve Wilson discussed the issue on the *Tremors 4* DVD commentary, noting that during the store scene that takes place after the muling station attack "it was raining so hard that the actors couldn't hear each other half the time. I couldn't hear them at all standing where I was. We eventually had to replace all the dialogue in the scene, but in the wide shots you'll see the floor is soaking wet, water was pouring through the roof of the tent."[1]

As with most films, *Tremors 4* was not filmed in the order seen on screen, with the film's opening silver mine sequence actually shot towards the end of the shoot at the infamous Bronson Caves, directly under the Hollywood sign. Used in hundreds of productions, the exterior is perhaps best known as the Batcave in the 1960s *Batman* (1966–68) TV series, with the *Tremors* crew re-dressing it to resemble a working mine while adding fake walls to the interior.

Production manager Jon Kuyper always worked hard to ensure the vision of the film's creators ended up on screen, but compromises sometimes had to be made. "The Stampede guys are flexible, they understand limitations and they have a really loyal team around them. Their director of photography, production designer, or, in my case, the production manager, could advise them on different aspects and there were no ideas that Steve, Brent or Nancy wouldn't listen to. I'm not saying they would always agree with them, but they'd take the time to listen."

As the film's action moves to the newly-built town of Rejection, a steam train can be seen passing Chang's Market, something Kuyper tried to organise for the shoot. "I said, 'Steve, I'm going to do my best to get you a train, but I don't know how unless we're shooting in a train yard, and we're not.' You deal with the train authority if it's a live track, or if it's not a live track [you have to figure out] how to get a train on it. I did the best I could to deliver a train and at one point I said, 'Steve, I don't think I can get you a train.'"

Following a discussion between Kuyper and Wilson, the latter came up with the solution of hiring a steam tractor engine, the type found in many frontier towns. "It looks like a train and they would drive around to run the mill and other things," continued Kuyper. "We ended up finding one a long way from Los Angeles and there was this collector who came down with this engine, it was beautiful, and we parked him on our set for two or three weeks. His salary was not cheap, but it paled in comparison to our wood budget to keep that thing going."

To get the most from the investment, Wilson ensured the steam engine made cameo appearances in various scenes throughout the film, including the moment Hiram Gummer's stagecoach arrives to deposit him in front of the store.

"To me *Tremors 4* was the most complete," said Gross of the sequels. "We went back to our roots I think in the best possible way, in that there were women and children who were in jeopardy. As powerful a movie as *The Thing* is, a wonderful film both the original and the remake, it's a bunch of guys. Get a few women and children in there and you're really fighting for something. And people are very much on your side. I think that's what was so very powerful about the first film."

Shots of Hiram and Juan travelling to the silver mine saw production move to the former mining town of Calico, near Barstow in California, before more scenes filmed at Bronson Caves were slotted in. The film's first major action sequence takes place at night, when Hiram, Juan and the miners are attacked by the newly discovered Dirt Dragons beside the campfire. Though the creatures were originally due to be full-size models, the sequence eventually used a combination of miniatures and CG effects.

Miniature experts Robert and Dennis Skotak were also heavily involved in the later muling station sequence. The attack on Juan saw KNB utilise their full-size version of the Graboid, while Kevin Kutchaver digitally inserted miniature tentacles into the creature's mouth. "We wanted to build the whole set so it was raised up 12-feet, so that puppeteers could get underneath and have the Graboids come up and attack, but the budget wouldn't stretch to that," said Linda Drake. "So Steve and Brent re-wrote the script and instead of the Graboids coming underneath, they'd come through the sides with their tongues and start pulling the boards away. When Black Hand Kelly sees these things pulling the boards away, that's a miniature on set."

During the shoot, Robert Skotak was aware that the film's tight budget was always a consideration. "Originally we were going to do it for three takes and there were four boards, so 12 sheets of balsa wood. Steve Wilson said, 'How about if we just do three boards, so it's only nine pieces that I need?' In other words they were counting pieces of wood, knowing that would cost an additional $50. That's how tight it was budgeted and how well planned it was."

The small budget also affected the amount of footage that could be shot, with the prohibitive cost of a second unit meaning it was left to the main unit to capture everything on film, much to the frustration of the team. "We couldn't afford a second unit because it was a union film," said Linda Drake. "If you hire a second unit you have to have a second director of photography, a second camera assistant, a whole other unit that includes the camera assistant, a second assistant and a loader. You have to hire another four or five people."

"Unfortunately it can be very limiting, especially when you want to do something as simple as inserts for visual effects, things like Graboids popping out of the dirt," said Jon Kuyper. "Instead of doing it in the ground we would do it on a raised platform filled with dirt. We would have a controlled environment and we'd light it similarly to what we were doubling out in the field. We might shoot it at a different frame rate to give the illusion of it being larger. All you really need to do that is an operator and a camera assistant and maybe one or two guys on the lights. We've got those guys present on set, why can't we have them go 20-feet away and help out with this little unit?"

The lack of a second unit occasionally led to the crew taking the production's second camera, a back-up that could be used if one of the main cameras had a technical problem, to capture footage they'd otherwise miss. "Whenever there was something else to be shot, I would take the other camera with one of the camera assistants who was also a director of photography and we would run off and say, 'Let's get this stock shot here, these mountains look really good, I'm sure our editor can use it to cut in an establishing shot,'" said Drake. "We had shots where the Graboids are grabbing the old covered wagon, we did close-ups of the wheels being pulled, just wherever we could get second unit stuff."

The union may not have endorsed the practice, but it ensured important footage could be captured on film. "Virgil's background is documentary and he's a real can-do, practical guy," said Kuyper. "When he would say, 'Hey, we can go grab this sunset while these guys are lighting', why couldn't he take a camera and go do it? He got flack from his own union and I'd step in. We weren't trying to cheat anyone or get away with anything, it was just a more improvisational atmosphere, especially on these movies where there's a lot of material to get in a very short period of time. When you see the opportunity you just go for it."

With it being a western, horses played an important role in *Tremors 4*, requiring the presence of the American Humane Association on set to ensure their safety. "The horses were in a corral and Steve wanted them to run right in front of camera and away, but the horses saw the camera crew and ran in the opposite direction," said Drake. "The animal representative said, 'You're scaring the horses, they don't want to do this.' The trainer said, 'Well, I can stand over there and get them to go in the other direction' and I told Steve, 'That's fine, we'll just paint him out.' We had the animal trainer there calling the horses and we got the shot, we just painted him out digitally."

Bad weather continued to hamper the production, even when it moved away from the main town set. By the end of the shoot the team were filming at Vasquez Rocks in the high desert, an area that regularly suffered from flash floods, one of which separated the crew from civilisation. "One of our rental vehicles was washed away and we had to end up getting it later," said production manager, Jon Kuyper. "We were basically trapped there; luckily we had the caterer, so at least we had hot food. I seem to remember when the sun came up it had stopped raining and the water had receded enough to get out, so we were able to get out at the last minute, but it was a little hairy there for a while."

POST-PRODUCTION

"Post-production is almost always the last thing that anybody thinks about and the editor is almost always the last person hired," explained *Tremors 4*'s editor, Harry B. Miller. "It always tends to be a last minute decision. When they were interviewing me it was only a couple of weeks before they were going to start shooting, there was very little time for me to be involved. They sent me the shooting script and on my own I often try and look at previous work that the people have done, so I watched the first three *Tremors* films and thought the idea of moving back in time and doing a western was really great."

With filming taking place on location, Miller waited while on-set script supervisor, Jennifer Farmer, kept a note of each take, circling each one that Steve Wilson and Virgil Harper liked. "On occasion they give a note, 'preferred take' or 'this cuts to this', but usually I have to watch the dailies and make sense of what they shot and how I would put it together," noted Miller. "Once they finish shooting I usually have a week to put together my editor's cut, with a temporary soundtrack and sound effects with music."

Following the editor's cut, Miller sat with Wilson for the next 10 weeks preparing the director's cut, reviewing sequences and changing some performances. "Steve was a terrific collaborator. He had some specific ideas of ways he wanted certain things to work, and I had made decisions in my editing that he could look at and say 'Well, that works' or 'That doesn't work quite as well as I'd like, let's try this.' I think he really liked my first take on putting the movie together and then we worked very hard solving some of the problems we had with making it a more complete film."

Miller and Wilson ensured that time was taken to work on building up the film's characters, particularly the interaction between Hiram and his new neighbours. "We paid attention to Hiram's development and how he changes [through the] experience of meeting and working with these people; we were much more concerned about him having a coherent character arc," stated Miller. "You want visual effects to look good, but it's more about the characters."

One sequence that came together in post-production featured Hiram, Juan and Christine escaping the muling station by horse and cart while being chased by a Graboid. As they cross a small bridge, the Graboid can be seen underneath, "jumping" from one side to the other. "They shot the live action for that scene, building the space underneath in miniature before animating the

Graboid going across," said Miller. "They then composited that under the bridge to the live action production that we'd shot."

"We were very happy with that, the miniature worked out really well," said Robert Skotak. "We went there and took pictures of it and we had to invent a certain amount that's different than what is actually there, but it's pretty darn close. We made a different bridge structure to make it a little more interesting. Kevin Kutchaver did the composites of the film and did a great job. Most of the composites were nicely done."

One of the final pieces of the jigsaw was the score, which saw the return of composer Jay Ferguson to the *Tremors* franchise for the first time since *Tremors 2: Aftershocks*. "I was thrilled to be invited back for *Tremors 4*," Ferguson enthused. "The whole idea of the story going retrograde gave it a new musical twist. And again, more puppets! I remember Nancy and Steve coming to my studio for playbacks. My studio is set in an avocado grove in Santa Barbara, and Nancy especially loved avocados. I would play a few cues, look around and she would be somewhere in the trees grabbing fruit. On second thought, I think they may have hired me for the avocados."

Wilson and Miller were so impressed with Ferguson's score that they increased the length of some sequences to allow more of it to be used in the finished film. "It's rare that music influences the editing of a film, but I think I added enough in certain scenes that [they extended them], which is very flattering to a composer," admitted Ferguson. "I can't say enough about Steve, who was a music fan and gave great input. A lot of film people, being visually oriented, don't have a vocabulary for communicating musical ideas. Not the case here. He referenced everything from Morricone to Elmer Bernstein and was a big influence. Harry was also great to work with, giving the film a nice rhythm."

Though he rarely visited film sets, Miller made an exception for *Tremors 4*. "If I'm around while they're shooting it hurts my perception of the movie; if I know what a set really looks like it breaks the illusion of what it looks like on film. They were filming outside LA and I thought it would be fun to take my six-year-old son, Winn. I was scared I'd walk in front of the camera and screw up a take. The director shouted, 'Action!' and after a pause Michael Gross looked directly at me, put his finger up to his mouth and said, 'Shh!' I'm like, holy shit what have I done? It turned out that was the part of the scene and he was supposed to look right towards that camera. I said, 'OK Winn, let's go home'."

RECEPTION AND RELEASE

Premiering on Sci-Fi at 8pm on the evening of 2 January 2004, five months after the broadcast of the final episode of *Tremors: The Series* on the same network, and arriving on DVD soon after, *Tremors 4: The Legend Begins* has the dubious honour of being the least successful sequel in the franchise.

Thanks to a combination of changes in the DVD industry and a lack of promotion to retailers and consumers, what should have been a bold new direction for *Tremors* ended up stopping the franchise in its tracks. "*Tremors 4* didn't do quite as well as the others," admitted Steve Wilson. "Ironically, not because it was a western. Some fans were disappointed at not having Burt, while others love it and say it's their favourite."

The main issue for the film was that the previously buoyant DVD rental market had started to collapse in 2003, meaning Universal saw little point in advertising the film in stores. In addition, the Walmart chain of discount stores, responsible for 50% of all DVD sales in the USA, made the decision not to carry any titles that weren't preceded by a blockbuster hit or a major advertising campaign. Almost overnight, 50% of the potential market for *Tremors 4* disappeared, leaving many casual viewers unaware it existed.

The decision on how to market the film, from posters inside Blockbuster stores to magazine adverts, sat with Universal Studios Home Entertainment. "We were very involved in every aspect, not only in the development and delivery but also in marketing, distribution and sales," said Louis Feola. "You have to evaluate the best way to talk to your customers because you have various in-store materials you create, but not everything revolves around posters. It changes as you move along; obviously the Sci-Fi channel does a lot of 'tune in' promotion and that takes the place of some of the marketing. Also, Sci-Fi was commercially interrupted and a DVD is not."

"They always rent and they sell and in fact they still rent today," said Universal's Patti Jackson with reference to the *Tremors* back catalogue on DVD and Blu-ray. "With the advent of Netflix, they're still popular. Things changed in the video market and rentals changed to sell-through; that's when the prices went way down, you had to sell more to make a living. *Tremors 4* did not do as well and I think it was absolutely about the change in the marketplace."

"Sales typically tail off," added Feola. "It's the nature of things, sales angle down. I think you get a little bit of audience fatigue. You're trying to be inventive, you're trying to be creative, to engage the audience."

For Michael Gross, it was clear that the lack of promotion and support from Universal was the nail in the coffin for the *Tremors* franchise. "It was the tree falling in the forest and nobody was there to hear it. You do your best job but you didn't feel that somebody had your back to say, 'We're going to go to bat for you on this thing, we're going to make sure everybody knows.' There were people who did not know there was a *Tremors 4*. I would say, 'Have you seen the fourth one?' and they said, 'Is there one?' Perfect example. We cared, but not a lot of people were behind us. They wanted the die-hard *Tremors* fanatics and I felt as if we were the somewhat unappreciated bastard child of Universal."

Tremors 4 may not have been the success everyone hoped for, but the film remains an important one in the career of Jon Kuyper. "Shooting a period western with horses, steam tractor engines, period costume and building a town in the middle of Southern California; the thought of that for that price, even today, strikes me with fear. I used to teach a production class at

UCLA and I would go back to *Tremors 4* more often than any other movie to show what you can do if you really think about it and your filmmakers are your partners."

Though Universal Studios Home Entertainment's Louis Feola had commissioned a *Tremors 5* script from Steve Wilson and Brent Maddock in 2004, the franchise stalled that same year. "By then we'd finished the script for *Tremors 5* because Universal assumed this would go on forever," said Wilson. "They then pulled the plug and it never got made. It was a fun script: Burt goes to Australia."

CHAPTER ELEVEN
BEYOND PERFECTION

One intriguing aspect of the fictional *Tremors* universe has been the writers' decision to explore the effect that the existence of Graboids might have on the town of Perfection's economy.

Tremors 2: Aftershocks' return to Perfection Valley, specifically to Earl Bassett's trailer, proved the existence of a Graboid-themed arcade machine created in the aftermath of the events of the first film. A few years later in *Tremors 3: Back to Perfection* and *Tremors: The Series*, the sight of Chang's Market full to the brim with merchandise, including Graboid mugs and Graboiccino coffees, makes it clear that as scary as the creatures might be in the flesh, small plastic versions are a great addition to any mantelpiece.

In the real world, fans wanting to recreate scenes from their favourite *Tremors* movie with Burt Gummer figures, build their own town of Perfection from a model kit or buy their children a plush, stuffed, Graboid have been thwarted by Universal Studios, the owners of the brand copyright. "I still get emails asking where people can buy Graboid action figures," said Steve Wilson. "I feel there's some sort of cloud over Brent [Maddock] and me because there was supposed to be action figures for *Short Circuit*, but something went wrong. According to the studio, Number Five was the third best-known character for school kids behind Mickey Mouse and Bugs Bunny."

The release of *Tremors 4: The Legend Begins* in 2004 effectively marked the end of Universal Studios' attempts to exploit the *Tremors* brand. "The video division was making money hand over fist doing little advertising, and for *Tremors 3* and *4* they did no advertising whatsoever and still made a lot of money," continued Wilson. "They thought that was a good thing, so they didn't need to come up with a Graboid toy."

Universal's decision not to release official merchandise meant that fans were left with a choice of buying only VHS tapes, LaserDiscs, DVDs, or HD DVD with viewers of the latter enjoying different content depending on which part of the world they lived in. Alongside the first film, the North American/Region 1 DVD release contained a comprehensive Making Of documentary with footage from the Amalgamated Dynamics, Inc workshop and the Lone Pine location, the unused opening sequence featuring Old Fred and Edgar, cut scenes, actor profiles and more. Fans who bought the European/Region 2 DVD could watch the film and the Making Of documentary, but none of the extra or deleted footage.

For *Tremors 2* and *3*, the Region 1 and Region 2 releases had no extra features, though the Region 1 *Tremors 4* DVD benefited from a commentary by Steve Wilson alongside a short Making Of featurette. A *Tremors* Attack Pack collected all four DVDs into one set for both Region 1 and 2, with the same extras as the individual releases. The first film debuted on Blu-ray in 2010, with the sequels following in 2013. *Tremors: The Series* arrived on Region 1 DVD in 2010 as a three-disc set, with the episodes placed in their correct order rather than Sci-Fi's broadcast order. The films and series are also available to watch on streaming services such as Netflix and to download from iTunes, depending on which country viewers live in.

In 2000, record company Entrada released a promotional CD featuring nine tracks from Ernest Troost's *Tremors* score, though this is difficult to purchase outside occasional listings on eBay. Troost has also made a suite from his score available to stream from his website at ernesttroost.com.

In the years that have passed since the release of *Tremors 4*, Stampede Entertainment has been approached time and again by fans wanting to buy mementos of Perfection. "We've investigated options [for merchandise] but we don't have the rights," sighed Steve Wilson. "We're always asked why we don't do a comic book, but it's because we can't. Universal has actually said no to some of these ideas and they have no interest in getting involved in another business; unless it's an enormous franchise that will then turn around and pay them somehow, it's not worth their lawyers' time to even figure out the deal."

Comic books did make an appearance in Chang's Market in *Tremors 3: Back to Perfection*, as Burt Gummer studies a rack of titles including 'Graboids', 'Shreikers' [sic] and 'Graboids versus Shreikers' [sic] from US comic book company, Dark Horse Comics. In 2013, Dark Horse's Associate Editor, Jim Gibbons, explained on his blog that Universal commissioned the company to create three fake covers from artist Chris Quilliams. According to Dark Horse's Randy Stradley, following the release of the film, a number of comic shop owners contacted the company looking to buy stock of the *Tremors* comic book.[1]

In April 2002, it was announced that a *Tremors* computer game was in development for the PS2, Xbox and PC by Swedish developers, Rock Solid Productions. Gameplay elements were said to include "finding creative methods to avoid walking on the ground, hiding characters' body heat signatures and battling with ranged and melee weapons against various types of Graboids", while Shriekers were also said to be involved in the story. The project folded in 2003 with no explanation.[2]

Attendees to the 2006 San Diego Comic-Con were greeted with the announcement of *Tremors* figures from SOTA, a company known for producing toys based on horror and cult films. The planned Series 4 range would have included a miniature Burt Gummer aiming a rifle at a Graboid, and a prototype was displayed at the convention with a release date of Christmas 2006 and a price tag of $34.99. Sadly, the toy range folded before the figure made it into production.[3]

One of the most fascinating locations for fans on the internet has been Stampede Entertainment's own website, stampede-entertainent.com. Run primarily by Steve Wilson, the site includes a wealth of information spanning 25 years of filmmaking. An important stopping off point is The Ultimate *Tremors* FAQ, comprised of dozens of frequently asked questions relating to each of the films and the TV series. Here, fans have the opportunity to ask anything and everything *Tremors*-related, from the song playing while Val and Earl clean Melvin's septic tank (Fahrenheit's "You are the One") to the model type of Tyler's jeep (a 1960s Jeep Gladiator).

Nestled away in the Fan Extras section is a photo gallery that's an eye-opener for anyone keen to own a piece of *Tremors* memorabilia. The gallery proves the existence of items such as Perfection paperweights, Graboid oven mitts, a Burt Gummer ashtray, a Shrieker hat, a Graboid keychain, a Perfection license plate frame and a *Tremors 3* survival kit, most of which were created as props for the films or as promotional items sent to the press.

The site also reveals the existence of a short book, 'How To Survive Perfection', created by Sci-Fi and sent to members of the press to promote the launch of the *Tremors: The Series*. "When I got assigned to the TV project I came up with a bunch of ideas I thought would be cool for the show," said Al Burstein, formerly a member of staff at Sci-Fi who had written and produced promotional spots for the series. "One of them was a book that was a *Tremors*-centric spoof of those pocket survival guides. I thought about the show's location, the movies, the creatures and the different scenarios people might find themselves in around Perfection."

Illustrated by Brenda Brown, the 20-page dossier includes a map of Perfection alongside eight chapters including "How to Kick an AssBlaster's Ass" and "How to Make a Hand Grenade from Cactus, Rocks, and Common Bodily Fluids". "I looked at some of those survival guides that were popular at the time to see what kind of scenarios they talked about," continued Burstein. "Then I tried to think of *Tremors*-specific situations and clever, fun solutions; 'How to Survive Perfection' was the natural title."

Also tying into the short-lived TV series, Sci-Fi at one time dedicated a section of their official website to all things *Tremors*.

Fans could take a tour of Perfection with an animated map and meet the locals with handy biographies, while an online first-person shooter game called "Shriek and Destroy" allowed visitors to assume the role of Burt Gummer as Shriekers attacked the town.

A "Monster Guide" offered a brief overview of Graboids ("Graboids hatch from eggs which can lie dormant for as long as 300 years, and possibly even longer"), Shriekers ("Shriekers' prolific reproductive skills make them so dangerous that the US government has decreed they are not a protected species, and should be killed on sight"), and Ass Blasters ("If you are unable to mask your body heat from an AssBlaster [sic], attempt instead to sate its hunger with high-calorie foodstuffs until such time as it becomes dormant"), while a lengthy "Scientific Analysis of the Graboid Species a.k.a. The Graboid Guide" went into greater details about the background of the various creatures.

Some episodes were also given their own entries in "Burt's Journal", a diary supposedly written by Burt Gummer after each encounter. Though most entries were written from Burt's perspective, Tyler Reed took over for episodes in which the survivalist didn't appear, writing him a letter for the "Sounds of Silence" and offering an "Excerpt from the unpublished autobiography From NASCAR to Nowhere: The True Story of Tyler Reed" for the events of "The Key".

The *Tremors* section of the website is now long gone, but some elements can be retrieved with the use of the Wayback Machine at archive.org/web.

Despite the lack of new *Tremors* material for over a decade, online forums such as *Tremors* Underground (burtgummer.proboards.com) offer fans the opportunity to discuss various plot points from the films and TV series, share news, promote cinema screenings and TV reruns around the globe, profile actors and focus on the sort of minutiae that might otherwise be ignored.

The internet is also home to unofficial *Tremors* fan fiction that explores aspects of life in Perfection. *Tremors: The Series* inspired a new unofficial adventure for Burt, Tyler, Rosalita and the other townsfolk in TekeoMiona's "Daughter of Hokumunja", in which Twitchell sends Burt and Tyler to a remote island to kill a worm and help broker a peace deal, while other fan fiction is based around incidents from the films.[4]

LONE PINE FILM MUSEUM

Tremors fans wanting to search for some of the locations seen in the first film should make their way to the Lone Pine Film Museum, an establishment that celebrates over 100 years of filmmaking in the Eastern Sierra Nevada region.

As well as featuring memorabilia from the many westerns shot in the Alabama Hills, including the dentist's wagon and a signed script from Quentin Tarantino's *Django Unchained* (2012), *Tremors* fans can get up close and personal with a full-size Graboid head, a Shrieker from *Tremors 2*, a miniature of Chang's Market used in *Tremors 4*, an original script, one of Michael Gross' own Atlanta Hawks caps and numerous other mementos from the films. Staff are happy to point fans in the direction of local *Tremors* landmarks, just make sure you stay close to some rocks at all times.

The museum is also home to the annual Lone Pine Film Festival, which takes place each October on Columbus Day Weekend. The festival invites those involved in making films and TV series in Lone Pine to discuss their time in the area and to meet their fans. The festival celebrated its 25th anniversary in 2014 and played host to British filmmaker, John Jessup, who is making a documentary about the area's film connections due for release in 2015 entitled *A Show Down at Lone Pine*.

Full details about Lone Pine Film Museum, which is open year round, seven days a week, can be found at lonepinefilmhistorymuseum.org, while the Lone Pine Film Festival is online at lonepinefilmfestival.org. Follow the progress of *A Show Down at Lone Pine* at creativejohnny.co.uk.

TREMORS IN THE MEDIA

As befits a cult movie, *Tremors* has been referenced in various media over the years, from subtle nods to more overt mentions.

Described by Variety's Joe Leydon as "*Night of the Living Dead* meets *Tremors*", James Gunn's tongue-in-cheek 2006 horror comedy, *Slither*, features two obvious call-backs to the 1990 film.[5] Set in the small town of Wheelsy, Gunn's camera lingers for a moment on the Earl Bassett Community School, while two of the characters indulge in a game of rock-paper-scissors before making decisions.

Screenwriter Kevin Lehane, the scribe behind the 2012 sci-fi comedy *Grabbers*, which finds a small Irish community under attack from alien creatures, has admitted that *Tremors* "is the real spiritual godfather" to his film and that the script's first draft featured a scene from *Tremors* that the producers couldn't get clearance for. Lehane is adamant the Grabbers of the title weren't named after Graboids.[6]

In the decade since *Tremors 4: The Legend Begins* aired on Sci-Fi, the channel, now renamed SyFy, has continued to premiere original features that pit humans against monsters. Deciding to invest their small budgets in copious computer-generated effects, films such as 2010's *Mongolian Earth Worm* and 2013's *Sharknado* are the modern equivalent of the type of films *Tremors* gently spoofed, but with none of the same wit or style.

The creators of 2003's *What's New, Scooby-Doo?* episode, "The Fast and the Wormius", showed their affection for *Tremors* with the design of its giant worm, a creature that bears more than a passing resemblance to a Graboid.

Players of the massively multiplayer online role-playing game (MMORPG), *World of Warcraft*, encountered a *Tremors* reference in the 2007 expansion pack, *The Burning Crusade*. One of the game's many quests, A Job for an Intelligent Man, requires that the player kills sand worms, a reference to the scene in which Earl asks Val, "Is this a job for an intelligent man?" to which Val replies, "Well, show me one and I'll ask him."[7]

In the United States, Kevin Bacon was hired to promote Google TV via a short advert in which the actor took on the role of the world's biggest Kevin Bacon fan. As well as doing an impression of Val McKee's "This valley's just one long smörgåsbord!" and "They're under the ground!" lines from *Tremors*, the advert features the film's poster and a statue of a Graboid emerging from the front lawn.

Meanwhile, in the United Kingdom, 2013 saw mobile phone network EE launch a major advertising campaign led by Bacon, in which the actor again referenced his film roles. Seen on TV and in cinemas, one advert found Bacon playing heightened versions of characters from his films as they planned a night at the movies, only for "*Tremors* Bacon" to be left out because he's said to be "deep underground".

CHAPTER TWELVE
THE ROAD TO TREMORS 5

With a 14-year track record of successful video and DVD sales to the franchise's name, the immediate commissioning of a *Tremors 5* script in 2004 following the release of *Tremors 4* made good financial sense for Universal Studios Home Entertainment. With Michael Gross now free from his *Tremors: The Series* contract, the release of a new instalment every three or four years would have kept both the fans and the accountants happy.

"We did commission a *Tremors 5* because I always wanted to be ahead of the game and try to anticipate that it would be a success and developing a script is not a very great risk," said Universal Studios Home Entertainment's Patti Jackson.

The request for a new screenplay in 2004 forced Brent Maddock and Steve Wilson to consider ways to keep the franchise fresh while still giving fans something recognisably "*Tremors*". Their solution was to take Burt Gummer to a new continent. "[Universal] hired us to write the script and paid us," said co-writer, Maddock. "It would have been fun and fresh, the idea of going to Australia and working with the Aboriginal culture. We wouldn't even have had to go to Australia to shoot it, we could have gone up to the Mojave desert, hired three or four Aborigine actors and brought them to LA."

"Burt goes to Australia and he meets a young guy whom he moulds into a version of himself," added Wilson. "He's a little bit of a lone mercenary, the one guy you can call now and he's tired of being called. [Graboids] don't crop up very often; if they did people would deal with them. He goes there and all the incarnations appear to almost thwart Burt as he tries to be as prepared as he can be. The rest of it is rock-'em, sock-'em action all the way through. It had more, and bigger, guns. The ultimate challenge for Burt."

Unfortunately, an enemy far greater than any Precambrian life forms thwarted Maddock and Wilson's ambitions: economics. In order to make a fifth film a viable proposition for Universal, the budget would have to be lowered even further than its predecessors.

"The DVD rental market changed quite a bit after *Tremors 4*, getting narrower and narrower in terms of its profit margins," explained Jon Kuyper, who, as well as being the film's production manager, was later in charge of physical production for Warner Bros.' direct-to-DVD division. "There's an intrinsic cost to making a movie, a certain point at which you can't make one for less unless you're willing to give up certain elements, such as visual effects, practical effects, shooting days, locations or actors; there's a laundry list of things that you're just going to have to do without if you're going to go under a certain number."

In Kuyper's experience, there was effectively a line in the sand where it was impossible to take any more money out of a film's budget without the quality being sacrificed. "What comes next? The marketing, music and other ancillary budgets associated with the cost of a film. In order for the studio to make it work with their profit and loss statements, they needed to shrink the overall financial footprint of these movies in order to get them greenlit, and there was a point not too long afterwards where you couldn't afford to make a movie at that budget with the advertising, music and all these other things."

For Kuyper, the idea of further reducing the already tight budgets of the effects-heavy *Tremors* films would have resulted in the concept being compromised. "I think *Tremors* was definitely a movie that, if you took some of the more expensive elements out of it, the practical and visual effects, it wasn't *Tremors* anymore. They always had to 'one-up' the previous film and when it came to *Tremors 5* I would imagine that at a certain point they said, 'Can we take it to the next level?' With the shrinking budget it was probably deemed, 'No.'"

Unlike scripts for the first four films, which went through numerous drafts before shooting began, Wilson and Maddock only had a chance to complete one for *Tremors 5*, subtitled *Gummer Down Under*, before the project stalled.

Long-time Stampede collaborator, Virgil Harper, had an opportunity to read the script and felt he had seen many of the elements before. "When I read it I said, 'It's the same old, same old now', the same sort of set-ups just in a different country. I'd come right off *Tremors 4* and they'd all of a sudden planned *Tremors 5*. The originality had run out of it for me. We never really got a chance to talk it out because they killed the project before it ever got off the ground."

By the end of 2004, the possibility of a fifth *Tremors* film was looking extremely unlikely. While there had been some mentions of a new script in the limited publicity surrounding the release of *The Legend Begins*, *Tremors* fandom soon realised that nothing was on the horizon, a situation confirmed by Steve Wilson via multiple responses on the Stampede Entertainment website.

Things took an intriguing turn in 2008, when, according to a fan question on the website, there was talk of the *Gummer Down Under* script being resurrected. In October 2009, Wilson stated that there had been "some brief, guarded interest in *Tremors 5*. Hollywood politics being what they are, we must be secretive about the players ... *Tremors 5* may not be completely dead. But it's only un-dead, not alive. (And if it's 2019 as you read this, and there has still been no *Tremors 5*, this answer is then "Yes, but it died again.")."[1]

In 2011, Wilson had more to say on the subject. "I don't know how all the rumours came about, but I do know about this one. A producer came to us and said he could get the money, or some of the money, to make *Tremors 5*. He was a fan and saw the value of the franchise, so he contacted us and we contacted Universal." Although Wilson and Brent Maddock weren't part of the negotiations, the pair had been informed that no agreement could be reached between Universal and the anonymous producer. "He eventually decided it wasn't worth pursuing and Universal let it drop where they've always let it drop, which is: *Tremors 4* didn't perform quite to the number they expected, therefore *Tremors 5* will not be made. I've been online ever since telling fans that no, it's not happening."

"This guy was an independent producer who thought he could raise the money," said Maddock. "As writers we said, 'Yeah that makes sense.' A constant in our careers is us saying, 'That makes sense, why aren't they doing it?' Then you'd get this garbled response from the studios, if you got a response at all. Take any group of lawyers and they can come up with reasons why you shouldn't drink water or breathe the air. They'd say, 'We own the copyright, why would we give it to someone else?' and we'd say, 'You're not doing anything with it!'"

Said Universal Studios Home Entertainment's Patti Jackson, "There was a period of time where the budget was forced down so low that it made sense for an outside producer with funding take a look at it, but that didn't work out."

"It was baffling, I don't even go there because you just end up getting pissed off," mused Maddock. "Why is there no *Tremors 5*? I have no idea. Would it at least have made its money back and a little bit of a profit? Of course it would. I haven't read the script in years; I'm sure we could rewrite it now and do even better. The only explanation I got from the DVD people was, 'We're only making movies that are sequels to recent theatrical successes.' Although in the middle of all this they hired us to write an update of *Smokey and the Bandit*, it was contemporary but it was essentially the same story. They paid us to write the script and that didn't fit the rules. So I never got a clear answer."

Crowdfunding platform Kickstarter burst onto the scene in 2009, offering anyone with a creative project the opportunity of appealing directly to fans to help fund it. "Even before Kickstarter existed, fans were coming to us offering us money to make the movie," said Wilson. "Ron, Nancy and I had a discussion, but the difficulties with the script and of doing a Kickstarter project with a property that is owned by the studio caused us to decide not to pursue it. We would need a lot of money to make even a small *Tremors* movie."

"Today it's about box sets, selling stuff through Walmart and a cable run, because overseas DVD sales have just tanked," said Cristen Carr Strubbe, crew member on numerous *Tremors* productions. "I still get my *Tremors* residuals cheques every three months; I've worked on some really impressive movies and *Tremors* is the gift that keeps on giving. Clearly there's still an active rotation for it out there."

"It's great if people are hungry for the next one," continued Maddock. "I think that as creative guys, you're always looking for your voice. What is it you do that isn't copying someone else? It would be fun to do *Tremors 5* because it would be our voice, a combination of Steve and me and that would be satisfying. This new world of the internet is making movie companies feel sort of how record companies felt 10 years ago, it's kind of exciting and it could be really fun to find a way to do something."

"*Tremors 5* is still not likely," said Wilson in 2013. "As the script sits longer and longer, other issues develop. The script was built around Michael Gross and was designed as what we call a 'hand off' picture, meaning we would attempt to revitalise the franchise by the old guard handing off the action to newer, younger people. It was designed that way because Michael was the only one really coming back. It's been quite a few years now so the cold questions are ones such as 'Is Michael too old to be the lead?' What do we do about that?"

"I don't wait for the phone to ring," said Michael Gross in 2013 with regards to a potential fifth film. "I'm just happy with our quartet, I think it was a good place to end and so if it never happens again that's great. It was lightning in a bottle, we caught it, enjoyed it, it lit up the room for us for a long time and for a lot of fans, and for that I'm extremely grateful."

REMAKE, REBOOT OR SEQUEL?

Friday the 13th. The Texas Chain Saw Massacre. A Nightmare on Elm Street. Halloween. Carrie. The list of classic horror films remade decades later by studios desperate to cash-in on brand recognition is a trend that shows no sign of abating, with one rumour circulating online for years that *Tremors* is a likely candidate for the remake treatment.

For Jim Jacks, the one-time Universal executive who helped bring *Tremors* to the big screen in 1990, the idea of a remake didn't appeal. Speaking a few months before his death in January 2014, Jacks explained "it'd be hard to surpass the original, I kind of like it the way it is. It would probably have to have a slightly different take on it to make it even more of a horror movie. It just wouldn't be as much fun. If it was me running a studio, I'd say, 'Let's quit while we're ahead.' If they want to do a fifth direct-to-video movie that might be fun."

Gale Anne Hurd, another member of the team responsible for the first film's success, also made it clear that the possibility of a fourth sequel could be a good way to celebrate the anniversary. "Because it has such high and positive title recognition, it wouldn't surprise me at all; for a 25th anniversary that would be amazing."

There was a glimmer of hope for Wilson and Maddock's old *Tremors 5* script in December 2013, when Patti Jackson was interviewed for this book. "In the world of filmmaking, production budgets have gone down, and *Tremors* is not a particularly low-budget franchise to make," Jackson said. "I'm doing a new *Dragonheart* film for a little under $3m; the original was $80m and our dragon is so much superior. Because of new filmmaking techniques, incentives around the world and absolutely terrific CG, if I can get *Tremors* down to a reasonable budget I have a shot at getting a greenlight."

Jackson's attempts to revive the 10-year-old script seemed to be gaining momentum by 22 March 2014, when Michael Gross attended a screening of *Tremors* at American Cinematheque's

Aero Theater in Los Angeles. "There's a script out there that was written 10 years ago ... it needs work ... I don't know who's going to be involved, pray God somebody like Steve Wilson and Brent Maddock are," said Gross in response to an audience member's question about a fifth film. "I don't know that's going to be the case, there's been some bad blood here and there and I don't know what's going to happen. They seem to think if something like this happens, it will happen in September ... but the greenlight has not been given yet."[2]

Nothing more came of Gross' comments until Kevin Woods at Joblo.com wrote on 22 July 2014 that he had visited the website of *Lake Placid: The Final Chapter* (2012) director, Don Michael Paul, who had recently posted some news: "After I finish up *Company Of Heroes: The Fourth Reich* I will be headed to Johannesburg, South Africa to reboot the *Tremors* franchise for Universal. Big year ahead and I'm excited to keep it going with the support of all you genre movie lovers out there." Following the site's revelation, Paul's blog post was deleted with no more reference to his work on the franchise.[3]

Anyone searching the internet for news relating to *Tremors 5* in August/September 2014 was met with little information, though a tweet by South African actor, Brandon Auret (*District 9*, 2009), stated: "Had our first cast read through today for *Tremors 5*. Awesome cast and crew."[4]

In late-September 2014, Michael Gross posted photos to his Facebook page revealing he was travelling to South Africa for a new film project, with speculation mounting that the location could be standing in for Australia, as per the original *Tremors 5* script.[5] On 26 September, South African actor, Daniel Janks (*Generation Kill*, 2008), announced on Facebook: "So today started at 03:45 for a 04:15 pickup for my second call on *Tremors: Bloodline*. Spent the day caked in blood an [sic] goop running away from graboids and having a blast of a time."[6]

After posting a handful of teasing Facebook images, including footage of a 1969 Bell Helicopter flying across the South African terrain, Michael Gross revealed on 14 October that

Universal Studios would be releasing an official statement the following day that "promises to reveal why a gentleman actor from *Family Ties*, *Curb Your Enthusiasm* and *Suits* ends up in South Africa cavorting with warthogs and other exotic fauna."[7]

As promised, on 15 October, Universal Studios Home Entertainment issued a press release:

> The fifth heart-pounding installment in the action-packed sci-fi comedy-adventure franchise, *Tremors 5* began principal photography in South Africa on September 22, 2014. With even more deadly creatures on the loose, *Tremors 5* continues the films' hallmark combination of adrenaline-laced suspense, explosive action and tongue-in-cheek humor. Michael Gross returns for his fifth appearance in the *Tremors* films alongside new cast member, *Scream* film series star Jamie Kennedy in this original release from Universal 1440 Entertainment, a production entity of Universal Pictures Home Entertainment. *Tremors 5* will be released on Blu-Ray™ Hi-Def, DVD and Digital HD in 2016.

Revealing that *Scream* actor, Jamie Kennedy, would be taking on the role of Burt's new right-hand man, the tech-savvy-Travis, the statement went on to explain that the new film "travels halfway around the world to South Africa, [where] the Graboids and the Ass Blasters are not only bigger and badder but *Tremors 5* introduces an additional unexpected surprise that raises the stakes in the battle for survival."

Though cast and crew details were limited, the release did note that the script was by *Tremors 3*'s John Whelpley and confirmed Don Michael Paul as director, while Ogden Gavanski (*The Scorpion King 4: Quest for Fire*, 2015) was announced as producer.

As consumption of films and TV series increasingly moves towards streaming services such as Netflix, it's interesting to note one small piece of information revealed by Universal's *Tremors 5* press release, namely that the film will be available to own on "Digital HD". Just as Universal exploited VHS, DVD and TV for previous *Tremors* films, the fifth film will be available to purchase digitally before being streamed at 1080p high definition on TV, computers and tablet devices. As technology changes, so the *Tremors* films adapt.

Reaction to the news soon spread around the internet, with film websites positive about the return of Burt Gummer and the *Tremors* franchise. On his Facebook page, Michael Gross reacted to news that the film would be another direct-to-video release: "You would think, with all the enthusiasm for *Tremors* and the dime-a-dozen horror films that appear so often on the local multiplexes with no-name casts, that this latest sequel would have a chance at the big screen. At this time, however, it is only scheduled for DVD and Blu-Ray release."[8]

The absence of any mention of Stampede Entertainment from Universal's original statement was addressed on 16 October, when a press release was published on the former's website:[9]

> As we approach the 25th anniversary of *Tremors*, we have news about *Tremors 5*.
>
> Most fans are aware that Universal Studios has announced production of a new DVD sequel, being shot in South Africa. For all of us at Stampede, this is a bittersweet development in our long connection with the franchise, since we, the creators, are not involved.
>
> Stampede has always been interested in reassembling the original *Tremors* creative team to produce a fresh new theatrical sequel in the *Tremors* voice. We attempted rights negotiations with Universal for an independent theatrical film in 2012. However, the studio passed on the option, preferring to continue the franchise with DVDs at some future date.
>
> Early in 2014, Universal Home Video indicated that they were budgeting another sequel based on a 2004 script written by Brent Maddock and S.S. Wilson. While they pointed out that they had "no further contractual obligation" to Stampede, they did offer us Executive Producer positions. But

they also made it clear that in this new even-lower budget project, the Stampede partners' participation would be severely restricted, with little control over cast, director, special effects, locations, or indeed any aspect of production.

It was always only our full involvement as creators that gave us the means and incentive to reinvigorate and expand the *Tremors* universe with *Tremors 2, 3, 4* and the series – despite the significant increasing budget limitations. Without meaningful creative control allowing us to continue to guarantee the integrity of our *Tremors* vision, we sadly declined to be involved.

The entire Stampede Team extends a big THANK YOU to the loyal fans who have clamored for this movie for so long. For your viewing pleasure, we hope it's good!

The Stampede Partners:
S. S. Wilson, Brent Maddock, Nancy Roberts, Ron Underwood.

After 25 years, four films and a TV series, the creators of the *Tremors* franchise had finally succumbed to the falling budgets and changing priorities of Universal Home Entertainment. Ironically for a team that had fought so hard to gain creative control over their original *Tremors* script, the same deal that had led them to sign rights to the concept and characters over to Universal in 1989 now saw them walking away from a project they were still fighting for as recently as 2012. Their 10-year-old script was finally in production without them.

Michael Gross responded to Stampede's statement on Facebook: "I spoke with both the Stampede and NBC Universal producers. Both were committed to making the best possible sequel, but could not come to terms about the details. I was not privy to those details, only to what was told me by each side, so I felt a bit like the child caught between divorced parents. Like most children of divorce, nothing would make me happier than to see a reconciliation and a renewal of their vows."[10]

Following a Facebook announcement from Gross that Saturday 18 October was his final day of filming on the sequel, actor Daniel Janks posted more news on Facebook of his work: "Saturday night saw my last call on *Tremors: Bloodline*. What a jol! I had the best time being slimed, chased by monsters, flying helicopters and looking like a Cuban drug lord. Great to work with SA talent like Brandon Auret, Sello Sebotsane, Ian Roberts, Pearl Thusi, Rea Rangaka, as well as Michael Gross and Jamie Kennedy from the states. Don Michael Paul, you're a legend sir."[11]

Although making it clear he had signed a non-disclosure agreement with Universal, Gross offered some more nuggets on Facebook about the plot of *Tremors 5* that could be construed as spoilers:

- Filming lasted a total of 25 days, between Monday 22 September and Saturday 18 October 2014
- Fans are unlikely to see Perfection in the new film, but Michael Gross believes El Blanco is still alive
- Graboids and Ass Blasters will return but there will be no Shriekers. Due to the African location there are said to be fascinating and bizarre evolutionary "off-shoots" of the original creatures
- Burt once again wears an Atlanta Hawks cap, this time it's the Retro Slouch Adjustable edition
- One of Burt's latest weapons is the FN MAG, a machine gun that fires 750 to 1000 rounds per minute, and is perfect for Graboid hunting
- Burt loses some of his original weapons and resorts to "cobbling together what is at hand", including a single-action Colt sidearm which he derisively calls a "pop-gun"
- Practical effects will still be used for the creatures, but there will be more computer-generated imagery than previous films

Information continued to be drip-fed by the cast during 2015, with the title *Tremors 5: Bloodline* being adopted by the online journalism community without official confirmation from Universal. Jamie Kennedy explained to *Fangoria* in February that "it's been 15 years since the last worm, and it's a whole new world; the worms aren't just in Nevada anymore. The new one is set in South Africa; we shot down there, and it was awesome. From the little bit I saw, the CGI looks awesome."

When asked whether the Graboids would be CGI or "live-action", Kennedy responded "it's a mix. I don't know what I'm allowed to say about that [laughs], but I have to tell you, I'm really excited about the movie. It felt big, and there was a lot of action while we were filming it. It was a very intense shoot, so I think it could be really cool, and the *Tremors* fan base will like it a lot. It could be a real reinvigoration of the franchise."[12]

By March, the title was now being referred to as *Tremors 5: Bloodlines*, Universal Home Entertainment utilising the official *Tremors* Facebook page to offer fans an opportunity to vote for their choice of artwork for the DVD and Blu-ray cover. Version one depicted Travis and Burt Gummer standing on African terrain and almost being consumed by the gaping mouth of a toothy "Graboid" (similar to the creature seen on previous *Tremors* DVD covers), while the second showed a variation but now rotated at an odd angle, with the creature now back under the ground and Travis and Burt surrounded by elephants, a truck and a helicopter.

Also in March, Michael Gross was interviewed by *Famous Monsters of Filmland* magazine about his return as Burt Gummer. Gross elaborated on the situation between Universal and Stampede Entertainment, admitting that the prospect of making *Bloodlines* without the original creators was "frightening" and that the shoot was a "bittersweet" one for the 67-year-old actor. "It's really cutting the cord. And that was not easy, because I felt there had been a divorce in the family and I was the child in the middle. Long story short, Stampede had the will and the passion, but they did not own the property. So it was either sit out this dance and they'll reinvent the franchise without Burt, or here's a chance to do Burt again."[13]

The feature also quoted original *Tremors* director, Ron Underwood, who revealed that he had been approached to direct the latest sequel. "I would have done it if Brent [Maddock] and Steve [Wilson] were involved with it on a day-to-day basis," admitted Underwood. "It was being done on a smaller budget; it felt like it was difficult to maintain what we felt was important."[14]

Without the Stampede team guiding the production, Gross admitted that off-screen interactions could be "a little uncomfortable" as the actor, the sole returning member from the previous instalments, attempted to "protect the franchise" from a new production team. "Because we had a different director who hadn't done this before, there were certain things we would disagree with, and I'd say, 'Burt can't say that, because it's not factually true.' So there's a real balancing act without somebody like [the original writers] Steve or Brent there to ultimately say, 'No, that can't be done.'"[15]

Interviewed a few months before *Tremors 5: Bloodlines* was revealed to be in production, *Tremors 4*'s production manager, Jon Kuyper, advised caution for any new production team hired to oversee the development of a new film in the franchise. "I was very dubious going to watch *Star Trek* when J.J. Abrams had taken it over and I walked out of the theatre going, 'OK, he proved me wrong', but I think [*Tremors* is] unique. It wasn't just how well [Stampede] knew the franchise and the tone of these movies, it's how they always thought about their audience. I think it would be very, very difficult to make a movie in the true *Tremors* way without the Stampede people. I sure wouldn't try and do it."

According to Michael Gross, fans can be confident the *Tremors 5* production team did "the best job we could with what we had," and that the film is "still *Tremors*, but it's different," while leaving the door open for a future sequel.[16]

Viewers will discover just how different the latest iteration of the *Tremors* franchise is when it receives its DVD premiere in October 2015.

EPILOGUE
TREMORS AT 25

Looking back on their *Tremors* legacy, both Steve Wilson and Brent Maddock have positive, if mixed, feelings.

"The high point was certainly getting to make *Tremors*, being out in Lone Pine with all of those people making a movie," said Maddock. "They were all fun to do, even the sequels which were intense pressure. One of the running jokes was we'd have a discussion for three or four minutes about something and say, 'Whose money did we just spend having this talk?' Somebody figured it out per minute, that just cost $900, because the clock is ticking the whole time."

"We can't complain because on *Tremors* one to four we had all the control a filmmaker could hope for," Wilson added. "The video division at Universal, Patti Jackson in particular, were just wonderful to work with and we made the movies we wanted to make, within the budget constraints."

With their dream of having creative control over the films fulfilled, it was *Tremors: The Series* that led the pair to question the way the franchise was being developed. Losing control of the series was frustrating, particularly as they were only beginning to get to grips with the format when the axe fell. "The TV show was the toughest thing to get through emotionally," admitted Maddock. "That's when you wanted to change your name or move to Minnesota."

"That part of the giant odyssey was a bit of a disappointment, but overall it's been great fun," added Wilson, speaking before the news of *Tremors 5* broke. "Who knew back in 1990 that we'd be doing something for 15 more years? Nobody in Hollywood controls their characters, except an extremely rare person like George Lucas."

Away from *Tremors*, Wilson and Maddock continued to write together, collaborating on a script for a third *Short Circuit* film in 2008. "We developed a sequel idea with David Foster and pitched it around town, but we couldn't sell it," said Wilson. "Dimension Films said they wanted to do a reboot, but that it had to have a kid in it. Here we were back at square one after 30 years. We thought that if we could come up with a more adult version, playing the scientist and security guys straight, it would be more effective and scarier. So, for free, we went off and wrote them a script of what we thought it should be. They said we were 'too close to our own material' and that it 'really needs to be re-imagined'. We thought we'd reimagined it pretty well: it had cell phones and everything!"

Brent Maddock took a sabbatical from screenwriting after the disappointment with the aborted *Short Circuit* remake, tired of spending so much time on projects that never made it to the screen. "I haven't done anything for a few years, partly because I felt burned out; I said to Steve, 'I'm fried'. For all those movies, whether it's *Tremors* or *Heart and Souls* or whatever, there are three or four other screenplays you've written, all of which you've worked on just as hard, that don't get made. Some of them are quite good, and it's heartbreaking when they don't get made. Some of them deserve not to be made, even though you worked hard but you never quite cracked it. I got to a point where I needed a break and that I couldn't think about screenplays anymore."

For his part, Steve Wilson turned to novel writing, publishing his first book, the award-winning *Tucker's Monster*, in 2010 before following it up in 2013 with *Fraidy Cats*. In 2014, Wilson and Maddock joined forces once again with Nancy Roberts to develop new projects for the screen, some of which may bear fruit in 2016 and beyond.

As a result of creating the soon-to-be-five films and a TV series, those involved have also spawned an ever-growing fan base.

"People, even little kids, love it; I'm certainly proud to have been a part of it," said Kevin Bacon of his association with *Tremors*. "In America it's a film that's really loved in the heartland, the centre of the country, and when I go there and I'm walking through an airport it's a movie a lot people come and talk to me about."

"It's wonderful to see their enthusiasm," said Michael Gross of those who approach him to discuss Burt Gummer. "Kids look at me now with the grey hair and no moustache and they go, 'That can't be Burt', but I've got the photos to prove it. I talk about the fact that Burt never shoots another human being and that [the monsters are his enemy], the people are all on the same side. Then there are the otherwise normal human beings who say they've watched *Tremors* 50 times. There are some rabid people out there and it's great to be a part of their history and to bring them so much enjoyment."

"I get letters and video covers from people who are autograph hunters," said Maddock. "Signing autographs is a strange thing. It's very touching and encouraging to know people really like what you've done, or some of it. You forget about it because you're not waking up every morning thinking about *Tremors*, you're trying to think about the next thing."

TREMORS 25TH ANNIVERSARY CAST AND CREW REUNION

On 26 March 2015, Hollywood welcomed *Tremors* back to the silver screen for one night only to celebrate a quarter of a century of giant underground worms. Jointly organised by Taylor White of LA's Creature Features store and the team behind *Famous Monsters of Filmland* magazine, the Hollywood ArcLight cinema on Sunset Boulevard was the destination for fans of the 1990 film, who gathered to watch a big screen presentation of *Tremors* in the company of more than a dozen cast and crew.

Following pre-screening drinks for VIP ticket holders, panel host David Weiner likened the event to a "high school reunion" and explained that the number of cast and crew who had responded to the invitation far exceeded any previous event, leading to there being a panel both before and after the film.

For the first panel, director Ron Underwood joined writers Steve Wilson and Brent Maddock, producer Nancy Roberts, and actors Finn Carter, Michael Gross, Conrad Bachmann, Robert Jayne, Richard Marcus and Charlotte Stewart to explain the genesis of the film. It was Bachmann who summed up the feelings of many of those on the panel when he explained how thankful he was to be there 25 years after filming had ceased: "This is the one film that nails me wherever I go. Usually [people will say], 'You look familiar, I know we've met before' then all of a sudden, 'Are you Dr. Jim from *Tremors*?' Because it runs [on TV] every other minute."

Cast and crew gather for the 25th anniversary screening
© Jonathan Melville

The second panel featured Ron Underwood, Steve Wilson, Michael Gross, Finn Carter, cinematographer Alexander Gruszynski, production designer Ivo Cristante, creature designers Tom Woodruff, Jr. and Alec Gillis, actor John Goodwin and visual effects supervisor

Robert Skotak. The panel discussed subjects ranging from the building of Perfection to Finn Carter's lack of expertise as a pole vaulter. Ron Underwood revealed that originally the water tower was going to collapse with Rhonda atop it, while Miguel was to have died when the Caterpiller fell into the Graboid trap as the residents left Perfection. Steve Wilson also explained that budgetary cuts decided upon before the shoot began meant the character of Mindy was almost removed from the script, before being reinstated at the last minute.

Finn Carter closed the event with an emotional speech, noting that the film came about thanks to the cast and crew pulling together in Lone Pine on "an ego-less, collaborative set, where we all worked together in a remarkable way" that resulted in an end product she couldn't have predicted based on her first reading of the script.

THE LEGEND BEGINS AGAIN?

From their 2015 vantage point, Brent Maddock and Steve Wilson's view of the modern film industry is not altogether positive. "Hollywood has become more a business of spectacle, it's astonishing to me to see the number of gigantically expensive, overblown movies coming out one after the other," said Maddock. "I recently had the experience of going to the movies, watching three or four trailers in a row and thinking, 'It's all the same movie!' The lighting is the same, the tone is the same, the music is the same, the elements and tropes are the same. There's nothing wrong with big movies, it's just I relate more to independent low-budget films."

According to Maddock, Hollywood's current "state of semi-chaos" has some potential opportunities for today's filmmakers, and the *Tremors* franchise. "Periodically you need a crisis because we're going to go in a new direction. You can make a movie with your friends on a digital camera and put it online and charge people five bucks to watch it. If we owned *Tremors* we could do that ourselves. We'd have to do a super low-budget version, even lower than the movies."

Though absent from the Los Angeles anniversary screening due to filming commitments on his New York-set TV series, *The Following* (2013–15), Kevin Bacon's allegiance to *Tremors* is stronger than ever thanks to a recent re-watch of the 1990 film. "I don't look at my movies after I've seen them, maybe once with an audience and once by myself, but I went back to look at *Tremors* for a specific reason and it really holds up, I was really surprised with it," said the actor. "It's a beautiful looking movie and I think it's got the right tone and set pieces. I was really happy with it."

When pushed on whether he'd be interested in a return to the franchise, Bacon was unequivocal in his response: "I would love to, but not as a *Tremors* 6, 7 or 8. My feeling would be to revisit it as a new movie, it wouldn't be a remake of the old one, but it would be a reboot. This guy is one of the few characters I've played that I'd be interested in seeing where he is 25 years later. Who does that guy grow into? There's a lot of possibilities about what could have happened in his life in 25 years. For me it always comes back to the character and that would be fun to explore. But Universal doesn't seem to be interested, so it's moot."

The announcement of *Tremors 5: Bloodlines* as a traditional direct-to-video release, almost certainly with a budget lower than any of its predecessors, not only throws doubt on Maddock and Wilson's vision of a reimagined theatrical sequel, but also upon Kevin Bacon's suggestion that he would like to revisit the character of Valentine McKee 25 years on.

Tremors fans find themselves in a unique position for the franchise's silver anniversary, able to look back on four films and a TV series while wondering how a brand new production team will approach the legacy that precedes them. Concerns raised by Stampede's statement regarding their non-involvement in the latest film were addressed in an October 2014 Facebook post from Michael Gross: "Hollywood sequels are quite often made without their original creators, but I particularly felt the absence of writers S.S. Wilson and Brent Maddock in this latest adventure.

Without them, we wouldn't be here, and a future outing with the entire team would be most welcome."[1]

Whether or not Gross gets his wish will depend on the success of *Tremors 5: Bloodlines* plus Universal Studios Home Entertainment's willingness to proceed with further sequels, not to mention their ability to offer Stampede Entertainment the level of control they enjoyed on previous instalments. Should Kevin Bacon and Michael Gross get their way, a brand new cinematic offering could be on the cards for the franchise. At the same time, with the surge of popularity in high-quality television, from *Game of Thrones* (2011–) on HBO, *The Walking Dead* (2010–) on AMC and the likes of *House of Cards* (2013–) on streaming services, perhaps there could even be a future for *Tremors* back on the small screen.

Any new version would first require the blessing of Universal Studios, who had faith in a team of creatives over 25 years ago as they moved from a cinema release to VHS success, DVD/cable premieres and a TV spin-off. The evolution of the *Tremors* franchise has always been impossible to predict, with that uncertainty now likely to continue as a new adventure enters the canon and Hollywood accountants eagerly await the financial results. At the same time, fans will soon discover whether *Tremors 5* is a bona fide *Tremors* film or simply a film borrowing the *Tremors* name.

What is certain is that the original *Tremors* remains one of the most popular films of the 1990s, both a horror film that's scary and a comedy that's funny, a combination that baffled marketing men and delighted audiences. As modern filmmakers continue to explore the opportunities afforded to them by new technology, using increasingly complex computer generated imagery to create their worlds, *Tremors*' resolutely old school feel has a timeless and rustic charm that befits a film set in rural USA.

Like the tourists who made their way to Perfection each week in the TV series, viewers still have a desire to visit the small Nevada town via repeated screenings on DVD and Netflix. The world of *Tremors* and its sequels is rarely safe, with death just around the next boulder, but with Burt Gummer, Val McKee,

Earl Bassett, Grady Hoover, Desert Jack or Tyler Reed never too far away, there's something oddly comforting about this corner of the desert that can't be spoiled by the presence of subterranean creatures, government agents or, perhaps most dangerous of all, studio executives.

© Al Burstein

APPENDIX

The following is an abbreviated cast and crew list for the first four *Tremors* films, with an attempt to list some of the talent for *Tremors 5* gleaned from around the internet in June 2015.

TREMORS

Release Date: 19 January 1990 **Screenplay:** S.S. Wilson and Brent Maddock **Story:** S.S. Wilson, Brent Maddock and Ron Underwood **Director:** Ron Underwood

Selected crew: Associate Producer: Ellen Collett **Line Producer:** Ginny Nugent **Executive Producer:** Gale Anne Hurd **Producers:** S.S. Wilson and Brent Maddock **Production Designer:** Ivo Cristante **Cinematographer:** Alexander Gruszynski Second Unit **Director of Photography:** Virgil Harper **Production Coordinator:** Cristen Carr Strubbe **Visual Effects Supervisor:** Robert Skotak **Creature Designs:** Tom Woodruff, Jr. and Alec Gillis **Casting:** Pam Dixon **Editor:** O. Nicholas Brown **Music:** Ernest Troost **Senior VP of Production and Head of Acquisitions for Universal:** Jim Jacks **Special Thanks:** Nancy Roberts

Cast: Kevin Bacon (Valentine McKee), Fred Ward (Earl Bassett), Finn Carter (Rhonda LeBeck), Michael Gross (Burt Gummer), Reba McEntire (Heather Gummer), Robert Jayne as Bobby Jacoby (Melvin Plug), Charlotte Stewart (Nancy Sterngood),

Tony Genaro (Miguel), Ariana Richards (Mindy Sterngood), Richard Marcus (Nestor Cunningham), Victor Wong (Walter Chang), Conrad Bachmann (Dr. Jim Wallace), Bibi Besch (Megan Wallace), Sunshine Parker (Edgar Deems), Michael Dan Waggner (Old Fred), John Goodwin (Howard), John Pappas (Carmine)

TREMORS 2: AFTERSHOCKS

Release Date: 9 April 1996 **Screenplay:** S.S. Wilson and Brent Maddock **Director:** S.S. Wilson

Selected crew: Producers: Christopher DeFaria and Nancy Roberts **Executive Producers:** S.S. Wilson and Brent Maddock **Production Designer:** Ivo Cristante **Director of Photography:** Virgil Harper **Production Manager:** Cristen Carr Strubbe **Second Assistant Director:** Hilbert Hakim **Creature Designs:** Tom Woodruff, Jr. and Alec Gillis **Music:** Jay Ferguson

Cast: Fred Ward (Earl Bassett), Christopher Gartin (Grady Hoover), Helen Shaver (Kate Reilly), Michael Gross (Burt Gummer), Marcelo Tubert (Señor Ortega), Marco Hernandez (Julio), José Ramón Rosario as José Rosario (Pedro), Thomas Rosales (Oil Worker)

TREMORS 3: BACK TO PERFECTION

Release Date: 1 October 2001 **Story:** S.S. Wilson, Brent Maddock and Nancy Roberts **Teleplay:** John Whelpley **Director:** Brent Maddock

Selected crew: Producer: Nancy Roberts **Co-producer:** Anthony Santa Croce **Executive Producer:** S.S. Wilson **Production Designer:** Ken Larson **Director of Photography:** Virgil Harper **Casting:** Craig Campobasso **Unit Production Manager:** Tom

Keniston **Creature Designs:** Tom Woodruff, Jr. and Alec Gillis **Visual Effects:** Kevin Kutchaver and Linda Drake **Music:** Kevin Kiner

Cast: Michael Gross (Burt Gummer), Shawn Christian ("Desert" Jack Sawyer), Susan Chuang (Jodi Chang), Charlotte Stewart (Nancy Sterngood), Ariana Richards (Mindy Sterngood), Tony Genaro (Miguel), Barry Livingston (Dr. Andrew Merliss), John Pappas (Agent Charlie Rusk), Robert Jayne (Melvin Plug), Billy Rieck (Buford)

TREMORS 4: THE LEGEND BEGINS

Release Date: 2 January 2004 **Story:** S.S. Wilson, Brent Maddock and Nancy Roberts **Teleplay:** Scott Buck **Director:** S.S. Wilson

Selected crew: Producer: Nancy Roberts **Associate Producer:** Linda Drake **Executive Producers:** S.S. Wilson and Brent Maddock **Production Designer:** Simon Dobbin **Director of Photography:** Virgil Harper **Unit Production Manager:** Jon Kuyper **Creature Designs:** Tom Woodruff, Jr. and Alec Gillis **Visual Effects:** Kevin Kutchaver and Linda Drake **Editor:** Harry B. Miller III **Music:** Jay Ferguson

Cast: Michael Gross (Burt Gummer), Sara Botsford (Christine Lord), Billy Drago (Black Hand Kelly), Brent Roam (Juan Pedilla), August Schellenberg (Tecopa), Ming Lo (Pyong Lien Chang), Lydia Look (Lu Wan Chang), Sam Ly (Fu Yien Chang), J.E. Freeman (Old Fred)

TREMORS 5: BLOODLINES

Release Date: October 2015 **Script:** John Whelpley **Director:** Don Michael Paul

Selected crew: Producer: Ogden Gavanski **Executive Producer:** Lisa Gooding **Line Producer:** Alan Shearer **Cinematography:** Michael Swan **Film Editing:** Vanick Moradian **Casting:** Jeff Gerrard and Gillian Hawser

Cast: Michael Gross (Burt Gummer), Jamie Kennedy (Travis Welker), Natalie Becker (Lucia), Brandon Auret (unknown), Lawrence Joffe (Basson), Ian Roberts (unknown), Pearl Thusi (unknown), Daniel Janks (unknown), Zak Hendrikz (Riley), Ernest Ndhlovu (Ndebele Chieftan), Emmanuel Castis (Dr. Michael Swan), Jarrod Pinto (unknown), Sello Sebotsane (unknown), Rea Rangaka (unknown)

ACKNOWLEDGEMENTS

Most of this book is based on brand new interviews with more than 50 people who worked on the *Tremors* films and TV series in some capacity between 1990 and 2004. The majority generously offered their time for Skype chats, happy to oblige a UK-based author working with an 8-hour time difference to Los Angeles, while others took time to reply via email. Thanks to the following for their help and enthusiasm:

Kevin Bacon, John Badham, Steven D. Binder, Victor Browne, Al Burstein, Yancy Calzada, Craig Campobasso, Shawn Christian, Susan Chuang, Ivo Cristante, Christopher DeFaria, Pam Dixon, Linda Drake, Tony Garnett, Louis Feola, Jay Ferguson, Tony Garnett, Christopher Gartin, Alec Gillis, Donn Greer, Alexander Gruszynski, Hilbert Hakim, Virgil Harper, Gale Anne Hurd, Dr. Kate Hutton, Patti Jackson, Robert Jayne, Gladise Jimenez, Tom Keniston, Kevin Kutchaver, Jon Kuyper, Lela Lee, Barry Livingston, Lydia Look, Reba McEntire, Harry B. Miller III, Ariana Richards, Lise Romanoff, Helen Shaver, Jack Sholder, Christopher Silber, Robert Skotak, Charlotte Stewart, Cristen Carr Strubbe, Ernest Troost, Marcelo Tubert, John Whelpley and Tom Woodruff, Jr.

Special thanks to S.S. Wilson, Brent Maddock, Nancy Roberts, Ron Underwood and Michael Gross for their tireless support of this project. Without them there would be no *Seeking Perfection*.

Sadly, three of my interviewees passed away before the book was published, Marcia Strassman, Tony Genaro and Jim Jacks. I'd like to take this opportunity to mention their good humour and willingness to offer their time. The *Tremors* family misses them.

I'd also like to thank Taylor White at Creature Features (visit creaturefeatures.com and if you're ever in Burbank, CA, check out his store) and the team at *Famous Monsters of Filmland* magazine for organising the March 2015 25th anniversary screening of *Tremors* in Los Angeles. It was a privilege to sit in the front row at the ArcLight Hollywood and listen to the cast and crew reminisce about their work on *Tremors*, while it also supplied me with some extra material for this book. Thanks also to journalist and panel host, David Weiner, for his fantastic *Famous Monsters of Filmland* feature on the *Tremors* movies and his support for *Seeking Perfection*.

For helping with research I'd like to thank Ben Sampson, who trawled various Los Angeles library files for information on the films' press coverage, and Chris Langley at the Lone Pine Film History Museum for his expert knowledge on *Tremors* locations.

Thanks to Julia Overlin for her transcription skills and to Angela Hamilton for helping out when deadlines were tight.

Editorially, I'm indebted to Mairi Cumming, Ross Maclean, Rob Girvan, Ian Hoey, Douglas McNaughton and Dorothy Connachan, who each took time to read my words and critique them.

Thank you to Ben Morris for designing the book's cover, Kayla Stuhr for animating the book's trailer and Emília Rovira Alegre for the trailer's atmospheric music.

A final thank you to Claire Connachan for listening to me talking about writing this book for a few years, before I spent 2013 to 2015 actually writing it – giving up part of your holiday to read about giant underground worms is something few people would do.

REFERENCES

PROLOGUE

1. Naval Air Weapons Station China Lake website, http://www.cnic.navy.mil/regions/cnrsw/installations/naws_china_lake.html

CHAPTER ONE

1. Official Ray Harryhausen website, http://www.rayharryhausen.com/biography.php
2. Appelo, Tim, "These Are the Top 25 Film Schools in the United States", *The Hollywood Reporter*, 30 July 2014, http://www.hollywoodreporter.com/news/top-25-film-schools-united-721649
3. Official *Tremors* website, http://tremors3movie.com/crew_trem2.swf
4. Official *Tremors* website, http://tremors3movie.com/crew_trem2.swf
5. Thompson, Anne, "Risky Business", *LA Weekly*, 19 November 1989
6. *Short Circuit* on Box Office Mojo, http://boxofficemojo.com/movies/?id=shortcircuit.htm
7. *Ghost Dad* trivia on IMDb, http://www.imdb.com/title/tt0099654/trivia?item=tr1868260

CHAPTER TWO

1. Negative Pickup Deal on Wikipedia, http://en.wikipedia.org/wiki/Negative_pickup_deal
2. Bernstein, H, "Hollywood's craft workers under pressure to take cuts", *LA Times*, p. 1, January 24, 1989
3. Wasko, Janet, "Challenges to Hollywood's Labor Force in the 1990s." In *Global Productions: Labor in the Making of the*

"Information Society", edited by Gerald Sussman and John A. Lent, 173–189. Cresskill, NJ: Hampton Press, 1998

4. Yeomans, Adam, "Trying To Get A Better Grip Unions Are Making Inroads Into The State's Film Industry", *Orlando Sentinel*, July 24 1989, http://articles.orlandosentinel.com/1989-07-24/business/8907234383_1_florida-organized-labor-producers
5. The Projection Booth, 28 January 2015, http://projection-booth.blogspot.co.uk/2015/01/episode-203-tremors.html
6. Finn Carter panel interview, 25th Anniversary *Tremors* screening, ArcLight Hollywood, Los Angeles, 26 March 2015
7. Charlotte Stewart panel interview, (as 6.)
8. Conrad Bachmann panel interview, (as 6.)
9. Sammarco, pNut, "From *Tron* to *Legacy*: The History of Computer Generated Imagery in Cinema", Perylg Productions, 14 November 2013, http://peryglproductions.wordpress.com/2013/11/14/from-tron-to-legacy-the-history-of-computer-generated-imagery-in-cinema/
10. Dirks, Tim, "Greatest Visual and Special Effects (F/X) – Milestones in Film", AMC Filmsite, http://www.filmsite.org/visualeffects11.html

CHAPTER THREE

1. Langley, Chris, "Silent Six-Guns in the Sierras", *Lone Pine in the Movies: Celebrating the Centennials*, Riverwood Press/Lone Pine Film Museum, 2012
2. Weiner, David, "Oh Criminently! Reba Reminisces About Tremors, Guns & Graboids", *Famous Monsters of Filmland*, p. 33-35, May/June 2015
3. Pierce, Scott, "Maleficent Director Has One Degree of Separation from Kevin Bacon Thanks to *Tremors*", MoviePilot, 23 May 2014, http://moviepilot.com/posts/2014/05/23/maleficent-director-has-one-degree-of-separation-from-kevin-bacon-thanks-to-tremors-1444458?lt_source=external,manual#!8OtYH
4. John Goodwin panel interview, 25th Anniversary *Tremors* screening, ArcLight Hollywood, Los Angeles, 26 March 2015
5. Conrad Bachmann panel interview, (as 4.)
6. Lone Pine Chamber of Commerce website, History of the Lone Pine Area, http://lonepinechamber.org/history
7. Lone Pine Chamber of Commerce website, The Great Earthquake of 1872, http://lonepinechamber.org/history/the-great-earthquake-of-1872/

8. US Beacon website, Lone Pine CA, http://www.usbeacon.com/California/Lone-Pine.html

CHAPTER FOUR

1. Richard Marcus panel interview, 25th Anniversary *Tremors* screening, ArcLight Hollywood, Los Angeles, 26 March 2015
2. Robert Jayne panel interview, (as 1.)
3. Shannon, Jody, "Beneath Perfection", *Cinefex* no. 42, May 1990, p. 36
4. Cinefex no. 42, p. 36
5. Cinefex no. 42, p. 44

CHAPTER FIVE

1. Finn Carter panel interview, 25th Anniversary *Tremors* screening, ArcLight Hollywood, Los Angeles, 26 March 2015
2. Interview by Larson, Randall D., originally published in *Soundtrack Magazine*, Sept 1997 and March 1998 issues
3. Galbraith, Jane, "Indie Hurd Prepares Action, Sci-Fi Pix" *Variety*, 19 April 1989
4. *Hollywood Reporter*, "Universal Picks Up Hurd's '*Tremors*'", 3 August 1989
5. Cohn, Lawrence, "Hurd Juggles Indie, Studio Work With Trio of New Pix, *Daily Variety*, August 14 1989, p. 10
6. Thompson, Anne, "Risky Business" *LA Weekly*, 19 November 1989
7. The Making of *Star Wars: The Empire Strikes Back* By Rinzler, J. W.
8. *Tremors* on Box Office Mojo, http://www.boxofficemojo.com/movies/?id=tremors.htm
9. *Tremors* review, *Variety*, 17 January 1990
10. Wilmington, Michael, "Wormy Thrills, Fear and Humor Burrow Up in '*Tremors*'", *LA Times*, 19 January 1990
11. Stringer, Ron, *Tremors* review, *LA Weekly*, 19 January 1990
12. Fuchs, Cindy, "Wannabe Worm" *Philadelphia City Paper*, January 26 – February 2, 1990
13. Musto, Michael, "Scum Came Running" *The Village Voice*, 29 January 1990
14. Canby, Vincent, "Underground creatures and dread events" *New York Times*, 19 January 1990

15. Harrington, Richard, "Tremors: As the Worms Turn" *The Washington Post*, 22 January 1990
16. Mulkerrins, Jane "Kevin Bacon interview for *The Following*: 'my career went down the toilet", 22 January 2013, http://www.telegraph.co.uk/culture/tvandradio/9806535/Kevin-Bacon-interview-for-The-Following-my-career-went-down-the-toilet.html
17. Ashlock, Jesse, Q&A: *X-Men*'s Kevin Bacon, Details, HuffPost Live, 1 June 2011, http://www.details.com/culture-trends/movies-and-tv/201106/kevin-bacon-actor-footloose-xmen

CHAPTER SIX

1. Rose, Tiffany, "Interrogation: Grilling Bacon; He may be a big Hollywood star, but that doesn't mean Kevin Bacon can get away with telling us porkies. We turn up the heat and demand some home truths" *Sunday Mirror*, 20 April 2003
2. Feldt, Mark, "The History Of The VHS Movie Industry", Knoji.com, 28 February 2012, https://entertainment-industry.knoji.com/the-history-of-the-vhs-movie-industry/
3. Fonda, Jane, "30th Anniversary of My First Workout Video", JaneFonda.com, 24 April 2012, http://www.janefonda.com/30th-anniversary-of-my-first-workout-video/
4. Ganapati, Priya, "June 4, 1977: VHS Comes to America, *Wired*, 4 June 2010, http://www.wired.com/2010/06/0604vhs-ces/
5. Henderson, Stuart, *The Hollywood Sequel, History and Form 1911–2010*, Palgrave Macmillan, 2014, p. 76
6. Bridges, Andrew, "Some shocker this fund-raiser" *LA Times*, 8 March 1996
7. *Tremors 2* review, *Entertainment Today*, 5 April 1996
8. Bernstein, Abbie, "*Tremors 2* review", *Hollywood Drama-Logue*, June 20–26 1996
9. Brass, Kevin, "Video Invasion: B Film Makers Battle A-List for a Place on the Shelf", http://articles.latimes.com/1996-04-19/business/fi-60235_1_video-title

CHAPTER SEVEN

1. Hettrick, Scott, "U Rattling Tremors" *Variety*, 11 August 2000
2. S.S. Wilson talks to UK *Tremors*, http://www.angelfire.com/movies/krccc/sswilson.html

3. Michael Gross wins Best Actor for *Tremors 3*, Stampede Entertainment website, http://www.stampede-entertainment.com/tremors3/videoaward/

CHAPTER EIGHT

1. Stampede Entertainment website, The Lost Monsters, http://www.stampede-entertainment.com/wrmkllr/lost/index.html
2. Stampede Entertainment website, reference to start of filming on *Tremors 4*, http://www.stampede-entertainment.com/faq/faq.php?category_id=8&cat_name=Questions%20about%20Tremors%20The%20Series&pop=0
3. Boston, Chuck, "Encore Hollywood aims for Perfection", CGChannel.com, 21 July 2003, http://www.cgchannel.com/2003/07/encore-hollywood-aims-for-perfection-in-tremors/
4. Boston, Chuck, "Encore Hollywood aims for Perfection", CGChannel.com, 21 July 2003, http://www.cgchannel.com/2003/07/encore-hollywood-aims-for-perfection-in-tremors/
5. King, Susan, "Sci Fi's '*Tremors*' Has Perfection on Its Side" *LA Times*, 23 March 2003, http://articles.latimes.com/2003/mar/23/news/tv-coverstory23
6. Ryan, Mike, "Dean Norris on 'Men, Women and Children' and the Chances of Seeing Hank Schrader on '*Better Call Saul*'", Screen Crush, 9 October 2014, http://screencrush.com/dean-norris-men-women-children-better-call-saul/

CHAPTER NINE

1. Garcia, Frank and Phillips, Mark, *Science Fiction Television Series, 1990–2004: Histories, Casts and Credits for 58 Shows*, McFarland & Co., reprint 2012
2. Boston, Chuck, "Encore Hollywood aims for Perfection", CGChannel.com, 21 July 2003, http://www.cgchannel.com/2003/07/encore-hollywood-aims-for-perfection-in-tremors/
3. (see 1.)
4. (see 1.)

CHAPTER TEN

1. Wilson, S.S., *Tremors 4* commentary, Region 1 DVD

CHAPTER ELEVEN

1. Gibbons, Jim, "The Short Story Behind the *Tremors* comics", Enemy of Peanuts, 9 March 2013, http://www.enemyofpeanuts.com/2013/03/09/the-short-story-behind-tremors-comics/
2. "Christofer Sundberg Talks to UK *Tremors*", 8 January 2003, http://ps2.gamespy.com/playstation-2/tremors/
3. Schwartz, Mike, "Lost Toys – Now Playing Series 4", Cartoon and Horror, 19 May 2010, http://www.cartoonandhorror.com/2010/05/lost-toys-now-playing-series-4.html
4. TekeoMiona's "Daughter of Hokumunja", FanFiction.net, 26 April 2013, https://www.fanfiction.net/s/7952734/1/S1E15-Daughter-of-Hokumunja
5. Leydon, Joe, "*Slither* review" *Variety*, 19 March 2006
6. Brown, Todd, "Writer Kevin Lehane talks *Grabbers*", Twitch Film, 18 July 2013, http://twitchfilm.com/2013/07/writer-kevin-lehane-talks-grabbers.html
7. List of Pop Culture References in Warcraft/BC, http://www.wowwiki.com/List_of_pop_culture_references_in_Warcraft/BC

CHAPTER TWELVE

1. Stampede Entertainment's *Tremors 5* FAQs, http://www.stampede-entertainment.com/faq/faq.php
2. Michael Gross talks *Tremors 5*, 23 March 2014, https://www.youtube.com/watch?v=A1rjpt3BuZE
3. Woods, Kevin, "It seems that a *Tremors* reboot is in the works at Universal", 22 July 2014, http://www.joblo.com/horror-movies/news/it-seems-that-a-tremors-reboot-is-in-the-works-at-universal-214#p8puAbkU02sjDaJP.99
4. Brandon Auret on Twitter, 18 September 2014, https://twitter.com/BrandonAuret/status/512652021984268288
5. Michael Gross on Facebook, 24 September 2014, https://www.facebook.com/ActorMichaelGross/photos/a.729466040429468.1073741827.728990673810338/796282410414497/?type=1
6. Daniel Janks on Facebook, 26 September 2014, https://www.facebook.com/danieljanks/posts/10154639272745384
7. Michael Gross on Facebook, 14 October 2014, https://www.facebook.com/ActorMichaelGross/photos/a.729466040429468.1073741827.728990673810338/806948622681209/?type=1

8. Michael Gross on Facebook, 18 October 2014, https://www.facebook.com/ActorMichaelGross/photos/a.729466040429468.1073741827.728990673810338/807725255936879/?type=1&reply_comment_id=808892165820188&total_comments=8
9. Stampede Entertainment Press Release, 16 October 2014, http://www.stampede-entertainment.com/about/news.html
10. Michael Gross on Facebook, 18 October 2014, https://www.facebook.com/ActorMichaelGross/photos/a.729466040429468.1073741827.728990673810338/808396199203118/?type=1&reply_comment_id=808912829151455&total_comments=3
11. Daniel Janks on Facebook, 20 October 2014, https://www.facebook.com/danieljanks/posts/10154738005140384
12. Gingold, Michael, "Q&A: Jamie Kennedy Talks "BUDDY HUTCHINS," "TREMORS 5" and More, Fangoria, 26 February 2015, http://www.fangoria.com/new-qa-jamie-kennedy-talks-buddy buddy-hutchins-tremors-5-and-more/
13. Weiner, David, "*Tremors* Family Ties: *Tremors 5 Bloodlines*", *Famous Monsters of Filmland*, p. 36–39, May/June 2015
14. Weiner, David, "*Tremors*: Remembering Perfection 25 Years Later", *Famous Monsters of Filmland*, p. 10–20, May/June 2015
15. (as 13.)
16. (as 13.)

EPILOGUE

1. Michael Gross on Facebook, 18 October 2014, https://www.facebook.com/ActorMichaelGross/photos/a.729466040429468.1073741827 073741827.728990673810338/808396199203118/?type=1&comment_id=808461275863277&reply_comment_id=808912829151455&total_comments=3&comment_tracking=%7B%22tn%22%3A%22R9%22%7D

If you've enjoyed this book, please take a minute to leave a review on Amazon or a comment on Goodreads.

Alternatively, please consider tweeting your thoughts using the #TremorsGuide hashtag, or leaving a comment on the *Seeking Perfection* Facebook page.

* * *

For the latest news on *Tremors* and *Seeking Perfection: The Unofficial Guide to Tremors*, visit tremorsguide.com to sign up for the free newsletter.

Visit the Facebook Page at facebook.com/tremorsguide

Visit the Twitter feed at twitter.com/tremorsguide

Printed in Great Britain
by Amazon.co.uk, Ltd.,
Marston Gate.